THE NAVAJO NATION

A Visitor's Guide

THE NAVAJO NATION

A Visitor's Guide

Patrick Lavin
Joan Lavin

HIPPOCRENE BOOKS, INC.
New York

For information, address:
HIPPOCRENE BOOKS, INC.
171 Madison Avenue
New York, NY 10016
www.hippocrenebooks.com

Library of Congress Cataloging-in-Publication Data

Lavin, Patrick.
The Navajo nation : a visitor's guide / Patrick Lavin, Joan Lavin.
p. cm.
Includes bibliographical references and index.
ISBN-13: 978-0-7818-1180-4
ISBN-10: 0-7818-1180-5
1. Navajo Indians—Antiquities—Guidebooks. 2. Southwest, New—Guidebooks. I. Lavin, Joan. II. Title.

E99.N3L38 2008
917.9104'540899726—dc22 2007052589

Printed in the United States of America.

Dedicated to the memories of

Edith Binet and Shirley Montbleau

ACKNOWLEDGMENTS

We are grateful to many individuals whose encouragement and help have made this book possible. First and foremost we thank our daughter, Edie Lavin, for the generous use of her time in helping shepherd this book to publication. Secondly, we are indebted to Mary Francis of Many Farms, Arizona, whose counseling on the Navajo language was extremely helpful. She helped make a difficult task much easier, particularly in providing the appropriate diacritical markings for Navajo words. Without her help it would have been a thorny undertaking. We also wish to thank our editors, Priti Gress and Garrett Gambino, at Hippocrene Books, whose perceptive editing smoothed out some serrated edges. The many historians and writers we consulted will be evident throughout the book and are acknowledged in the bibliography.

CONTENTS

FOREWORD

The Navajos form the largest Indian tribe in the United States, today numbering about a quarter million. They have not always been a large group; they numbered fewer than 10,000 when they returned from exile to their homeland in 1886. Several hundred years ago their ancestors migrated southward from what is now northwestern Canada. In the southwest they learned from the Pueblo how to farm and later acquired livestock from the Spanish. Their initial contacts with the Americans in the 1800s were, by and large, adversarial. After a series of encounters with the U.S. Army in the 1860s they were conquered and forced to relocate farther east at Bosque Redondo in New Mexico territory. In 1868 they signed a treaty with the U.S. government allowing them to return to part of their homeland, which then became the Navajo Indian Reservation.

Navajo is not their own word for themselves. In their own language they are *Diné*, "The People." *Navajo* is, of course, a Spanish word, and this spelling, rather than the anglicized spelling with an *h*, is followed in this book. The Navajo are brilliant in their ability to create impressive and multifaceted art. Nowhere is this more evident than in the beauty of their silversmithing. Navajo rug weaving is recognized far and wide, not only because of its creative qualities, but also because of its unique stylistic variances.

The Navajo Nation encompasses 25,000 square miles in northeastern Arizona, northwestern New Mexico, and southern Utah. However, *Diné' bikéyah*, the Navajos' country, extends well beyond these boundaries. The area has some of the most awesome scenery in the world. In every direction there are spectacular views of distant mesas, expansive plateaus, and towering mountains. Navajo country is the ultimate southwestern landscape.

With this introduction, we begin an exploration of Navajoland and the Navajo people. *The Navajo Nation: A Visitor's Guide* provides what the visitor to Diné' bikéyah should know: attractions, accommodations, routes, and a guide to hiking and camping. It is also about the Navajo people: their history, culture, language, and religion.

Have some fun on your travels by learning a few Navajo words whenever you stop. Navajo speakers will appreciate your interest, chuckle at your efforts, and then will go out of their way to help you pronounce the words and phrases you wish to learn. The language section of this book will help you get started. As you come across Navajo words in this book and on your travels, please note that there is a guide to correct pronunciation in Part III.

PART I

A SHORT HISTORY OF THE DINÉ

CHAPTER 1

THE LAND AND ITS PEOPLE

The Navajo Nation is the largest American Indian nation in the United States with an on-reservation, enrolled population of approximately 168,000 and another 80,000 members living in towns nearby. Spanning 16.2 million acres (nearly 27,000 square miles), the Navajo reservation occupies the south-central portion of the Colorado Plateau, a region located well above the lower parched basins of Nevada, southern Arizona, southwestern New Mexico, and the Rio Grande valley from Albuquerque southward.[1] In contrast, the Rocky Mountains to the east climb to great elevations, blocking the frigid Canadian air masses that sweep southward along the Great Plains during the winter (Goodman 1971). By and large the plateau climate is remarkably diverse—more tolerable summers, much colder winters—supporting a broad variety of vegetation.

Diné' Bikéyah: Navajo Country

Today, the Navajo people occupy Navajo country (*diné' bikéyah*), a special portion of land that the United States government set aside for them in 1868. Diné' bikéyah, the largest reservation of its kind in the United States, is roughly 16 million acres in area (excluding the smaller Hopi reservation

1. "Navajo Nation Profile." Navajo Nation Washington Office. Retrieved August 25, 2003, from www.nnwo.org/nnprofile.htm.

lying completely within it). It takes in sections of northeastern Arizona, northwestern New Mexico, southern Utah, and some disputed territory in Colorado. There are three satellite areas separated from the main reservation: Ramah, Canoncito, and Alamo Navajo, bands occupying unattached sites in New Mexico. Although physically detached from the main reservation, these three areas participate in Navajo tribal government (Goodman).

From the daunting formations of Monument Valley to the sweeping sandstone walls of Canyon de Chelly, Navajo country is a geographically breathtaking southwestern landscape. Among its many spectacular sites are Monument Valley, the Painted Desert, Window Rock, and the Petrified Forest. Monument Valley has come to symbolize the West's dramatic beauty. Its spires, buttes, and mesas have been featured in numerous western films. John Ford shot the classic *Stagecoach* at the site and over the next several decades used the site as a backdrop for many other movies (Bryant 2003).

Few have described the area's unrivaled beauty better than Tony Hillerman: "Everywhere you look there are dramatic views of distant, angular mesas, expansive plateaus, and wide, pale-green valleys. . . . In every direction the treeless Navajo horizon stretches out before you in a landscape of tawny dunes, orange-and-pink canyons, and faraway blue mountains rising more than 10,000 feet" (Hillerman 1991: 199).

Diné' bikéyah is indeed high country. There are five principal mountainous regions within Navajoland, ranging in elevation from 4,000 feet (near the east rim of the Grand Canyon) to over 14,000 feet in Colorado's San Juan Mountains. The Chuska Range—including the Chuska, Tunicha, Lukachukai, and Carrizo mountains—stretches between Shiprock and Gallop along the New Mexico–Arizona line, peaking at 9,784 feet at Roof Butte. Near the center of the reservation, Black Mesa is an extensive "island prominence" with a circumference of 250 miles and elevations as high as 8,210 feet. The Zuni Mountains roughly parallel Interstate 40 between Grants and Gallop, New Mexico. Navajo Mountain, with a summit of 10,416 feet, is located on the Arizona-Utah line east of Lake Powell. The San Juan Mountains, by far the highest, rise to over 14,000 feet in southwest Colorado. Extending in a general southeast-to-northeast direction across the reservation there are three major areas of relatively lower elevations (below 6,000 feet): the Painted Desert, Chinle Valley, and the San Juan Basin (Linford 2000).

Two tributary watersheds of the Colorado River—the San Juan River to the north and the Little Colorado River in the west-central region—irrigate most of the reservation. A small part of the westernmost limits of Navajoland drains directly into the deep canyons of the Colorado River, which in turn empties into the Gulf of Cortez. The eastern sectors of Navajoland lie in the Rio Grande watershed, which flows into the Gulf of Mexico (ibid.).

They Call Themselves *Diné*

More fascinating than the enchanting landscapes they occupy are the Navajo people themselves. *Navajo* is not a Navajo word. In their language they are *Diné,* which means "The People." Supposedly, *Dineʼé,* an old plural of *Diné,* is the more correct Navajo term, but *Diné* is the more accepted usage (Kluckhohn and Leighton 1962). The exact origin of the term *Navajo* is uncertain. The seventeenth-century Franciscan friar Alonso de Benavides speaks of the Navajo as "the Apache of the great planted fields" (Spicer 1997, 211).

Athabaskan Language Family

The Navajo are kin to the Apache, and linguistic anthropologists tell us that their languages both belong to the Athabaskan language family. Both tribes had previously lived in the interior of northwestern Canada and Alaska before migrating southward centuries ago. Some historians believe they had been pushing southwestward from their northwestern habitat since the 1300s and were still in the process of this migration when the Spanish arrived in the sixteenth century. Although Navajos and Apaches share a common ancestry, the tribes went their separate ways before the seventeenth century (ibid.). As they drifted apart, the Navajo adapted to cultural and environmental changes. Borrowing from other cultures they encountered, they acquired sheep and horses from the Spanish and became some of the best herdsmen and horsemen in the Southwest. The Navajo also learned how to work silver from the Spanish, and over the years they polished their craft to become among the finest silversmiths in the world. From the Hopi and the Pueblo tribes, they acquired the skills of desert agriculture and weaving, and Navajos are nationally known for their exquisite handwoven rugs.

Archaeologists believe that Athabaskan-speaking people migrated from Asia to North America some 11,000 years ago. Their descendents—the Apacheans—began venturing further south centuries later. Before the arrival of the Spanish, the Athabaskan speakers, who were becoming the Navajos, had moved into the Southwest. They settled on a rugged stretch of land east of present-day Farmington in northwestern New Mexico. They called their new home *Dinétah* ("among the Diné") and it was here, beyond the Pueblo frontier, that much of the early Diné culture evolved. In this new land, northern ways became southern ways.

The Diné came to the Southwest and created their culture from diverse sources: from their Athabaskan roots; from the neighboring Pueblo, Paiute, and Pai tribes; from the Spanish; and more recently from Anglo-American society. New peoples became Diné, and new clans were created to describe their kinship: *Naakall Dine'é* (Mexican Clan) and *Naasht'ezhi Dine'é* (Zuni Clan). After centuries of such incorporations, sixty individual Navajo clans exist today (Trimble 2000).

The Diné lived at Dinétah in small groups from the 1500s through the late 1700s, supporting themselves by hunting and sometimes by farming. Then, intimidation from Spaniards, as well as conflicts with Comanches and Utes, forced them to move out of the Dinétah area. Few Diné live in the area today; however, Dinétah continues to be a powerful lure for Navajos captivated by their history and heritage. Dominated by the distinctive peak Gobernador Knob, Dinétah is home to a variety of painted and carved ceremonial art (Iverson 2002a).

Navajos are generally referred to as a tribe—a term that is usually used to describe a group of individuals who are politically and economically united. Tribal cohesiveness, however, was a more recent happening for the Diné. Although they had a shared language, ceremonial system, and clan-based kinship for more than two centuries after their first contact with the Spanish, they did not share tribal realization until the mid-nineteenth century. Most of the characteristics of their culture—those now considered distinctly Navajo—evolved during this two-hundred-year period (Kluckhohn and Leighton).

The Navajo engaged in almost constant warfare—first they fought the Spanish, then Mexicans, and then Americans from the middle of the seventeenth century. The United States government finally subjugated them in 1863–64.

CHAPTER 2

RELIGION AND MYTH

According to Navajo tradition, First Man and First Woman had emerged into *Dinétah* from the Third World on what is now Huerfano Mountain in New Mexico. It was here that Talking God revealed how to build a hogan, the round Navajo home. It was here also that Coyote tossed a blanket-full of stars into the heavens, creating the Milky Way. First Man and First Woman found the infant Changing Woman on top of Gobernador Knob, not far from Huerfano Mountain. This is where the Holy People performed the first puberty ceremony for Changing Woman. Here also, Changing Woman gave birth to the Twins who would liberate this Fourth World of its monsters (Trimble 2000).

Navajo religion is based on reciprocity: favor for favor, gift for gift. Gods gave the *Diné* the earth and everything on it—land, water, and livestock—so the Diné must give in return by caring for these gifts and performing prescribed rituals. Their religious belief represents a superb example of acculturation. They superimposed much of the Pueblo creed and ritual upon the more primitive Athabaskan beliefs. Like the Pueblo, the Navajo have elaborate rites for every phase of life and have special reverence for the growing season. However, while borrowing from the Pueblos, they still have managed to maintain much of their own beliefs and ceremonial functions. Beyond Pueblo influences, the Navajo creation myth is quite similar to that of the Apache, and according to some sources there is striking similarity to corresponding Mongolian beliefs (Beck 1971).

The number of Navajos who adhere to the Christian faith is sizeable in some areas of the Navajo reservation. At the same time, most who profess to be Christians continue to observe Native beliefs and practices as well.

Christianity preaches of far-off lands and places, which some Navajos have difficulty envisioning—their own stories tell of the four sacred mountains, at least one of which is visible almost everywhere in Navajo country. The Christian Bible speaks only of a male God and of a society where authority and responsibility centers chiefly in men—the Navajo have Changing Woman, arguably the principal Navajo divinity, and their esteem of the female role is personified in their social organization and religious lore. The picture of a god who is entirely good is hard for the Diné to understand, for their whole outlook insists on duality—all beings having an evil as well as a good side (Kluckhohn and Leighton 1962).

Navajo Creation Myth

The Navajo's own story of their origin begins with an account of the emergence of all life forms through a series of worlds. This myth is the Diné counterpart to the Genesis account of the Bible. Given that the Navajo have not rationalized their mythology into a canonical theology, there are some variations of the origin myth and dissimilarities between the origin myth and other myths. Anthropologist Clyde Kluckhohn writes: "Whatever the discrepancies, the origin myth still gives definite form to many Navajo notions and things. It is also the final warrant of authority for carrying out many acts, ritual and secular, in prescribed ways" (Kluckhohn and Leighton, 194). The emergence story is a religion of many tales. These tales and legends orally carry the basic worldview of the Navajo people from ritual to ritual, from generation to generation. They may vary from one generation to another, but these tales are intrinsically a part of Navajo history and culture (Linford, 2000).

One variant of the origin myth describes how First Man (*Áltsé Hastiin*) and First Woman (*Áltsé Asdzáá*) are formed in the Black World of Insect Beings, but are forced out of the Black World due to quarreling among the Insect Beings. They move to the Blue World, where Blue Birds (*Dólii*), Blue Hawks (*Ginitsoh Dootl'izhí*), Blue Jays (*Jigí*), and Blue Herons (*Taltl'ááh Ha'alééh*) lived with other Insect Beings. This is where First Man and First Woman discover terrestrial animals, including Wolves (*Ma'iitsoh*), Wildcats (*Nashdoilbáhí*), Badgers (*Nahashch'id*), Kit Foxes (*Ma' iiltsooi*), and Mountain Lions (*Nashdoitsoh*). Once again, quarreling among beings causes another move, this time to the Yellow World. The ill-behaved Coyote was the source of many problems that eventually brought about a great flood, forcing First Man and First Woman to relocate to the present world.

First Man and First Woman surface in the present world, only to find it entirely under water. Eventually succeeding in coming to terms with the monster who ruled the waters, the waters recede and the world known to Navajos today begins to take shape, exposing the four sacred mountains that mark the traditional boundaries of *Diné' bikéyah*: San Francisco Peaks (*Dook'o'ooshid*) in the west, Blanca Peak (*Sis Naajini*) in the east, Mount Taylor (*Tsoodzil*) in the south, and Mount Hesperus (*Dzil Na'oodilii*) in the north.

As the creation myth unfolds, it describes how the sun, moon, and the stars first appeared in the sky, day and night came to be, and the year divided into seasons. This was also the time when First Man and First Woman arrive in the vicinity of what is now called Huerfano Mountain in New Mexico.

Changing Woman and Other Supernatural Beings

During this time, Changing Woman (*Asdzáá Nadleehí*) is born: discovered on top of Gobernador Knob (*Ch'ool'i'I*) by First Man and First Woman. When Changing Woman reaches puberty, the Holy People (*Diyin Dine'é*) conduct a ceremony (*Kinaaldá*) for her. Talking God (*Haashch'éítti'í*) conducts the final night ceremony, when he presents the twelve hogan songs (*Hooghan Biyiin*) still used today (Iverson 2002a).

The story goes on, telling of how Changing Woman falls asleep by a waterfall, where she is visited by the Sun. She becomes pregnant and gives birth to twin sons, naming one Child Born of Water (*Tóáíbajishchíní*) and the other Monster Slayer (*Nayee' Neizghání*). Then, while out hunting, the Twins meet Spider Woman, who teaches them special prayers, coaching them on how to survive the long, difficult, and dangerous journey to reach their father, whose identity their mother has refused to reveal to them.

Journeying to the Sun's home, Child Born of Water and Monster Slayer enlist the assistance of a worm and a water bug who take them past the many obstacles they encounter along the way. Blocking their entry to the Sun's home are a great snake, an enormous black bear, big thunder, and big wind. By chanting the prayers Changing Woman had taught them, the Twins safely gain entrance. The Sun, however, tells the Twins that he can't admit being their father, because he does not wish his wife to know that he has impregnated another woman. After some pleading, the Sun finally acquiesces, telling the Twins he would admit to being their father if they would agree to undertake a sequence of hazardous physical ordeals. After the Twins manage to survive these, the Sun, true to his word, admits that he is their father (ibid.).

The Twins are invoked in most every Navajo ritual. Their adventures establish many of the Navajo ideals of young manhood. They serve especially as models of conduct in war and can arguably be considered Navajo war gods. While the Twins slay most of the monsters they encounter, they do not kill all the potential enemies of mankind: hunger, poverty, old age, and dirt. The Navajo believe these survive because they exhibit their purpose in human existence. The exploits of the Twins, as well as those of other supernatural beings, sanctify as holy places many features of the Navajo landscape. The lava fields, for example—spectacular and eye-catching even in modern Navajoland—are the bloodstains left behind from monsters slain by the Twins (Kluckhohn and Leighton 1962).

Changing Woman, the Sun, and the Warrior Twins are the four supernatural beings who seem to play leading roles in the religious thought and lore of the Diné. In the background are First Man and First Woman and others prominent in the stories of life in the lower worlds. The Diné believe that First Man created the universe (ibid.), but another version, attributable to Christian influence, mentions a being called *be'gochidí* as the creator. Still another version of the origin story portrays Changing Woman as having much to do with the creation of the Earth Surface People. She organizes a meeting with the Holy People to decide how the wind, lightning, storms, and animals will function in harmony with each other. This gathering has become Blessing Way, a ritual, which occupies a key position in the Navajo "religious system" (ibid.). Changing Woman is also important for her role in creating the four original Navajo clans: *Kiiyaa' áanii* (Towering House clan), *Hashtł'ishnii* (Mud clan), *Todich' ii' nii* (Bitter Water clan), and *Honághánii* (One Walks around You) (Iverson 2002a).

Navajo tradition has two classes of personal beings: the earth inhabitants, living and dead (these are the ordinary human beings), and the "Holy People." The latter are not holy in the sense of possessing moral sanctity; they are "holy" as in "powerful and mysterious," of belonging to the sacred as opposed to the profane world. They travel about on sunbeams, on the rainbow, on the lightning. They have great powers to aid or harm earth people, but one should not call them gods. In general the relationship between Holy People and ordinary people is very different from the Judeo-Christian theological connection between God and man.

Medicine Men: Singers

The traditional Navajo system of religious belief was not written down, resting solely in the hands of practitioners of the religion: the Medicine Men. These specialists, more properly known as "Singers," apprentice for years as trainees to elder Singers. Confirmation as a Singer usually takes several years, after the trainee has demonstrated his skill by conducting a full ceremony on his own. Tradition requires that ceremonies be conducted in a traditional hogan. For this reason, most Navajos living in modern "ranch style" dwellings also maintain an octagonal or hexagonal hogan adjacent to the home.

Major ceremonies are "multi-night" affairs. The Blessing Way ceremony, for instance, is a two-night event, while the Night Chant will run for nine nights. Each ceremony is a grouping of songs punctuated by prayers and periods of quiet. The songs are generally renditions of Navajo legends. Sand paintings, also known as "dry paintings," are also an important part of the process. Medicine men shape depictions of important parts of relevant legends on a smooth bed of sand, using sands and finely crushed rock of myriad colors to help implore the help of supernatural beings.

The Navajo ceremonial routine is approved and communicated in a large collection of mythology consisting of two essential parts: the general origin myth, including the story of the Emergence, and the origin legends of the ceremonies themselves, which branch off the origin myth at various stages. There are a great many Navajo ceremonies, about half of which are rarely seen today or are extinct. While some ceremonies can be conducted year-round, others are seasonal. Some ceremonies are intended to benefit strictly the individual while others are conducted for the benefit of the "tribe."

No ceremony is regarded as minor, but the Emergence *(hózhóóji)* narrative is considered the most universally understood ceremony. Commonly referred to as the Blessing Way, this ceremony unites and controls all others. According to well-informed sources, "It is the backbone of Navajo religion, and all other rituals derive from it. The Blessing Way is concerned with assuring peace, harmony, and all things good in life, and every ceremonial chant, including those of the Evil Way group, includes a Blessing Way song" (Linford 2000, 20).

Kluckhohn and Leighton call attention to the fact that all Navajo "rituals" are socioeconomic events; that is, they are procedures for securing food, restoring health, and ensuring survival. They go on to state that all ceremonial practice is based on an accompanying myth, which tells how the rite started and how it should be carried out. According to Kluckhohn and Leighton, there are some contradictions among various versions of the original myth and between the origin myth and other myths. This, they suggest, is because the Navajos have not rationalized their mythology into theology. However, the origin myth still gives definite form to many Diné notions of things. It is also the final affirmation of authority for carrying out many acts, ritual and secular, in prescribed ways (Kluckhohn and Leighton).

Customs and Taboos

There are seemingly endless customs and taboos among the Navajos. They generally arise from convictions about beings and powers that are negative in character. Coyotes, bears, snakes, and some kinds of birds must never be killed because they are supernaturally potent animals (Linford). Of all the figures in Navajo life and mythology, Coyote (Masii') is the most contradictory and charming animal. Coyote is regarded as a god, as well as a trickster and evil spirit. A Navajo omen, also considered as a taboo, warns that if a coyote crosses your path, you should turn back and not continue your journey. If you keep traveling, you will be in an accident or be killed.

Bears also figure largely in an important ceremony, the Mountain Way, and several taboos are associated with this animal. For example, do not make fun of a bear or it will make you sick. Incidentally, it was also once considered taboo for a young man to look at or speak to his mother-in-law. To do so could cause blindness.

The hogan is the primary traditional home of the Navajo people and is considered sacred to those who practice the Navajo religion. The religious song "The Blessingway" describes the first hogan as built by Coyote with help from beavers to be a house for First Man, First Woman, and Talking God. Many structural taboos are associated with the hogan and its use. Should a death occur in the structure, the body is removed through a hole cut in the north wall or buried in the hogan with the entry sealed to warn others away. The spirits or ghosts that inhabit the hogan where someone has died are called *chindis* (Kluckhohn and Leighton; also see www.navajocentral.org/navajotaboos_nature.html). One does not call out the dead person's name for fear the chindi might respond to the call.

Any kind of sexual contact and even walking down the street or dancing with members of one's own or father's clan are prohibited. These are among the literally thousands of deeds that are taboo (*báhádzid*).

Taboos are multiplied during critical periods in an individual's life. A pregnant woman is supposed to observe many taboos. Her husband must share some of them for fear his wife and unborn child be injured. As with other Native American tribes, the number four is significant to the Navajo. It has significance in their creation story and in everyday life. There are four worlds, four basic colors, four sacred stones, and four sacred mountains.

Many families still have medicine men that perform ceremonies to restore *hozjo*—a sense of harmony, balance, beauty, and prosperity—the highest ideals of the Navajo. Among the most common ceremonies still practiced are the *kinaalda,* a girl's puberty rite, and the *nidaa,* or squaw dance, a four-day ceremony performed in the summer (www.vibrani.com/Kinaalda.htm, 1988).

Young Navajos are brought up to fear many forces in the supernatural world, but they are also taught ways of coping with them. In most cases, there are ways to affect a cure after the threat has struck.

The Navajo Fear of the Dead

In previous times, Navajos had a great fear of the dead and would have a trader or missionary handle the burial whenever possible. But if a white man could not do it, then one person had the task of preparing the body. People also avoided the grave, day or night. Navajos who performed this necessary task became unclean and needed a four-day purification ceremony performed by a medicine man before returning to society. As mentioned above, if a Navajo died in his or her hogan, the body remained there and all the openings of the structure were tightly sealed. The hogan was shunned. It was considered extremely unlucky to use any timber from this abandoned hogan as firewood or for cooking, and it was said that a malignant spirit would haunt those that did. Thus, the hogan and its timbers rotted away, and after many years, the whole structure returned to Mother Earth (Evans 2005).

CHAPTER 3

CIRCLES OF PERSONAL RELATIONS

A Navajo's "relatives" traditionally include more than the members of his biological and extended families. "Outfit," clan, and linked clan are important extensions of the circle of relations (Kluckhohn and Leighton 1962). The importance of relatives to the Navajo can scarcely be exaggerated. The worst that one may say to another person is, "He acts as if he didn't have any relatives" (ibid., 100).

The basic unit of economic and social cooperation is the biological family, consisting of husband, wife, and unmarried children. The line of descent is traced through the mother. In the past, Navajos practiced polygamy but seldom had more than two or three wives, and these were often sisters. The federal government maintained a constant vigil to suppress the practice. Where a husband had more than one wife, each wife with her children usually occupied a separate dwelling. If a man had married a woman who had a daughter from another marriage, he may also have married the daughter when she became mature.

Young men sometimes married women with children older than themselves. Evans describes how a young man could marry an older woman because she had a flock of sheep and perhaps a good-looking daughter in the bargain. Financially, it was an ideal situation for the man, as it provided two blanket weavers instead of one (ibid.). There have been cases where parents of the groom would barter livestock and horses for an acceptable bride. There is not much bargaining done nowadays, although the custom is sometimes observed.

Navajo Marriage Ceremony

The Navajo do not follow a particular formal procedure when getting married. Many couples obtain a license from the county clerk; others meet and decide to live together, set up housekeeping, and are considered married by their neighbors. The Navajo marriage ceremony is simple, but looked upon with as much religious commitment as an Anglo-American wedding. Guests are not formally invited, but word is sent out that a wedding, a "sing," or other type of gathering is to be given by a family on a certain day. Those who wish to attend show up. The first part of the ceremony consists of sprinkling sacred corn pollen toward the four points of the compass within the hogan; then the heads of both bride and groom are anointed with pollen. There is much singing and praying, led by the medicine man, with guests joining in. During the main part of the ceremony, the bride and groom eat cornmeal from a ceremonial wedding basket that has been blessed. The pair does not reach for the sacred meal themselves; a pinch of it is placed between their lips by the medicine man. Later everyone is given a taste of the meal (ibid.).

A Navajo woman was just as free to divorce her husband as he was to divorce her, and she did so just as often. In many cases, the wife was the breadwinner and owner of the flocks and herds. If she decided her husband was incompatible, she divorced him by simply setting his saddle and other belongings outside their hogan. If a husband initiated the divorce, he would just go away, leaving his wife the hogan, thus ending the marriage (Evans 2005).

Ownership and Inheritance

One of the complexities in understanding a different culture lies in differing concepts of private property, ownership, and inheritance. Among the Navajo, certain belongings are "communal property," in which no individual or family has vested or exclusive rights. Water resources, timber areas, and patches of salt brush (which serve livestock in lieu of mineral salt) belong to all the people, and certain conventions are observed regarding this type of property. It is improper to cut wood within a mile or so of someone else's dwelling. A person must use only his customary water hole, except when it dries up or when he is on a journey. Any attempts by

Navajos to imitate white practices with respect to wood and water rights are bitterly challenged within the Navajo community.

Kluckhohn and Leighton write that in the Navajo tradition, farm and rangeland "belongs" to a family. The dominant Navajo idea of ownership of such land has been well called "inherited use-ownership"; that is, the man who "owns" farm- or rangeland can only control it for a limited period, and no "owner" can give away or otherwise alienate land from his family. Furthermore, in this matrilineal society the real owners "are the wife and children, and the husband is hardly more than a trustee for them" (Kluckhohn and Leighton, 106).

Advent of Spanish Culture

The Navajo were a small, insignificant tribe eking out a living from basic agriculture, augmented by hunting, raiding, and gathering, when the Spaniards set foot in North America. Then as now, they made their home on the mesas and canyons of the Colorado Plateau—land desired by few others. Tribes already there—the Hopi, Zuni, Southern Paiute, and Pai—were sparsely spread out over much of northeastern Arizona and southeastern Utah. Diné herders gradually took possession of the extensive space left to them and, "transforming," as Navajo journalist Marshall Tome wrote, "the land into this place that is all of us and we are all of it" (Trimble 2000, 135). Today, Navajo homesteads dot much of the landscape, inconspicuously spread across the open country.

It is generally acknowledged that Diné territory in the late 1500s was in the vicinity of Huerfano Butte (south of Farmington, New Mexico), extending east to the Rio Grande and west to Chinle Valley. Most of it, however, was hunting and raiding range (Linford, 2000). Little was known of the Diné themselves until the later seventeenth and early eighteenth centuries. The Spanish saw almost nothing of the Navajo, and their lack of interest lasted until about 1626, when they gave them a name. Some historians suggest that this lack of interest may have been because Spaniards did not recognize the difference between Navajos and the several bands of Apaches that were frequently encountered at the Taos and Pecos trading centers. In the early 1600s, however, the Spaniards had become aware of at least one settlement of Athabaskans living north of the Jemez Pueblos, between the Chama and the San Juan rivers. They referred to them as Apaches of "Navaju."

Father Alonso Benavides wrote about the Navajos in his reports, and, in 1627, the Franciscans became adequately interested in "Apaches of Navaju," desiring to establish a mission in Santa Clara, the Tewa village on the west side of the Rio Grande below San Juan. The Franciscans, however, did not succeed in bringing any Navajos under the mission system during the 1600s (Spicer 1997).

Additionally, intelligence reports to the Spanish Viceroy in Mexico City, during the period from 1706 to 1743, provide the first glimpse of the Navajo people. According to these reports, the Diné lived in small, compact communities where agriculture was their basic economic quest. Sheep and goats, and to a lesser extent horses and cattle, had already been obtained from Spaniards by trade, raid, or indirectly through the Pueblo Indians. Woolen blankets and dresses for women were woven; men dressed in buckskin (Kluckhohn and Leighton).

While various types of livestock were fundamental to the evolution of Diné society and economic growth from the beginning, sheep mattered most. Sheep and goats, which had been brought into the Southwest by the Spanish, provided a larger and more dependable food supply. This was an essential element of Navajo population growth. Furthermore, livestock animals, wool and mohair, hides, and woolen textiles revolutionized the Navajo economy in another way. They supplied a steady source of saleable and exchangeable wealth and allowed the acquisition of metal tools and other manufactured articles. Surpluses were now commonplace, and the practice of disposing of extras by intra-tribal and inter-tribal gift and exchange quickly came to an end. With the expansion of trade, demands for a wide variety of goods from the European world grew (Iverson 2002a).

The Navajo: Raiders, Not Fighters

In the late eighteenth and early nineteenth centuries, references to the Navajo became more numerous. These references dealt mostly with warfare as both sides (Navajo and Spanish) preyed on the other regularly. The Navajo were primarily raiders, not fighters; they were no match for the military cultures of the Plains Indians—the Utes and Comanches. Navajos were only interested in taking food, sheep, horses, and other booty and waged war chiefly in reprisal. An especially ugly feature of these hostilities was the enslavement of Navajo captives. The Spanish began the practice in the seventeenth century and, although illegal, the custom thrived openly. It was justified by the spiritual benefit the victims would receive by their exposure to the Christian faith. The slave raids escalated the frequency and intensity of Navajo reprisals.

Knowledgeable sources tell us that it is difficult to say, with any degree of certainty, which European ideas reached and were accepted by the Navajos during the Spanish and ensuing Mexican period. What is evident is that major changes in the Navajo way of living occurred between 1626 and 1846. However, these changes were mainly due to the increased contacts Navajos had with Pueblos during this period. For some years after the Pueblo Rebellion of 1680, Indians from Jemez and other pueblos took refuge in an area surrounded by the Diné. In the eighteenth century, numerous Hopi fled from drought and famine to live among the Navajo, especially in Canyon de Chelly. These Pueblo Indians not only taught the Navajo their own arts, such as weaving and the making of painted pottery, but they also acted as intermediaries in passing on various European skills (Kluckhohn and Leighton).

Horses greatly increased the mobility of the Navajo, aiding tribal expansion and the scope and frequency of their contacts with other peoples. The horse provided the means whereby the Diné could reach wide-ranging areas, "swapping buckskin, buffalo hides, and baskets for Ute beadwork and elk skins in the north, for Hopi cotton mantles and ceremonial articles in the west, and for fruits and maize and turquoise along the Rio Grande" (Fergusson 1980, 68–69). This trade exposed them to other lifestyles and environments. Moreover, the character of social relationships within the tribe itself changed because of the horse. Hogans and outlying sheep camps could now be supplied with food and water more readily, and attendance at ceremonials and meetings became relatively easy for the first time.

The Spanish-Mexican period was deeply important in Navajo life. Contact with Spaniards, Mexicans, and the many different native communities transformed the Navajo from a minor to a leading tribal participant on the southwestern stage. The Diné had demonstrated that cultures are more likely to flourish through continuing contact rather than in isolation. Even contact through conflict with other groups was a plus. By the time Americans appeared, the key elements of Navajo culture had been well established (Iverson 2002a).

CHAPTER 4

SPANISH CONQUEST AND ACCULTURATION

Spanish explorer Francisco Vásquez de Coronado entered the Southwest in 1540 searching in vain for the fabled Seven Golden Cities of Cibola. When he entered present-day New Mexico, there were small groups of nomadic people in the country west of the Rio Grande Pueblo villages. Some historical sources suggest they were the ancestors of the Navajo. It is not clear how far these people extended northward and westward. According to Spicer, they were either confined to tributaries of the San Juan River (such as Gobernador and Largo Canyons), or they were dispersed over a wide area—southward as far as Acoma and westward to the Hopi villages. Spicer believes the latter seems more likely in view of the fairly wide distribution they had attained within the area by about 1700 (Spicer 1997). Other historical sources have maintained that after Coronado, none of the Spanish explorers knew anything of the Navajo until Oñate in 1598.

The area that Coronado traversed was all but forgotten for nearly forty years after his expedition. However, the Spanish never lost interest in the lands still farther to the north, which they had begun calling Nueva Mexico. Renewed interest in Nueva Mexico led to four expeditions in the last two decades of the sixteenth century, including the first colonizing expedition by Don Juan de Oñate in 1598. His assemblage consisted of 400 men, 130 wives and children, several Franciscan friars and lay brothers, and several hundred Indian servants. A large herd of livestock was driven along to provide meat, and oxen hauled the eighty-three carts carrying essentials (Fergusson 1980). Oñate selected the Tewa village of *Ohkay Owingeh*, located in a fertile valley near the confluence of the Rio Grande and the Rio Chama, for the first colony site. He established the first Spanish capital of New Mexico there on July 11, 1598, and renamed the village San Juan de los Caballeros.

The arrival of Spaniards did not cause immediate conflict for Navajos because the initial Spanish presence in the Rio Grande valley lay well to the east of Navajo country. But the Spanish were committed to expansion, and conflict was inevitable. Spaniards often suspected Navajos of plotting with Pueblo communities against them. The Navajo did form alliances from time to time with other tribes. For instance, they joined with Jemez, Isleta, Alameda, Sandia, and Felipe in an unsuccessful effort to overthrow Spanish rule in 1650.

In the years leading up to the 1680 revolt, the Spanish had grown increasingly frustrated over raiding and the refusal of many Natives to fully acknowledge the legitimacy of the Spanish Crown and the Catholic Church. Navajos certainly raided Spanish communities from time to time for livestock and other material items. Navajo raids, however, were more often sparked by the capture of Diné individuals for the Spanish slave trade. In 1675 and twice in 1678, Spanish governors authorized military campaigns against the Navajo, destroying their crops and taking them captive. The number of Diné killed by the Spanish is impossible to measure. Most Diné did not directly join the successful Pueblo rebellion of 1680 that killed several hundred Spaniards and drove the others into exile, although a few did (Iverson 2002a).

Following the return of the Spaniards under Diego de Vargas in 1692, many Pueblo people, fearing reprisals, fled into hiding. After the failed attempt of the Jamez to resist Vargas in 1696, many Jamez (along with the Tewas and Keres who had joined with them) fled west beyond the boundaries of their known world into the eastern fringes of Navajo country. They settled among the Diné. For the next thirty-five to forty years, Navajos and Pueblos lived peacefully alongside each other in the Jemez Plateau area.

Anthropologists tell us this was a period during which the Navajo were very much influenced by their neighbors. It was here that the two cultures mingled and blended, allowing the Navajo to adopt Pueblo traits and customs. This intermingling affected Navajo culture in many ways, most important of which was the development of crafts such as weaving and pottery making and house building (Spicer).

Spanish Military Expeditions Against the Navajo

Hostilities erupted between the northeastern Navajo and the Spanish again in the early decades of the eighteenth century as the Diné of the east raided the reestablished Spanish settlements on the Rio Grande. In response, the Spanish carried out almost ceaseless full-scale military assaults against the Navajo. The first decade of the eighteenth century was marked by several "punitive" Spanish strikes into Navajoland.

In 1707, the Spanish military destroyed Navajo crops, killed a large number of Diné, and took still others captive. In February of 1709, the Navajo raided the vicinity of Santa Clara pueblo. This attack brought down an all-out Spanish retaliation. By the end of 1709, seven campaigns were launched, resulting in such destruction that the Navajo were forced to petition for peace. By the 1720s, however, policy makers in Madrid put into effect a reform program that curtailed both Spanish aggression and hence the Navajo retaliatory strikes against Spanish communities and Pueblo groups who had chosen to or were being coerced into fighting the Diné. Fifty years of unprecedented calm followed (Iverson 2002a).

Indisputably, Navajos needed Spanish protection from the Ute-Comanche coalition that, from 1709 onward, began raiding Diné settlements. These raids were likely carried out in response to occasional Navajo incursions northward and onto the plains. McNitt believes it was the Navajo's growing herds of stolen livestock providing a tempting prize to a hungry enemy (McNitt 1972). Comanches at this time had not moved southward to the Llano Estacado of present-day Texas but roamed the prairie near the head of the Arkansas River. Utes ranged directly to the west in a menacing half-circle.

This conflict, which continued into the 1750s, caused the Navajo to increasingly withdraw to the higher, more unapproachable elevations of the mesas. Here, they built fortified sites and lookout points from which they could defend themselves against a surprise attack. These sites extended southward from Gobernador and Largo canyons to the Chacra and Big Bead mesas. There was also a gradual movement of Navajos westward, which led to the establishment of important settlements, such as Bear Springs, or Ojo del Oso, north of Zuni, and others in the Chuska-Tunicha Mountains.

Navajos were settling in Canyon de Chelly as well, which was becoming a significant population center. They used its streams for crop growing. Its walls provided protection, and its vantage points permitted the Diné to spy on strangers from a long distance. As time went on, the Diné became increasingly more confident of their ability to repel unwanted intruders. As Iverson (2002a) noted, "friends and relatives from more than a hundred miles away would retreat to this citadel when enemies threatened. . . . Few were the raiding parties that had the temerity even to enter the canyons and fewer still those that dared stay long enough to do any real damage."

Province of the Navajo

By 1776 the region from Zuni northward to the San Juan River, and westward from the Rio Grande Pueblos to the Hopi villages, became known to the Spanish as the Province of the Navajo. Within the province the Navajo developed a new way of life, farming to an even greater extent than they had before. In addition, they were becoming accustomed to a new form of subsistence: they had acquired large flocks of sheep and hundreds of horses, to which they expanded by periodically raiding Spanish and Pueblo settlements. This livestock helped the Navajo adjust to a more or less settled lifestyle (Spicer).

Not all the Diné went west. The people of Cañoncito, who became known as the "Enemy Navajos" (*Diné Ana'aii*), allied themselves with Spaniards and Mexicans against other groups of Diné, accepting Spanish dominance in exchange for protection. Concessions, however, did not guarantee peace for the people of Cañoncito. Continuing Spanish incursions prompted a series of attacks and counterattacks at the turn of the nineteenth century. Treaties signed in 1805 and 1819 were not favorable to the needs of the Cañoncito people. Moreover, the later treaty surrendered to the Spaniards much Navajo land in the Dinétah, over which the people of Cañoncito had no legal jurisdiction. This treaty also permitted the Spaniards to appoint a Cañoncito headman, named Joaquin, as the area's "captain general." Navajo reaction to betrayal by Joaquin and his band was immediate and unmistakable: Diné Ana'aii became outcasts, shunned by the Dinétah Navajos (Iverson 2002a).

FIRST MISSIONS ESTABLISHED IN DINÉ' BIKÉYAH

Harassment by the Ute and Comanche made the Navajo more approachable when Father Carlos Delgado and Father Jose Yrigoyen journeyed to the rancheros of Dinétah in 1744 to explore missionary work. Some Navajos were willing to have their children baptized in return for a few trinkets and promises that they would be given livestock and clothing. These baptisms provided a source of encouragement for these and other missionaries during the next four years. Fray Juan Miguel de Menchero established a mission at Cebolleta in November of 1748.

A second mission was established at Encinal (several leagues to the southwest) under the custody of Fray Juan Sanz de Lezaún sometime later. Testimony taken from an investigation following a bloodless revolt in 1750 showed the Navajos at both missions had many gripes: they were doggedly opposed to being colonized and forced to live in pueblos, they had never invited the missionaries, and they had told Father Menchero from the start that "they were grown up, and could not become Christians or stay in one place because they had been raised like deer" (McNitt 1990: 28). The missions at Cebolleta and Encinal were abandoned soon thereafter. The Franciscans pulled up stakes and did not reenter this mission field until near the end of the nineteenth century, when they returned to open a mission in 1897 dedicated to St. Michael the Archangel near Window Rock (McNitt).

In 1805, the Spanish, determined to extend the reach of their authority deep into Diné' bikéyah, undertook a series of military operations against the Navajo. Spaniards pushed persistently all the way to Canyon de Chelly, where they proceeded to attack the Diné bastion. This clash led to the famous tragedy of Massacre Cave, where, according to Navajo tradition, a great many women, children, and elders were hiding in a high alcove in the adjoining Cañon del Muerto (the Canyon of Death), almost entirely hidden from the view of the troops below (Iverson 2002a). It is said that an old woman, who had been a Spanish captive, overestimated the security of her perch and began to yell insults, in Spanish, at the distant soldiers, inadvertently revealing their hiding place. The soldiers fired round after round in the direction of the cave, killing over a hundred of the Diné, and taking another thirty-five captive (Iverson 2002a).

Spicer (1997) considers that the most salient fact in the history of the contacts of the Navajo with the Spanish was the maintenance of complete independence on the part of the Diné through the whole Spanish period. The Navajo, he points out, were never subjected to the mission system, and he stresses that the Diné at Cebolleta did not subscribe to mission discipline, even for the two years the Franciscans maintained missions there. Navajos were never reduced to concentrated settlements. Further, not even the outward forms of political controls were extended to the Navajo. Ironically, the Spanish, who eventually destroyed the cultures of many Native groups in their conquest of the Americas, provided the Navajo with some key elements of their cultural uniqueness. Peter Iverson (2002a) stresses that these very conditions relating to the tribe's culture enabled it to become a major force in the Southwest.

Navajos in the Mexican Period: 1821–1846

Mexico gained its independence from Spain in 1821, bringing to a close three centuries of Spanish rule on the North American continent and making New Mexico, and by extension Navajo country, a part of the Mexican Republic. Politically, New Mexico was a province until 1824, when its status changed to that of a territory. It became a department in 1836 and remained so until the end of Mexican rule. Throughout the early years of the young republic, almost every institution that had held the Spanish frontier together disintegrated as the country plunged into civil war and bankruptcy.

Mexico's independence from the motherland was of little significance to the Diné. Navajo adversaries, who now took orders from a president in Mexico City rather than the king of Spain, even now warred against them. Slave raiding accelerated, notwithstanding that traffic in native slaves was illegal under Mexican law, as it had been previously under royal Spanish decree. Some would imply it had been practiced for so long that it had become an ingrained custom of the territory. Mexican slave raids drew the usual Navajo reprisals in the form of occasional murders and stock thefts.

Although the United States had not yet claimed the Southwest, American influence had already started to filter through the region during the final years of Mexican governance. It came in the form of trade after the removal of restrictions, which had, until the end of the Spanish period, prohibited all non-Spanish contact. The opening of the Santa Fe Trail in the early 1820s linked New Mexico to the central United States, providing the territory with an additional outlet for commerce. Navajo blankets, considered superior to those produced on treadle looms by Hispanic weavers in the Rio Grande villages, were in bigger demand than ever before (Iverson 2002a).

Hostilities continued throughout much of the Mexican period. In 1823, Jose Antonio Vizcarra led 1,500 troops and two regiments of militia on a seventy-four-day expedition across much of the land that would later constitute the Navajo reservation. Even though historians would call it the period's most ambitious mission, it failed to have any measurable success in reducing Navajo raiding. In 1835, Blas de Hinojos led a column of men from Santa Fe to Narbona Pass, where Navajos ambushed them, killing Hinojos.

Even a force of six thousand men led by Colonel Antonio Perez during the winter of 1836–37 failed to pacify the Diné. By 1846, a general state of war existed along the entire Navajo frontier. It is believed that Navajo hostility at this critical time weighed heavily to the advantage of General Kearny's approaching army. Without doubt, the Navajo threat was a factor in Armijo's failure to make even a pretense of resisting the American invasion when the final hour of decision arrived (McNitt).

CHAPTER 5

NAVAJOS IN THE AMERICAN PERIOD: AFTER 1846

A quarter century of Mexican rule in New Mexico ended in August 1846 when General Stephan Watts Kearny and his Army of the West marched over the Santa Fe Trail into New Mexico's undefended northern frontier and took possession of the territory. Three months earlier, the United States Congress had declared war on Mexico over matters in dispute between the two nations, which included a boundary squabble between Texas and Mexico and unpaid claims to United States nationals. The war ended on February 2, 1848, when Mexico and the United States signed the Treaty of Guadalupe Hidalgo. Under its terms, the Mexican government ceded to the United States more than 1.2 million square miles of territory, including much of present-day New Mexico, Arizona, Colorado, Utah, Nevada, and California, in exchange for $15 million and other considerations.

As the United States moved to exert control of its newly acquired territory, it faced the problem of making peace with the many independent Navajo bands scattered throughout northwestern New Mexico from Rio Puerco to the Hopi villages. The Diné lived in separate communities ranging in size from ten to forty families, each located within a defined area of agricultural and grazing land. Two or more of these bands sometimes united with one another for carrying out a raid, but the relationship was at all times temporary. According to Spicer, the Diné raided primarily against Pueblo and Mexican villages and it rarely involved more than a few such groups on any occasion. Raiding, writes Spicer, had become a normal means of livelihood for Navajos, adding that the "conduct of raids had become an institutionalized skill, giving rise to 'War Chiefs' who often paid little attention to the authority of the peacetime headmen" (1997, 215).

When General Kearny set up headquarters at Santa Fe, he found the various Pueblos from Taos to Zuni, as well as the Mexican population of northwestern New Mexico, ready and willing to ally themselves with American forces for a war against the Navajo. For a time nothing was done to bring the Diné to submission. Kearny, believing that peace treaties should be explored instead, dispatched Colonel Alexander W. Doniphan of the First Regiment Missouri Mounted Volunteers into Navajo country for a parley. Doniphan succeeded in convincing some Navajos to sign a peace treaty at Bear Springs, near present Fort Wingate, on November 21, 1846. It was the first of seven treaties negotiated between the Diné and the United States between 1846 and 1868. Among the Navajo leaders who put their mark to the treaty were Zarcilla Largo and Narbona, headmen, whose influence extended over less than a few hundred unwarlike Navajos. The agreement called for lasting peace, mutual trade, and return of stolen property from both sides.

Largo used the occasion to admonish "the new men," as Narbona had labeled Americans:

> Americans! You have a strange cause of war against the Navajos. We have waged war against the New Mexicans for years. . . . We had just cause for all of this. You have lately commenced a war against the same people. You are powerful. You have great guns and many brave soldiers. You have therefore conquered them, the very thing we have been attempting to do for so many years. You now turn upon us for attempting what you have done yourselves. This is our war. We have more right to complain of you for interfering in our war, than you have to quarrel with us for continuing a war we had begun long before you got here. (Iverson 2002a, 39)

Navajos Excluded under the Term "American People"

The Bear Springs Treaty was never ratified; it collapsed five days later when two Missouri volunteers were killed in a skirmish with the Navajo south of Socorro. They became the first American soldiers considered casualties of the war with the Navajo. Largo's hope for the Americans to allow the Navajo to settle their differences with Mexico vanished as the United States tightened its grip on its newly acquired territory. If the Bear Springs Treaty ought to be remembered at all, it would be for its indifference to the position of the Navajo within the new American order. Unlike Spaniards, New Mexicans, and Pueblos, they and the Apache were excluded under the term "American People" (Iverson 2002a).

Five military expeditions were launched into Navajo country during the next three years, expeditions that were often guided by "enemy" Navajos from the region of Cebolleta. In 1847, Major Robert Walker led an expedition into the heart of Diné' bikéyah, intending to defeat the Navajo once and for all. History recorded that Walker accomplished little. In 1848, Colonel John Macrae Washington was appointed military commander and provisional governor at Santa Fe. His troops marched into Diné' bikéyah in August 1849, reinforced by "a detachment of Pueblo Indians and Mexican militia" (Linford 2000, 8). At Chinle, Washington found three Navajo leaders, including Narbona, who were willing to talk peace. During the course of the parley, several Navajos, including Narbona, lost their lives in a fracas over a stolen horse. Witnesses of these senseless deaths were embittered by what they had seen. Narbona's son-in-law, Manuelito, a highly honored war chief of communities east of the Chuska Mountains, was particularly angry. Nonetheless, the negotiations at Chinle led to a treaty signed by several leaders, including Zarcilla Largo, signer of the Bear Springs Treaty.

The United States Senate ratified this treaty on September 9, 1850. It became known as the Treaty of 1850, and like the others, it achieved little. The Navajos understood it for what it was: an arrangement negotiated in rapidity and signed under duress. The essence of the agreement appeared in one clause: "The Government of the United States will establish such military posts and agencies, and authorize such trading-houses, at such time and in such places as said Government may designate" (Iverson 2002a, 40–41). It too failed to achieve peace. Raids continued as before, especially on the part of Navajos living in the eastern part of Navajo country, often under the leadership of war chief Manuelito.

Fort Defiance Constructed in 1851

After numerous unsuccessful attempts to come to terms with the Navajo, it became apparent to the War Department and the Territory of New Mexico that the problem of Navajo raids could not be settled with treaties, and that decisive military action would have to be undertaken. This led to the setting up of Fort Defiance in 1951, a military post in the heart of Diné' bikéyah. Navajos looked on this move by the United States military as an invasion of their homeland. Even so, in the beginning they offered no direct resistance to the soldiers stationed at the fort.

The early 1850s was also a time when Navajos moved to make peace with the American government under a fair set of conditions, including working with government representatives who they could trust or, at the very least, with whom they could communicate. A conscientious Indian agent could make a difference, but he faced an almost impossible assignment and was often caught among competing interests for native lands. Frequently, he had to contend with opposing factions within the tribe itself. The rapid turnover of personnel and the isolation of the job often caused problems.

Bungling and insensitive agents were far more numerous than those who could be considered committed and sensitive to the cause. Henry Linn Dodge was one such Indian agent who tried to make a difference. He was appointed to Sheep Spring, northeast of Fort Defiance, in June of 1853, where he set about persuading the Diné leaders to keep the peace. Dodge's personal efforts with Navajo leaders, and particularly with headman Zarcilla Largo, brought about a period of relative peace, but in 1856 Dodge was kidnapped and killed by Apaches on Haashk'aan Silá Mesa south of Zuni. Some believe that had Dodge lived, he might very well have made a considerable difference at this juncture of Navajo history. Without Dodge, an already tense situation became all the more volatile (Iverson 2002a).

Fort Defiance Incident Sparks Major Quarrel

In 1858, Fort Defiance witnessed the enactment of a drama that has often been described as "the murderous attack on Major Brooks' personal servant, a black slave named Jim" (McNitt, 325). His assailant was a Navajo who shot an arrow through Jim's back and then galloped off on horseback from the post. Zarcillos Largos, the headman who showed up at the post in answer to Brooks's call, was unpleasantly cool when the major demanded that the killer surrender at once.

According to one version of what happened, the old warrior quietly told Brooks that he was on his way to Zuni and would see to it upon his return. When the major expressed impatience at the delay, Largos told Brooks that he ought not be in such a hurry, for it had been six weeks since the major had killed headman Manuelito's cattle and horses, and he was still waiting to get reparation from the army. Brooks replied snappishly that he had no intention of making reparation to Manuelito, and, further, if the killer was not brought in, widespread war would be made against the Navajo people.

Brooks then told Largos that he had twenty days more to deliver up his slave's murderer; if in twenty days the man had not been brought in, war would begin. The Diné did not like Brooks, and they had no intention of surrendering one of their own to him. Instead, they killed a Mexican captive, brought him to the fort, and announced that they had apprehended the guilty party and were surrendering him in the interests of justice.

This deception infuriated the fort commander, Colonel Miles, who on that same afternoon directed the posting of Order No. 4, which read:

> Since the arrival of the commanding officer at this post (2nd inst.) sufficient time has been given to the Navajo tribe of Indians, to seek, secure, and deliver up, the murderer of Maj. Brooks' Negro: to atone for the insult to our flag, and the many outrages committed upon our citizens. They have failed to do so. Our duty remains to chastise them into obedience to our laws—after tomorrow morning war is proclaimed against them. (McNitt, 336)

And so the war began with Brooks threatening that it would continue until the Diné were willing to give up the actual murderer of his slave. Some seven or eight battles took place over the course of the four-month conflict, which ended with a treaty negotiated between the United States and fifteen Diné leaders at Fort Defiance at Christmas of 1858. One aspect of the treaty, which was perhaps the most insultingly bitter pill, came when the United States government insisted that the "enemy Navajos" from the Canoncito area had to be included as part of the Navajo Nation. Canoncito Navajos had continued to ally themselves with the Americans and had always been an obstacle in the way of Diné interests.

While the occupation of the Navajo territory at Fort Defiance caused resentment from the start, the presence of troops there fostered hatred. Now the Diné wanted to expel the army from their midst. Headmen like Herrero, who had worked for a peaceful solution, and others like Manuelito and Barboncito, who had never tried for anything but a continuance of the old way, joined forces for an attack on Fort Defiance itself.

The Navajo Attack on Fort Defiance

The Diné nearly succeeded in realizing their objective of ousting the army from Fort Defiance. On the morning of April 30, 1860, Manuelito of the Tohatchi area and Barboncito of the Canyon de Chelly area, with more than one thousand Navajo warriors, launched a carefully prepared plan of attack on the fort. The superior firepower, however, of the beleaguered three companies of the Third Infantry prevented the Diné from achieving an extraordinary victory. The army's artillery was too powerful against Navajo bows and arrows, and after a two-hour battle the Diné were in retreat. One observer in Santa Fe called it "the most daring attack by the Indians that has taken place since I was in the Army, and indicates a spirit that will become dangerous if not checked" (Iverson 2002a, 47).

The attempts to drive Americans out of Navajo territory had failed, but the raids continued, extending to the east as far as Santa Fe and to the south as far as Zuni. The intensity of the raids led New Mexicans to organize for retaliation; in a short time they took one hundred Navajo prisoners, mostly women and children, who were, in Spicer's words, "disposed of according to custom as slaves" (1997, 217).

Government Authorizes Exile for the Navajo

Although the Navajo were routed at Fort Defiance, it began to appear to them that the Americans were weakening in their resolve. In 1861, the fort, along with other forts in New Mexico, was abandoned as troops were withdrawn for the Civil War effort. The two-year absence of the military that followed had the Navajos believing they had succeeded in ousting the Americans. However, as Union troops regained control of the Rio Grande valley from the Confederates, a determined effort was launched to wipe out, by any means, the Navajo threat in the territory.

General Edward R. Canby, who was then the military commander of New Mexico, was resolute in ending Navajo rebelliousness. He formulated a policy for forcible separation of the Diné from other New Mexicans. He believed that removing them from their homeland and isolating them on reservations would make it a lot easier for the federal government to bring an end to their resistance. For the new Navajo home he chose the Mescalero concentration camp of Fort Sumner at Bosque Redondo, barren salt flats and wastelands on the Pecos. "In concert with isolating Native peoples, federal officials thought that it was high time to remake them in the American image" (Iverson 2002, 48).

The assignment of implementing the policy of forcing the Diné into exile went to Canby's successor, Brevet Brigadier General James H. Carleton. He in turn selected Colonel Christopher (Kit) Carson, mountain-man-turned-soldier, to carry out the order. Carlton instructed Carson to round up all Navajos, peacefully if possible, and move them to Bosque Redondo. Carson believed war with the Navajo was unnecessary, but he nonetheless undertook his orders with brutal severity. When the Navajo refused to move, Carson moved swiftly, carving a path of destruction and death. Thousands of Navajos were starving or freezing to death; countless others had died. Navajos were marched to Fort Wingate and then were forced on their infamous Long Walk (Iverson 2002a).

CHAPTER 6

THE ROUNDUP, LONG WALK, AND INCARCERATION AT BOSQUE REDONDO

On the deadline date of July 20, 1863, Colonel Kit Carson marched into the heart of Navajo country with a regiment of seven hundred New Mexico volunteers and began a methodical campaign of destroying all Diné means of livelihood. His soldiers scorched cornfields, contaminated water wells, and slaughtered livestock by the thousands. Although there were no major battles, Carson's military operation left the Navajo economy in ruins. Navajos began to spread out to find food—some to southern New Mexico and southern Arizona, some westward to Navajo Mountain, some to join the Apaches in White Mountain, and many women went to Jemez Pueblo. By the end of 1863, some were even showing up at Fort Defiance to surrender. The mountain-man-turned-soldier persisted in his pursuit and, early in 1864, led his troops into Canyon de Chelly, where they encountered a large number of Navajos. Marching through the canyon, he renewed his campaign to destroy all Diné means of livelihood. Exhausted, famished, and faced with annihilation, the Navajos reluctantly gave up.

After laying waste to Canyon de Chelly, an estimated eight thousand Navajos were rounded up by Carson's men and herded like cattle on the infamous three-hundred-mile walk from Canyon de Chelly to Bosque Redondo on the Pecos River (Fergusson 1980). They gave themselves up at Fort Canby and Old Fort Wingate, where they were organized into large parties for the march to their destination. The first party departed Fort Sumner on March 6, 1864. It consisted of 2,400 Dine, 30 wagons, 400 horses, and 3,000 sheep and goats. Only children and cripples rode in the wagons. By the end of April, 3,500 more Diné, in three separate parties, had made the same long march (Kluckhohn and Leighton, 1962).

Their treatment was harsh along the way. No one knows how many Diné left their homeland bound for the Bosque, but it is generally accepted that many died or disappeared along the way. If individuals complained, were too tired or sick to walk, or if they stopped to help someone else, they were shot and left for dead. One eyewitness recounts: "Two women were near the time of the births of their babies and they had a hard time keeping up with the rest. . . . Some army men pulled them behind a huge rock, and we screamed out loud when we heard the gunshots. The women didn't make a sound, but we cried out loud for them and their babies . . ." (Iverson 2002a, 55).

By no means did all Navajos surrender to Carson's men. Several thousand managed to stay behind, taking sanctuary in isolated strongholds near Black Mesa, the Grand Canyon, Navajo Mountain, and southern Utah. Life was severe, for they had to take cover, dwell in places barely accessible, and keep a constant vigil against white intruders. Those Diné who avoided capture played a vital role in the revitalization of the Navajo economy following the treaty of 1868. Although their lives had been disrupted, they had not been completely fragmented. Consequently, they were able to play a useful role in the land dispute that ensued between the Diné and the Hopi.

Those who endured the march were crowded onto the small reservation at Bosque Redondo, joining four hundred Mescalero Apaches already there. They were divided into twelve units, some six hundred to a unit, each with a headman. The twelve leaders of the new tribal divisions were to constitute a "chief's council" for dealing with the army officer in charge. General Carleton asked Archbishop Lamy to send over some padres to open a school. Soldiers were assigned to show the Diné how to build adobe houses and to help them get started raising crops on the farmland already prepared for that purpose.

The Human Suffering

History knows no more tragic displaced persons than the Navajo at Bosque Redondo. The place was abysmal: a flat, barren, and nearly treeless countryside, an empty landscape with no mountains around. Grubs gobbled acres of corn, drought caused three crop failures in succession, and disease and confinement reduced their numbers. A smallpox epidemic struck in 1865, and 2,321 of their number were dead within a few months. Deceitful storekeepers were selling them liquor and firearms and supplying them with rancid meat. Lastly, they had to endure the continuing attacks by Comanches and others who delighted in the Diné having nowhere to hide and no way to retaliate. Erna Fergusson wrote of their wretchedness:

> At the *Bosque Redondo*, Round Wood, the Navajos knew such exile as only the Hebrew poet could do justice to. Far from their deserts of colored rock, their rich valleys, piny hills, and snow peaks where the gods dwell, the People suffered every ill. They were hungry because they could not hunt, and the food they were issued was often bad and always insufficient. When they tried to farm they were plagued by drought and flood. The alkali water made them sick, and they were smitten with smallpox. They were cold because they had no sheep to give wool for blankets. Their old people died of sorrow and their children of undernourishment. They were filled with dread because of a tradition that the *Diné* (People) would perish if they went east of the Rio Grande. (Fergusson, 213)

For four years Navajos were crammed together in a solitary, closely supervised camp. Their way of life was completely altered, from that of roving herders to sedentary prisoners. The government called their new home a reservation, but to the defeated and exiled Navajos, Bosque Redondo was a wretched prison camp (Bial 2003). As time went by, their care at Fort Sumner deteriorated. The tribe made one dash for freedom but was rounded up by Apache scouts (a newly formed arm of the military) and was returned to the reservation. General Carleton's scheme of rounding up and imprisoning the Navajo caused little public outcry. As military commander of New Mexico, he declared martial law from 1861 to 1864, which prevented much condemnation of his policies. However, there were some who criticized Carleton's actions. Among them were Dr.

Michael Steck, commissioner of Indian affairs in New Mexico, and Judge Joseph Knapp, a judge of the New Mexico territorial Supreme Court. Both men were eventually forced to resign their positions because of their opposition to Carleton. Judge Knapp wrote to President Lincoln in 1864 denouncing Carleton for imprisoning the Navajo without trial or conviction, seizing their property without compensation, and setting up courts to try citizens for offences for which there were no laws. In an open letter to Carleton published in February 1865, by the *Santa Fe New Mexican*, the judge wrote that the general had never wanted peace with the Navajo and in a subsequent letter published in the same newspaper Knapp further asserted that Carleton had no authority to make war against the Navajo. He reasoned that individual Navajo people were personally liable for illegal acts, but that Carleton could not punish the Navajo people as a whole (Bial).

In 1867, quarrels among Navajos and soldiers resulted in the death of five soldiers. As the situation worsened, it became evident to the War Department that General Carleton's relocation program was a disaster. After an investigation by General Sherman, Carleton was removed as commander of the Department of New Mexico.

Navajos Allowed to Return to Their Homeland

In January of 1867, control over the Navajo was taken from the army and turned over to the Indian Service in the Department of the Interior. This was followed by the decision to allow Navajos to go back to a defined portion of their territory and to begin life again in their homeland (Linford 2000).

A treaty was drawn up and signed on June 1, 1868, by all the leaders who agreed to remain within a reservation—extending from Fort Defiance to a point on the San Juan River (at the mouth of Chaco Canyon) and from a point near Chinle to a line running north and south through about Fruitland. This was scarcely one-fourth of the territory through which the Navajo had formerly ranged. They also agreed to send their children to school, and the government agreed to furnish a teacher and schoolhouse for every thirty children. Individual land allotments, of as much as 160 acres, would be given to those asking for them. It had been agreed in the treaty that the government would, if necessary, issue rations while the Navajo were getting back on their feet. To enable them to restart their livelihoods, the government distributed 14,000 sheep and 1,000 goats to the 9,500 who showed up at the distribution center. Navajos were on the road to a new livelihood as independent herdsmen, and from it the blueprint of modern Navajo life emerged (Spicer 1997).

For native peoples, treaties were never voluntary. They never involved gain, but they always seemed to involve acquiescence and giving away land. Yet the signing of the Navajo Treaty on June 1, 1868, rather than tearing the heart out of the Diné, defined the heart of a homeland. In a ceremony held 131 years later at Northern Arizona University campus in Flagstaff on June 1, 1999, Speaker of the Navajo nation Edward T. Begay told the gathering: "What our leaders were able to accomplish at Hwéeldi was to give us a land, a home within the four sacred mountains, and a purpose as a people to live with our new partner, the United States, as a nation and a semi-independent entity within these borders" (Iverson 2002a, 37).

CHAPTER 7

EVOLUTION OF THE NAVAJO RESERVATION

The Diné returned to what formerly was their ancient land following their release from Bosque Redondo in late 1868. The years in exile left frightening impressions in their memories that would take years to remove; for now they were back on their old familiar mesas and canyons. They had agreed to live at peace with the United States. In return they were given a small part of their former rangeland and some livestock and corn to get started. They were promised schools; heads of families were permitted to homestead 160-acre tracts of their reservation. Few accepted, as individual ownership of land was an unfamiliar concept to Navajos. The treaty established a guardian and ward relationship, which gave the federal government a "paternalistic" role in deciding what was best for the Diné. Moreover, Diné' bikéyah was now federal land placed in trust under the terms of the treaty. On the positive side, their supervisor was a Bureau of Indian Affairs civilian instead of the military (Fergusson 1980).

The immediate period following the return of the Navajo to their traditional homeland was filled with hardship and misery, yet the Diné were determined to regain and resettle their lands and recover their culture and traditions. Essentially, they had to start all over and rebuild their economic base. Returned to Diné' bikéyah too late in 1868 to plant crops, and without any livestock, they had to rely entirely on government rations to carry them through the first winter. Rations were distributed first at Fort Wingate, and then at Fort Defiance. Some 2,500 Diné settled at Fort

Defiance; the others scattered throughout the newly created reservation, looking for their old homes.

Others chose not to go to Fort Defiance: about four hundred, including one of the treaty signers, Delgadito, headed for their home country to the north. They joined some of the "enemy Navajos" in the Cañoncito Navajo community. Cañoncito gained reservation status in 1949 after a series of land exchanges and purchases provided a contiguous unit. Today the community is known as Tóhajiileehí ("Where the Water Is Drawn up Out"). Another detached community was formed at Alamo (or T'iistsoh, "Big Cottonwood Tree"), west of Socorro. The Alamo Navajo community gained reservation status in 1946 when additional lands were purchased to consolidate the reservation. A third similar community was established at Ramah (or Tł'ohchiní, "Wild Onions") south and east of Gallup, near Zuni. Although removed from the main reservation, these three areas continued as Navajo communities and take part in Navajo tribal government (Iverson 2002a).

In the spring of 1869, the government distributed 14,000 sheep and 1,000 goats to the 9,500 Navajos who showed up for the distribution. Three years later, the government meted out another 10,000 sheep. With their livestock in hand, Navajos began spreading out beyond the limits of the newly surveyed reservation. Many had lived outside those boundaries before; returning to where they had previously lived was in violation of the treaty provisions. Others found the new limitations had nothing to do with good forage and followed their sheep and goats out into areas where there was feed. Crop failures and irregular rations during the first years on occasion tempted young Navajos into returning to the old ways of raiding (Spicer 1997).

It soon became apparent to the government that the Navajo were occupying some 6 million acres outside the reservation, nearly twice the amount designated by the 1868 treaty (ibid.). The treaty land award simply was not sufficient to support the growing Navajo population and the increasing herds of livestock. Furthermore, the overflow of Diné beyond reservation borders was the source of clashes with English-speaking "Anglos" who had settled on the borderlands of Navajo country. This led to a persistent struggle for land between the Navajo and the Anglo-American homesteaders who had streamed into northern New Mexico and Arizona (ibid.). Disputes erupted over where the Diné should live, where they should graze their livestock, and where they should hunt.

Anglos frequently accused Navajos of theft and trespass, and some hotheads took the law into their own hands in their efforts to impose their manner of "justice."

Historian Robert McPherson describes a number of violent incidents that occurred in the northern Navajo frontier in the closing years of the nineteenth century. Some Anglos who settled in the area were very uncivilized people who, according to McPherson, derived their greatest pleasure from making everyone around them miserable (Iverson 2002a). Drought and severe winters also plagued the Navajo and their stock, while at the same time the government forced their children to leave their homes and attend boarding schools in hopes of eradicating Navajo culture.

True to their nature, the Diné managed to thrive and preserve a sense of self-confidence. Steadily, and with resolve, they reestablished stable conditions, which led to a period of relative prosperity and steady growth of population. Fergusson (1980) describes how, in the ten years after the treaty of 1868, the Navajo population had reached thirteen thousand, and from then on there was a rapid rise. Livestock increased accordingly, and the Diné were beginning to achieve prosperity from trading in blankets and wool.

The grazing land was good with acres of tall grasses. Windmills, dams, and tanks had increased the water supply so that most families could raise vegetables and fruit. What else they needed, they got from the trader. There was one agent, one doctor, one teacher, and a few others who composed the government's oversight team. But, as Fergusson writes, time was not standing still, and the Diné went on multiplying. As they multiplied, so did the need for additional livestock to provide food and sustain their economy.

As the number of livestock increased, forage on poorer lands declined as the grass was consumed faster than it could renew itself. This led to intensive efforts by the government to deal with the problem. Government officials began exploring the possibility of a long-term approach for feeding and controlling the growing Navajo population. As early as the 1880s, the government had adopted two approaches to increasing the productivity of Navajo land. One was improving sheep raising and exploring new markets for wool and blankets; the other approach aimed at expanding the agriculture land.

The lands around Fort Defiance, Chinle, Tuba City, and Shiprock were improved with government funds. This increased, somewhat, the amount of irrigated farmland on the reservation (Spicer). Yet another approach called for the removal of Indians from reservation status and placing them into mainstream American society. The Dawes Act of 1887 was designed to do that in other parts of the United States. For the Navajo, however, the reservation not only stayed intact, but it expanded, and relatively few Diné took up the individual allotments of land offered by the government.

At the same time their reservation was being expanded, the Diné were being forced to surrender much of their best winter rangeland and many of their finest watering places to the advancing railroad. In 1876, the routes for the Atlantic and Pacific Railroad (later the Santa Fe) were pushed through the southeastern part of the reservation. Sections of Navajo lands were given up to the railroad and opened up for Anglo settlement. These sections contained some of their premium winter range.

The areas later added as a compensatory measure were unquestionably inferior. Manuelito, the "sub-chief" over the eastern part of the reservation, went to Washington to protest. He was politely informed that the newly added areas would be made available for homesteading to Navajos, as well as to Anglos, and that some new areas north of the San Juan River would be added to the reservation to compensate for the lands surrendered to the railroads (ibid.).

It was a time when corporations, headquartered entirely outside the west, dominated the economies of Arizona and New Mexico. These interests, in an attempt to exploit the natural resources of the area, were pushing for a reassessment of land policy within the Indian Office. (The Bureau of Indian Affairs was called the "Indian Office" from 1832 to 1947. The names Indian Office and Bureau of Indian Affairs appear to have been used interchangeably throughout much of the nineteenth and into the early twentieth century.) They claimed that the government had made a rather substantial error in allowing so many acres to be reserved for exclusive use by the Diné. Geological surveys were revealing that the Navajo land might yield significant financial returns from tapping its mineral resources. Discovery of oil near Mexican Hat, Utah, in 1879, attracted a great deal of outside commercial interest.

An 1891 federal law specifically permitted Indian communities to lease land for mineral exploration and development. At the beginning of the 1900s, the Navajo had no tribal council or business committee authorized to act on their behalf. Consequently, in their initial dealings with those outside interests, the Diné were confronted with an assortment of problems. They primarily had a language problem: lease contracts were embellished with endless, complex clauses that were difficult to comprehend. Few Diné knew English well enough to be able to decipher the meaning behind some of the intricate phrases. Second, there was the matter of individual, family, and community rights versus the potential for economic yield benefiting the tribe as a whole. A third issue centered on authorizing leases. Who had the authority to sign or refuse to sign such agreements? Should such a group represent all of the Navajo Nation as a whole or primarily or exclusively the immediate region of the proposed activity (Iverson 2002a)?

Growth and Expansion

The Navajo reservation has undergone many changes to its overall size in its 140-year history. The treaty of 1868, establishing the original reservation, set aside about 3.5 million acres for Diné use. This original reservation, half in Arizona and half in New Mexico, was enlarged from time to time, and now it includes about 15 million acres, reaching north to the San Juan River and west to the Colorado River. In the decades following the 1868 treaty, lands were added by presidential executive order. Congress had passed a law in 1871 that ended formal treaty making. The president, however, could still create reservations as well as add land to, or delete land from, an existing reservation, without congressional approval.

In 1878, General Sherman recommended to President Rutherford B. Hayes that the reservation's western boundary be moved twenty miles further west. Hayes did so on October 28, 1878; by executive order, he enlarged the reservation by nearly 1 million acres, moving the boundary westward to Glen Canyon, consistent with Sherman's proposal. Two more strips, almost equal in extent to the original reservation, were added in 1880 along the reservation's southern and eastern boundaries. In 1884, still more land was added—the Paiute strip, which carried the reservation north of Hopi country as far as the Colorado River, and an additional area that extended the northern boundary to the San Juan River.

President Chester A. Arthur signed an executive order in 1882 that created a joint-occupation reservation for both Hopis and western Navajos in present-day Arizona. It included the lands between 110° longitude on the east and 111° longitude on the west, and from 35° 30′ latitude on the south to 36° 30′ on the north (Brugge 1994). This area encompassed about 2.5 million acres. The reservation was set aside for the use of the Hopis (or Moquis, as they were often called at the time) and for other Indians that might be settled there at the discretion of the secretary of the interior. This order was intended more to protect the Hopis from encroachments by Anglos than to resolve rival land claims by the Hopis and the Navajos, and it did little to quell the constant complaining lodged by one tribe against the other or the struggle for land rights within the area (Iverson 2002a).

In 1962, a decision by a United States district court (*Healing v. Jones*) parceled the 1882 executive order reservation into two units: the Exclusive Hopi Reservation and the Navajo-Hopi Joint-Use Area, the latter primarily occupied by Navajo. This court action did not settle the debate over use rights within the joint-use area. Consequently, the United States Congress in 1974 enacted a law that led to the even division of the joint-use area into exclusive Navajo and Hopi areas. To compensate Navajos for having been displaced from land awarded to the Hopi, the tribe was permitted to purchase land along the external boundary of the Navajo reservation (Goodman 1971).

During the three decades following 1900, the Navajo population continued to increase and had reached forty thousand by 1930. The government continued to annex more land to the reservation to meet the needs of the expanding population. Through 1908, additions were made on the west and south, but in 1911, portions of land on the southeast were returned to the public domain (Spicer). Actions by Congress in 1933 and 1934 extended the exterior bounds of the Arizona portion of the reservation. In 1958, the Navajos exchanged an area near Page, in the vicinity of Lake Powell, for land in the Aneth area of Utah. Increasing the size of the reservation by executive order reduced the land conflict to some extent, but at the same time, the Anglo population was steadily increasing and Navajos continued to experience unwelcome pressures (Spicer).

"Coercive Assimilation" through Education

The 1868 treaty document *Naaltsoos Sání*, which returned 3.5 million acres of previous Navajo land to the Diné, also promised to provide an education for Native children. It pledged that for every thirty Navajo children between the ages of six and sixteen, a schoolhouse and teacher skilled to teach the elementary branches of an English education would be furnished (Article VI, from McCarty 2002).

In 1882, the Indian Bureau opened a boarding school at Fort Defiance. This school was fashioned on the pioneering efforts of General Richard Henry Pratt, who had founded the Carlisle Indian School in Pennsylvania in 1878.

Pratt believed that the role of education was to wean the Indian from his native traditions and replace them with the "civilizing" influences of white American culture. He strongly favored the total assimilation of the American Indian into the dominant culture, and he felt that the best and most efficient way to do this was to take Indian children away from their families and culture and immerse them in the language and culture of middle-class American society (Pratt 1987).

Another school was set up at Grand Junction in 1890. Between 1900 and 1913, additional schools were built at Tohatchi, Tuba City, Shiprock, Leupp, Chinle, Crownpoint, and Toadlena. Parental apprehension about the schools curtailed enrollment in the early years. The uncertainty regarding who would teach at such schools was another cause of anxiety: inadequate pay, poor housing, isolation, and lack of support discouraged most potential teachers. Schools turned out to be notorious for their English-only curriculum, strict discipline, inadequate food, overcrowding, and a manual labor system that required students to work half-days in the kitchens, boiler rooms, and fields. This allowed the government to operate the schools on a budget of eleven cents per pupil per day (McCarty). Disciplinary methods included ankle chains and solitary confinement. Fergusson (1980) gives the following version:

> [The schools] were designed to make Indians into whites, without considering the Indians' capabilities or needs. Children were taken, by force if necessary, to huge boarding schools, put through the standard courses, and required to do the menial work of the place. They were forbidden to speak their own languages, and religious toleration was interpreted to mean free election of any Christian faith. (218–219)

Many children fled the schools on foot, some perishing from exposure on the long trek home. Others succumbed to the brutality of the *siláo*, or police, sent to round them up and return them to school (McCarty). Navajos soon discovered that their children, after many years in boarding school, emerged ill-equipped to live either in the white man's world or among their own people. In 1887, the Indian Bureau passed a compulsory school regulation in an effort to counteract widespread absenteeism and general Indian indifference to schools. This brought about violence in several places in the western part of the reservation and at Round Rock north of Fort Defiance, where the superintendent was taken hostage when he attempted to enforce attendance (Spicer).

In an effort to boost school enrollment and impress some of the Diné leaders with the realities of contemporary American life, the Indian agent in charge persuaded some Navajo leaders to attend the 1893 Columbian Exposition in Chicago. What they saw greatly impressed them: they were overwhelmed at the size of the city and awestruck by the overall pace of contemporary industrial life. One Diné compared white people to ants. "They were," he said, "industrious, working all the time; they are thick, coming and going all the time." He was fascinated at how Americans went about discarding the old and embracing the new. It was, he said, like going from an old Mexican cart "to a Studebaker wagon" (Iverson 2002a, 93).

The expansion of Indian Bureau schooling coincided with the setting up of schools by missionary groups. Franciscan missionaries established the first Catholic school at St. Michael's in 1902. In their initial meeting with Diné headmen, the friars came face-to-face with Navajo antagonism toward having their children educated, particularly by white people. One prominent headman told the friars that, judging from his own observations, schooling harmed Navajo children more than it helped them. He called it a waste of time and effort, inasmuch as it did not equip the children for later life because it failed to prepare them for conditions they had to face when they returned to the reservation.

He went on to say that in the schools the children were taught an entirely different mode of living. They returned to their homes and soon became dissatisfied and unhappy at having to forego the comforts and conveniences to which they had grown accustomed during their school days. Before long, they were thoroughly disgusted with their lot. After only a few months in their home environment, one could scarcely recognize that they had ever seen the inside of a school building; if there was a change or difference in them at all, it was noticeable only in the fact that they were "usually more deceitful, more worthless, and less honest than those who had never gone to school" (Trockur 1998: 13). Despite their misgivings, St. Michael's was built, and others followed.

Presbyterians began operating a school in the area in 1904. Both of these schools steadily developed into schools giving both elementary and secondary education. From this time on, various religious groups entered the reservation, setting up missions, hospitals, or schools in different areas. By 1955, in addition to Catholic missions, seventeen different Christian sects were supporting missionary work among the Navajo. Some maintained schools and various social services; others engaged merely in evangelical work (Spicer).

Indian education continued to be provided by the Indian Bureau and by mission schools until the 1940s. From then on, the Bureau increasingly withdrew from this function, although it continued to operate schools in remote areas of the reservation (Luey and Stowe 1987). In 1947, the Navajo Tribal Council passed a compulsory school attendance law, similar to the measure that had previously encountered stanch resistance when enforced by the Bureau. School attendance steadily increased. However, the Indian Bureau did not provide enough schools for all Navajo children of school age until 1954, and then only with participation by the New Mexico and Arizona school districts (ibid.).

The 1960s experienced a national movement toward recognition and appreciation of ethnic groups in the United States. There was acknowledgment that such groups had been denied their constitutional rights and had been subjected to much unequal treatment, especially in the Anglo-centric schooling that had been provided by the federal government. This surfaced in the 1969 report of the United States Senate's Special Subcommittee on Indian Education. The report thoroughly censured the federal government's Indian education policy, describing it as "coercive assimilation" on the part of the dominant society. The report included a recommendation that Indian culture, history, and language be included as part of the school curriculum and that Indian parents become much more involved in the education of their children.

The subcommittee's recommendations for change resulted in legislation authorizing bilingual education and an English-as-a-second-language program for "Limited English Proficient" students. The 1960s brought confidence and a sense of cultural stance for the Navajos. Deborah House (2002) writes that when the Navajo Tribal Council Advisory Committee passed a resolution in 1969, officially calling for use of the term "Navajo Nation," Diné were claiming sovereignty. These were also the years when Navajos and other Native Americans were moving in the direction of self-sufficiency in education. As House points out, their leaders saw the need for establishing fundamental educational goals and distinguishing means for realizing them.

The Trading Post

The trading post began as an institution on the Navajo reservation soon after the return of the Diné from Bosque Redondo in 1868. It reached the zenith of its activity between 1900 and the 1930s, and steadily declined thereafter. As the name implies, trading post transactions, more often than not, involved barter rather than money. Normally established and owned by a non–Native American, the trading post was usually the only place of business for miles around. For all intents and purposes, it was a center for carrying on business transactions, but as historians point out, the trading post was also a facilitator of change for the Navajo, a people who frequently accepted change as a means of enriching their lives without surrendering cultural integrity (McPherson 2001).

Home industries were the heart of the Diné economy—the most famous being rugs, woven blankets, pelts, and jewelry. As early as 1883, traders bought more than 1.3 million pounds of Navajo wool and conceivably 300,000 sheep pelts. The advent of the trading post brought with it the potential for economic improvement, particularly for individual Navajos. Traders assumed a certain influence within the Diné tribal structure, pushing for a better quality of wool or encouraging artists to press forward from practical to artistic creations. Their decisions about the value of one's weaving or one's wool made a difference in Diné financial well-being (ibid.).

Trading posts served the same social functions as the earlier general store did in rural white society. The entire experience of reservation trading was laced with cultural meaning. When the customer entered the store, a lingering process was set in motion. He looked around; then sat down. Personal relations or the purpose of his business was not rushed. Eventually the customer approached the counter and started a light conversation with the owner, generally about upcoming social events (ibid.). The customer also took the time to exchange greetings with other customers and chat about news and gossip.

The trading post was a gathering place where friends and relatives would meet and where agents and traders could observe Diné expressions of opinion or grievances. One such observation, submitted by Agent Frank T. Bennett in 1869, compared the Diné with the Irish:

> They are more like the Irish than any people I can compare them with. Brave, hardy, industrious, restless, quick-witted, ready for either mischief, play, or hard work, they are people that can be guided into becoming the most useful of citizens, or, if neglected, the most troublesome of outlaws. . . . They are equally given to vices of stealing, gambling, and licentiousness when not employed, and to the virtues of the most indefatigable perseverance in farming, stock-raising, trading with their neighbors, the Moqui Pueblos, and weaving garments, when at work. (Iverson 2002a, 77)

Charles Crary opened and operated the first trading post about 1872, and thereafter the network of traders quickly expanded. Many of the traders were Mormons, members of the Church of Jesus Christ of Latter-day Saints who had migrated into Navajo country from the surrounding areas. They became multigenerational, ongoing family businesses that kept pace with the expanding marketplace. There were also non-Mormons who influenced, in a crucial way, the development and progress of Navajo society and economic well-being. Peter Iverson ranks the most important of these as Thomas Keam, Juan Lorenzo Hubbell, the Wetherills, and the Babbitt brothers. According to Iverson (2002a), the name Hubbell will always be associated with the community of Ganado (*Lók' aahnteel*, "Wide Reeds"), the base of the Hubbell empire.

Between 1900 and 1930, there emerged two types of trading posts servicing Navajoland. The first belonged to licensed traders approved by the Bureau of Indian Affairs—the store and inventory belonged to the trader while the land surrounding it belonged to the Navajos. Federal regulations provided rules for screening trader applicants, approving the opening of new posts, and regulating certain sale items. To be involved in the business, the trader "had to be of good moral standing, honest in his dealings, fair in establishing prices, concerned about his customers, and opposed to the sale and use of alcohol by the Indians" (McPherson, 66).

The second type of trading post avoided many government regulations by locating off the reservation on its adjacent borders. In the north, these trading facilities were found on the San Juan River to the western boundary and settlements along the Colorado and Little Colorado rivers. Before the 1890s, these posts flourished and were a never-ending source of aggravation to the Indian agents.

Most traders and their wives spoke Navajo; only a few depended on interpreters. From this commerce, a linguistic variation evolved called "trader Navajo," which emphasized the economic side of post life but missed the subtleties of more sophisticated speech. Regardless of linguistic ability, the universal sign of recognition was the handshake, "a warm slight touch rather than a vigorous, tooth-jarring pump" (ibid., 71). Navajos held the hand briefly and did not grip it tightly, since to do so boasted of one's physical strength and belittled the recipient.

In the early years of the twentieth century, incentives were introduced to promote Anglo business practices among Navajos and to instill in them the significance of commercial competition. The Shiprock Agency, founded in 1903 by William T. Shelton, sponsored its first regional fair at which trading posts promoted native crafts and traditional artifacts from their respective areas. This helped foster regional pride and competition while exposing Navajo crafts to the outside world. Until the 1930s, however, the Diné persistently continued to selectively choose those things that fit into traditional, cultural patterns. After the 1930s, a number of factors, including imposed livestock reduction, New Deal programs, service in World War II, and increased mobility, thrust the Diné into the wage economy of twentieth-century Anglo-America, crippling the economic partnership of Navajos and the trading post. The trading post, stunted but surviving, watched as many of its customers looked elsewhere for merchandise and employment. By the early 1970s, the golden days of the trading post were over (ibid.).

CHAPTER 8

THE AMERICANIZATION ERA

The Americanization era, as it became known, was slowly coming to an end in the closing years of the 1920s. It had begun with "Grant's Peace Policy," initiated by President Grant in 1869. Under the Grant administration, a board of Indian commissioners formulated the policy intended to correct the deplorable management of native affairs. Edward H. Spicer (1997) writes that it was more likely that Grant's Peace Policy was the upshot of a growing humanitarian sentiment. It gave rise to voices that were empathetic to the largely defeated tribes and their sufferings, voices that were also opposed to continuous military control of the native-white conflict.

One feature of Grant's initiative placed the education of native children into the hands of various religious denominations. This brought into existence a partnership policy between government and church whereby the churches (or their mission boards) were given responsibility for running native schools. The government, on the other hand, furnished funds for upkeep and maintenance of the buildings and other conveniences. With features pertaining to religious orientation, use of the English language, and curricula designed by religious leaders, the scheme, in effect, aspired to have Indian children embrace major elements of American society. As Trennert (1998) puts it: "they were to be 'civilized' through heavy doses of Christianity and education" (39).

Boarding School Concept Initiated

When the schools and missions in service under Grant's Peace Policy failed to produce any significant assimilation results, the government launched the boarding school model, believing it could accomplish the required results. Boarding schools took hold rapidly. Most were run under the supervision of the various religious denominations assigned under "Grant's Peace Policy," with Presbyterians having more supervisory responsibility than any other group. However, it was only a matter of time until the policy of placing education entirely in the hands of religious denominations became unpopular.

Congress looked into the matter and enacted legislation in 1897 that put an end to the government/church Indian education relationship. From this time, church-supported schools increasingly became independent of government financing. The boarding school program failed to fulfill the aims of its creators, chiefly because of its poor showing in the numbers of Indians who actually became bilingual. Two generations after the enactment of the program, fewer than 20 percent of Navajos spoke English, while at the same time their demographical numbers were rapidly increasing.

In the late nineteenth and early twentieth century, the government was still wrestling with the idea of removing Indians from reservation status and drawing them into mainstream American society as farmers and technicians. The Dawes Act of 1887 was designed, in part, to do just that. For the Navajos, however, the reservation not only stayed intact but expanded (McPherson 2001).

Struggle for Survival

Throughout the 1890s, the Diné struggled to survive. By some estimates, one-third of the population was then living outside reservation boundaries. The election of Grover Cleveland in 1884 brought the Democratic Party to power for the first time since the Civil War and produced a general turnover in agency personnel. The Democrats expressed sympathy with the increasingly popular reform idea of extending the Civil Service to the Bureau of Indian Affairs. However, party pragmatism got in the way, and again politicians handed out agency jobs to friends, supporters, and relatives, and again the Indian Office was beleaguered by the appointment of unqualified and incompetent personnel. As one government inspector observed in 1889, "the Indian Bureau has been made the dumping ground for the sweepings of the political party that is in power" (Trennert).

The Americanization policy had come under increasing criticism by the 1920s, culminating in a special study commissioned by the secretary of the interior and carried out under the aegis of the Institute for Government Research. It paved the way for far-reaching reform during the following decade. President Franklin D. Roosevelt, who assumed the presidency in 1933, appointed John Collier, a long-time advocate of cultural pluralism, as commissioner of Indian Affairs. Collier pushed through the Indian Reorganization Act in 1934, overturning sections of the unliked Dawes Act, which had tried to assimilate and acculturate Native Americans into mainstream American culture. But Collier is much less remembered for his advocacy of Indian cultural survival and self-determination than for his role in the infamous "stock reduction program" (discussed below) he spearheaded to remedy reservation land erosion. As Kit Carson became the living symbol to the Navajos of the calamitous Long Walk, John Collier came to represent all that was hideous about the "livestock reduction program" (McPherson, 116).

Nonetheless, it has to be acknowledged that the Collier commissionership marked a clear departure from the Americanization era with its "Indian New Deal." Enactment of the Wheeler-Howard bill in 1934 ended the land allotment era, authorized the creation of tribal constitutions, and focused heavily on permitting the tribes to preserve their cultural identity. However, native leaders successfully opposed some of the bill's provisions, especially the one recognizing tribal government. Past injustices, including a feeling that the government had not lived up to its treaty obligations, were partly to blame for the opposition (Trennert). The onset of World War II limited, to some degree, the reforming progress of the Collier administration. Like the New Deal generally, the Indian New Deal became subsumed under the war effort (Luey and Stowe 1987).

Livestock Reduction Program

The Navajos encountered two catastrophic events that affected them deeply. The first was their roundup at the hands of the United States military: their forced march of several hundred miles and their incarceration at Bosque Redondo in eastern New Mexico between 1864 and 1868. The second was the government imposed livestock reduction program of the 1930s, resulting in the forcible seizure and destruction of Navajo sheep and other livestock without Diné consent. This set off an economic war of attrition and slaughter comparable, in their tribal memory, to the horrifying 1860s Bosque Redondo nightmare.

The livestock reduction ordeal had its genesis in a survey carried out at the end of the 1920s, which alerted the government to an alarming soil erosion problem on reservation lands. The survey confirmed what already was suspected: Navajo livestock had increased to the point where there were too many animals on the reservation, and their number had to be significantly reduced if the grassland was to be protected from the effects of erosion and overgrazing. In 1931, Bureau of Indian Affairs officials convened to look into the problem and decided to implement a livestock reduction program on the reservation.

Early attempts to have the Navajos understand the gravity of the situation and persuade them to voluntarily undertake livestock reduction measures were pointless. Navajos saw their situation differently: if the government would only continue to increase their territory as it had done in the past, they believed that this, along with more rain, would fix the soil erosion problem. But a changing populace outside the reservation made enlarging the reservation difficult. The growing non-Native populations of Arizona and New Mexico (which had become states in 1912) had elected lawmakers who clamored against making public property part of Navajo country. Senator Dennis Chávez carried out a successful one-man crusade against additional Diné land in New Mexico (Iverson 2002a).

Concept of "Cultural Pluralism"

Following the election of Franklin D. Roosevelt in 1932, John Collier became commissioner of Indian Affairs. Collier, an unbiased advocate of Indian rights, embarked on a campaign to change the Indian Office from the way it operated. Committed to the concept of "cultural pluralism," he inaugurated a new era of Indian policy that gave rise to innovative approaches in education, health care, self-rule, and direct economic aid (Trennert). He succeeded in obtaining congressional approval for extensions to the reservation: two smaller ones on its northern and western boundaries and a larger extension on its southern boarder. Strong opposition by lawmakers from New Mexico blocked expansion to the east. Despite Collier's determination to improve the lot of Native Americans, the aggressive and paternalistic character of his reforms created almost as many problems as it solved.

In many instances, the Diné despised the reforms he crafted, with certain provisions leaving them bitter and suspicious of the government. Navajo observer Robert Trennert writes that even passages of the Indian Reorganization Act of 1934, the centerpiece of Collier's Indian New Deal program, were unpopular with many Navajos. This legislation ended the allotment era. It authorized the creation of tribal constitutions and focused heavily on safeguarding tribal cultural identity. It was strongly opposed on the reservation. Past injustices, including a feeling that the government had not lived up to its treaty obligations in the areas of health and education, partly accounted for the resistance (ibid.).

Collier's livestock-reduction program, carried out intermittently until 1941, was despised by most Diné, who felt it was carried out in a heartless and bullying way. Collier earnestly believed that what he was doing was in the best interests of the tribe. Boulder Dam, under construction in northwestern Arizona, also influenced the commissioner's decision. He felt that the workability of the dam was threatened by the vast amount of silt that continued to erode from Navajo lands and run off into the Colorado River (Iverson 1990).

Navajos Resented the Slaughter of Their Animals

While members of the Tribal Council agreed in principle with Collier's decision, they did not sanction the way in which the program was carried out. Iverson describes how it worked. Federal officials would call community meetings to clarify the rationale behind the program and to explain how it would be handled. Next, federal employees would arrive and demand a certain number of animals out of a flock or herd. They would seize the animals, take them over a knoll or down into a canyon or into a corral, shoot them, and leave their carcasses to rot. To many Navajos, these measures were repugnant (Iverson 2002a). Howard Gorman, tribal vice-chairman, lamented, "Such incidents broke a lot of hearts of the Navajo people and left them mourning for years." He added, "The cruel way our stock was handled is something that should never have happened" (ibid.). Navajos resented the slaughter of their animals, even though they were being paid at least a small amount for the livestock that was seized.

Navajos took particular offense to the slaughter of their sheep. Sheep were the essence of Navajo culture. Sheep were the traditional gift given to a performer for presiding over a sacred ceremony. Navajo children learned traditional tribal values and responsibilities by helping to care for their family's sheep herd (Luey and Stowe). Destroying their sheep was an assault on their culture, more so than on their economic well-being.

Robert McPherson captured this unique relationship while interviewing Navajos:

> In the time of myths, when the holy beings created the world, the landscape was foreordained to support the livestock industry. One of the four sacred mountains, *Dibé Ntsaa*, or Big Sheep Mountain, was "made of sheep—both rams and ewes." The holy beings associated with this mountain pour forth their wealth in livestock and are appealed to by herders for supernatural help in prospering. The gods work through this and other mountains to provide livestock to support the Navajos (104).

After 1936, livestock reduction took on the dimensions of a crusade as government agents forcibly took away animals without any explanation to their owners. To manage the program more effectively, the government divided the reservation into eighteen land management districts. In summarizing this restructuring, Iverson (2002) writes that within each of these districts federal officials estimated the grazing capacity of the area and then worked toward that combination of livestock: a goat counted as one sheep unit, a cow counted as four sheep units, and a horse as five sheep units, much to the bewilderment and bemusement of the Navajos. A family group consisted of "a single home economic unit, living closely associated in one or more grouped hogans or houses, which shares its livestock and agricultural income in common and recognizes one individual as the family head." The "family head" was "the person who exercises control of a family group either because of the responsibility placed upon him by blood relationship, moral or economic obligations, or otherwise" (Iverson 2002a, 155). Grazing permits would be issued to family heads.

This meant a complete change of lifestyle for Navajos, who had been well known for steadily increasing their flocks and for unregulated wandering over the reservation wherever forage was available (Spicer 1997). Navajos watched hopelessly: the whole modus operandi of government livestock management scared them. One elder lamented, "All was going well, and the people had increased their stock very rapidly, when along came John Collier and stomped his big foot on our sheep, goats and horses—and crushed them before our eyes" (Collier 2002, 27–28). These grazing regulations and their extensive definitions became the source of endless confusion and debate for all concerned. The cruel and heavy-handed way that government agents generally removed and slaughtered the animals turned many Navajos against the Indian Service agents.

In the face of a growing sense of powerlessness and increasing poverty, many Navajos continued to practice *hózhó*—that sense of balance, beauty, and harmony—to comfort them during these turbulent times. Other Navajos turned to the Native American Church, a newly formed religious congregation blending elements of Christianity with rituals of traditional native religions. Its members practiced peyotism (the ceremonial use of substances that induce hallucinations when ingested) as a means of communicating with God. This offered them a way to cope with a world that had been profoundly disturbed by the federal government. But in 1940, the Navajo Tribal Council passed a resolution outlawing the use or possession of peyote (Iverson 1990).

By 1946, livestock reduction had run its course, and in 1952 the Navajo Tribal Council wrote and put into effect its own grazing regulations based on the technical knowledge supplied by the Indian Bureau (Spicer). In the meantime, the Diné had endured not only the harshest of physical poverty and deprivation but had suffered appalling psychological turmoil as well. Today Navajo elders tell their children about the two times the tribe was devastated. The teachings about the Long Walk period have been passed down from generation to generation and mythologized. Livestock reduction, in contrast, with living witnesses remaining, lingers vividly in memory. The pattern in each instance is similar: surprise, betrayal, destruction, confinement, and the start of a new way of life (McPherson).

CHAPTER 9

NAVAJO ADMINISTRATION AND GOVERNMENT

Between the 1880s and 1920s, there was very little progress made in the way of Navajo political assimilation beyond what existed already. Most Navajos, having scattered widely after returning from Fort Sumner, continued to live in the manner of the old band social order. This consisted of social units composed of several extended families who ranged over a defined territory raising corn and herding their livestock. Navajos' physical distance from and limited contact with the outside world restricted American cultural influences—in those days conveyed for the most part through traders, missionaries, and teachers (Spicer, 1997). There was, moreover, a minimum of control by the Indian Service agent other than in the vicinity of Fort Defiance.

Today, the Navajo people have a large measure of self-government in the form of the Navajo Tribal Council, and they are answerable largely for administering the tribal code of law and the tribe's financial affairs. But the path to "self-government" has been difficult. It was marked by gyrations of official policy, from misunderstanding and confusion due to ignorance on the part of the white designers of the earliest versions of Navajo political organization, and from attempts to superimpose such versions when they were only partly understood by the tribe (Kluckhohn and Leighton 1962).

At first, army officers and the first civilian agents tried to work through the supposed headmen. When these men failed to obtain the desired cooperation, new headmen were created by governmental fiat. Of course, these pretense leaders had little or no control over their people. Their standing declined after 1900, and neither the Navajos nor the white administrators had much respect for them. For some time there were no really effective channels of communication (ibid.).

The first move of government-sharing came in 1915 when the Indian Service divided the Navajo reservation into five separate jurisdictions, with agencies in Tuba City, Leupp, Shiprock, Crownpoint, and Fort Defiance, each maintaining its own superintendent and staff. In 1917, Navajos were encouraged to organize into community groups to discuss problems and grievances and to facilitate interaction with Indian Service superintendents. In the early 1920s, however, outside oil interests—eager to tap the Navajo Nation's potential energy riches—urged the Interior Department to authorize the establishment of a central Navajo tribal council for the purpose of approving oil leases. The members of this first council were largely handpicked "yes-men"—not the most capable of leaders. They did not have the consent of a Navajo electorate; they worked as friends of the government. There was little or nothing in the way of a prescribed working relationship between the vast majority of Navajos.

The Navajo Tribal Council was the first body organized to act on behalf of the entire Nation. In 1925, "chapters" were established for various local areas, and it was hoped that these could be made into responsible local units. The system was entirely spurious and the federal government, as it had on previous occasions, made the mistake of insisting that "headmen" either agree with its program or be replaced. This led to many chapters becoming centers of antigovernment gossip and agitation. The Indian Service then timidly withdrew its backing and financial support, and most of the chapters collapsed (Kluckhohn and Leighton).

Passage of the Indian Reorganization Act

With the passage of the Indian Reorganization Act by Congress in 1934, Indian reservations, for the first time, were permitted to organize as political units rather than merely as an appendage of the federal government. The establishment of elective tribal councils gave some voice in reservation affairs to those Indian leaders who were willing to participate. In this regard, the law introduced an evolutionary factor, but government-appointed superintendents still held veto power over essential reservation affairs.

Navajos voted first in 1935 and again in 1953 not to accept the Indian Reorganization Act and, correspondingly, the measure of self-government it offered. Again in 1963, a reservation-based initiative failed after members found the process to be too unwieldy and a potential threat to their self-determination. Thereafter, a constitution drafted and adopted by the governing council failed to get the support of the members. Nonetheless, the Indian Service proceeded administratively, and under the legal principal of "inherent and un-extinguished" tribal authority, gave the council some control over tribal affairs (ibid., 159).

In 1936, a team headed by Father Berard Haile, from the Franciscan Fathers community at St. Michael's, undertook the task of searching the reservation for Diné with leadership ability. From the 250 names submitted to the Navajo Agency for consideration, seventy individuals were randomly chosen to create a constitutional assembly. The old council was then disbanded, allowing the new assembly to appoint a provisional executive committee to handle interim tribal business while a constitution was being drafted and a permanent tribal council chosen. Between 1934 and 1960, Navajos went on to build a tribal organization on the basis of this committee, precisely following the form outlined in the Indian Reorganization Act—including a constitution, universal adult suffrage, and political subdistricts.

With Indian Bureau support, the council assumed the management of reservation schemes such as logging and range development and by the 1960s had expanded its influence into the more isolated reservation communities. At the same time, renewed encouragement was given to the formation of local group organizations, or chapters, and election regulations were printed in the Navajo language (Spicer). In 1989, the Navajo Nation endured a nationally publicized standoff between council members supporting and opposing the council's all-powerful chairman. In the aftermath of the turmoil and through a series of amendments to Title 2 of its Governing Code, Navajos proposed reorganizing their government into three branches, renaming the "Navajo Tribal Council" the "Navajo Nation Council." Further changes carried out during the later part of the twentieth century led to a three-branch government: executive, legislative, and judicial. It provided for an elected tribal president, vice president, and eighty-eight council delegates representing the local administrative units, or chapters, making up the Navajo Nation. Council delegates were to meet a minimum of four times a year to deliberate at the Navajo Nation capital in Window Rock, Arizona. In addition to their duties as chapter representatives, council delegates were also to serve on one or more of eleven standing tribal committees.

The Judicial Reform Act, passed in 1978, led to some far-reaching reforms to the Navajo Nation court structure. Components of traditional Navajo law were integrated into the court system and a new division was added offering a distinctly Diné alternative for settling a variety of Navajo disagreements. The Navajo Nation Council revamped the Navajo Nation Criminal Code in 2000, eliminating jail time and fines for seventy-nine offenses. The traditional concept of *nalyeeh*, "the process of confronting someone who hurts others with a demand that they talk out the action and the hurt it caused so that something positive will come out of it," also became part of the criminal code (Iverson 2002a, 320).

At the same time, a forum for community-led, consensus-based dispute resolution was created to handle those offences where jail time and fines were removed. Instead of a single judge adjudicating guilt or innocence and imposing a sentence, resolution is achieved through a participatory process in which the affected parties work with a mediator to resolve their problems. Dubbed the peacemaker court, its approach has found overwhelming support from within the Navajo population. Commenting on its success, Navajo chief justice Robert Yazzie wrote in 2000: "[T]he prison approach to crime does not work. Western adjudication is a search for what happened and who did it; Navajo peace making is about the effects of what happened. Who got hurt? What do they feel about it? What can be done to repair the harm?" (ibid., 320).

Today, the Navajo Nation Council has grown into the largest and most sophisticated American Indian government in the United States. In 1968, the Diné celebrated the centennial anniversary of the 1886 treaty that returned them to Diné' bikéyah. In the following year, Navajos declared themselves to be the Navajo Nation. On both occasions, individuals and leaders from within the Diné community spoke proudly of their heritage and their path back to self-determination. In 1992, President Peterson Zah signed a sovereignty accord with the governors of Arizona, New Mexico, and Utah. This accord emphasized the importance of "a government-to-government relationship" and that the states and the Navajo Nation would deal with each other "in a spirit of cooperation, coordination, communication, and goodwill" (ibid., 321–322).

CHAPTER 10

WORLD WAR II ERA

President Franklin D. Roosevelt's directive in 1941 required all males over the age of twenty-one to register for the Selective Service. It applied to Navajos as they, like other American Indians, were citizens of the United States, having achieved that status through the Indian Citizenship Act of 1924. United States citizenship, however, did not secure voting rights for the Navajos, and, in 1941, state law in Arizona, New Mexico, and Utah still prevented reservation residents from casting a ballot (Iverson 2002a). Even without the vote, Navajos, like men and women throughout America, went off to war as servicemen and off-reservation war-effort workers.

They left the canyons, plains, and mesas of Diné' bikéyah to fight alongside other Americans at Guadalcanal, Tarawa, Iwo Jima, Saipan, Salerno, and countless other battlefields. About 3,400 Navajos enlisted in the army or navy, 540 served as Marines, and more than 10,000 went to work in war-related industries. This did not represent the total commitment, however, as many Diné were rejected because they had failed to pass military physical examinations. Tuberculosis and the lingering effects of trachoma, diseases that were prevalent on the reservation in the years before the war, prevented many from enlisting.

Among those who served in the war was a special group called the Navajo code talkers. Coming into focus in 1942, the Navajo code talkers used a special code based on the Navajo language and were able to transmit military messages that were impossible for the Japanese to decipher. The inspiration to use the Navajo language for secure communications came from Philip Johnston, the son of a missionary to the Navajos and one of the few non-Navajos who spoke their language fluently. He believed the Diné language had the essential elements to qualify it as the military's solution for an undecipherable code: it was an unknown language of extreme complexity, and its syntax and tonal qualities, not to mention dialects, made it incoherent to persons not thoroughly versed in the language. Its usage was limited to the Navajos of the American Southwest.

Johnston conducted a simulated experiment for Major General Clayton B. Vogel (the commanding general of the Pacific Fleet's Amphibious Corps) that demonstrated that the Navajos could encode, transmit, and decode a three-line English message in twenty seconds. Machines of the time required thirty minutes to perform the same task. Swayed by the results, Vogel convinced the Marine Service to recruit two hundred Navajos. The first twenty-nine enlisted at Fort Wingate in May 1942, and after a bus ride from the reservation to San Diego reported to the Marine base at Camp Pendleton.

Johnston may have come up with the idea of a code, but it was for the newly enlisted Diné recruits to work out the essentials. With the help of the twenty-nine recruits the task of creating code terms got underway without delay. The first task was to create a Navajo code talker's dictionary and numerous words for military terms. Where possible, Navajo words with a logical association to the desired military term were selected. Thus the Navajo word for *frog, ch'al,* became the code word for *amphibious*, and *ch' ah ligia* (white hats) became *sailors*. Similarly, *potatoes* became *grenades, eggs* were *bombs*, and *America* became *nihima* ("our mother").

Some military terms with no equivalent in Navajo were assigned their own code word. Several examples: *besh-lo* (iron fish) meant submarine, *dah-he-tih-hi* (hummingbird) meant fighter plane, and *debeh-li-zine* (black street) meant squad. The code talker receiving a message heard a series of seemingly unrelated Navajo words, which he initially had to translate into the English equivalents. He then selected the first letters of the English equivalent words in compiling an English word. For example, the Navajo words *wol-la-chee* (ant), *be-la-sana* (apple), and *tse-nill* (axe) all stood for the letter *a*. Following this approach the word *navy* in Navajo code would be *tsah* (needle), *wol-la-chee* (ant), *ah-keh-di-glini* (victor), and *tsah-ah-dzoh* (yucca).

Once a code talker completed his training, he was dispatched to a Marine unit in the Pacific war zone. He became part of an assault team, or an intelligence unit, operating behind enemy lines, relaying back vital information on enemy positions and troop movements. His duty often required hours of meticulous encrypting and decrypting of messages. It paid off; the Japanese, who were skilled code breakers, never broke the Navajo code. Lieutenant General Seizo Arisue, Japanese chief of intelligence, later conceded that the greatest obstacle the Japanese encountered in trying to crack the code used by the Marines was that of the code talkers.

They Saved the Lives of Countless Americans

Military commanders credited the code talkers with saving the lives of countless Americans and with helping in many successful engagements. Major Howard Connor, Fifth Marine Division signal officer at Iwo Jima, declared, "Were it not for the Navajos, the Marines would never have taken Iwo Jima." Connor had six Navajo code talkers working around the clock during the first two days of battle. Those six sent and received over eight hundred messages, all without error.

At the same time, elders back on the reservation lamented the government's livestock-reduction policy. They evoked bitter feelings about their people being jailed and their sheep being slaughtered. Even as their oral histories resonated with accounts of the "Fearing Time," that terrible period taking in the Long Walk and exile far from their beloved Diné' bikéyah, there were now the code talkers exemplifying the great warrior tradition of the Diné: defending the land and all of its occupants and demonstrating courage in the face of adversity.

They Returned Home Uncelebrated

In the aftermath of the war, the code talkers received essentially no public recognition for their accomplishments. In Iverson's words, "The Marines ignored them. They received no promotions or special medals. When they returned home, the code talkers had no welcoming parade. . . . They returned home uncelebrated by non-Navajos and undecorated by the military, despite their important contribution" (Iverson 2002a, 185–186). Why? In all probability it was because the military kept the code a classified matter until 1968. But even then the code talkers had to wait another thirty-three years before the Diné finally witnessed a belated but still significant recognition of these heroic men. Finally, in July 2001, four of the surviving code talkers and family members of the remaining twenty-five traveled to the nation's capital to receive the Congressional Gold Medal, the highest civilian award Congress can bestow. There were twenty-nine original code talkers, but a thorough research by Navajos Kelsey Begay and Zonnie Gorman disclosed that more than four hundred Diné had participated as code talkers. With strong backing from Senator Jeff Bingaman of New Mexico, Begay and Gorman succeeded in getting recognition for the remaining recruits. In November 2001, the other identified Navajo code talkers were given the Silver Congressional Medal of Honor in Window Rock, Arizona. Sadly, few of the recipients were still living. "*Bizaa yee nidaaz' baa*," Begay remarked during the ceremony: "They fought the enemy with their language" (Iverson2002a, 318).

The war was a broadening experience for all combatants, but for American Indians and Navajos especially, the war took them from the cloistered society of the reservation into the broader American society and beyond, to the cultures of Asia and Europe. Returning servicemen and defense-industry workers brought back cultural perspectives and skills to the reservation that Navajo leadership had previously lacked. World War II changed the Navajos forever. Not only did many patriotic Navajos support the war effort—both through military service and defense-industry employment—they learned more about the outside world, saw their economy altered by the influx of cash, and became aware of the need to understand mainstream society (Trennert 1998).

CHAPTER 11

DAWN OF THE MODERN NAVAJO NATION

The end of World War II marked the beginning of an era of transition in Diné life. New schools, new roads, new health care facilities, and new and revitalized forms of economic development all signaled the start of a period in Navajo life that furnished innovation and change (Iverson 2002a). In the years leading up to the war, there could be little doubt about Navajo identity, even if the future of the Diné remained uncertain. Navajos spoke their own language, resided within the general boundaries of the four sacred mountains, and raised livestock. A great many of the women were weavers. The trading post furnished supplies and a central place for individual communities.

Individual Diné lived in a world shaped on a daily basis by the presence, actions, and decisions of relatives. Most attended traditional ceremonies, lived in hogans, and used horses for transportation. In the 1940s and early 1950s, most of the Four Corners region was traversed only by dirt roads that followed the paths of dry washes and streams. There was no pavement west of Shiprock in New Mexico, or north of Cameron, Arizona. Driving from Cortez to Kayenta—a two-hour trip today—would have taken several hours or even several days, bursting through "sand traps" in the desert and skirting patches of quicksand in the canyons (Brown 1996). The children who attended school were few and far between; the schools where they enrolled required them to live away from home.

Because of the war, an impressive number saw themselves as both American and Navajo, and many enlisted in the war effort. About 3,600 served in the various branches of the military, and for many, the war was their first exposure to the world outside the reservation (Iverson 2002a). On the reservation, money sent home by Navajo servicemen temporarily helped the tribe's suffering economy. But at war's end, the return of thousands of unemployed veterans to the reservation caused an economic crisis. It was impossible for Navajos to prosper with a livestock-based economy, yet well-paid jobs off the reservation were out of reach to most because of their limited command of English and lack of education.

Winds of Change Blowing across Diné' Bikéyah

By 1960, fewer Navajo children spoke the Navajo language fluently. More and more Diné individuals were moving away from the reservation in seach of work. An increasing number of the tribe had become less engaged in or totally removed from the livestock industry. Fewer women wove. The Native American Church, combining elements of Christianity with rituals of traditional native religions, had gained an impressive following. More people lived in houses rather than hogans. The veterans, who had been immersed in the outside world, were convinced that Navajo society had to learn for its own good to deal more effectively with the non-Indian populace.

At the same time, there was a changing attitude among non-Indians toward traditional Indian ways of life. Relatives still mattered to Navajos, but a perceptible number of Diné felt less faithfully obligated to the link with extended families. At the end of the 1950s, new roads and new forms of transportation brought people beyond the confines of a nearby trading post to border-town communities. Even within the Navajo Nation, signs of urbanization were gradually appearing. Over time, parts of the reservation had come to resemble other small urban areas in the United States: fast-food restaurants, shopping malls, and supermarkets catering to tourists and local residents alike. However, large portions of the reservation remained wild and remote (Marcello 2000).

Concept of "Termination"

All Americans had worked together to win the war, and because Indians had played such a valiant role in the victory effort, many non-Indians concluded they deserved to be treated just like all other Americans and felt that Indian communities should no longer be separated or segregated from the majority of the population. This sentiment inspired a new federal Indian policy known as *termination*. This policy sought to terminate, or end, the federal government's financial responsibility for the well-being of Indians within their boundaries. Advocates of termination felt it would "free" Indians to join mainstream American society.

Most Indians, including Navajos, regarded it not as a reward but as a threat. They argued that their ancestors had signed treaties and agreements with the federal government, and therefore they were entitled to the unique legal status these treaties granted them. One of the earliest instruments of the termination policy was the Indian Claims Commission (ICC), which was authorized by Congress in 1946. The ICC established a temporary federal court in which tribes could sue the federal government for lost land and other damages. Resolution of, and compensation for, these claims was to be a preliminary step in ending the federal government's financial obligation to Indian groups (Iverson 1990).

Navajo-Hopi Rehabilitation Act

Sam Ahkeah was elected tribal chairman in 1946 and over the next few years he and other prominent Navajos, such as Jacob Morgan, pressured Congress about the urgent need for improved roads, schools, health care, and other concerns. Congress responded by passing the Navajo-Hopi Rehabilitation Act of 1950. This legislation was in keeping with the "termination" era, for it was designed to encourage Navajos to take charge of their own economic development. Through the act, the tribe received $88 million over a ten-year period for internal projects. Almost $25 million was spent to construct schools, but even more was directed toward improving reservation roads and highways. As road travel became easier, the development of industries on the reservation appeared feasible (ibid.).

Progress in Reservation Education

Improved roads gave Navajo children access to schools. At the end of World War II, the majority of reservation children were not enrolled in school. This troubled Navajos, who were coming to realize that education was key if they wished their children to survive and prosper. The obvious solution put forward was to develop a public school system on the reservation. However, state governments, using state tax revenues, had responsibility for funding public school systems, and residents of federal Indian reservations were exempt from paying state and local taxes. Given that the Diné did not pay property taxes to Arizona, Utah, or New Mexico (the three states over which the reservation extended), these state governments balked at the idea of building and running reservation schools (ibid.).

Congress came to the rescue in 1950 by passing two laws authorizing federal aid to public school districts that educated the children of military personnel. These laws were amended in 1953 to provide for the construction and operation of schools on Indian reservations as well. Navajos, benefiting from these laws, built the nucleus of state-operated public schools across the reservation. For the first time, thousands of Navajo children were able to attend school and still return home to their families at night. Some students, however, living in the remote areas of the reservation, were not so lucky. The absence of a nearby school forced many to continue attending boarding schools (ibid.).

More recently, Navajos have been calling for a greater role in administering the education of their children. In 2005, Navajo Nation legislators exercised sovereign powers to change their education code, creating an eleven-member board and a superintendent of schools. This was an initial step toward taking jurisdictional control of Navajo schooling from the states—Arizona, New Mexico, and Utah.

While education had emerged as the foremost priority in the decades following World War II, health care and economic development closely followed. Inadequate health care restricted the ability of many Navajos to find work. Sickness, particularly tuberculosis, was a significant crisis calling for more physicians, nurses, and centrally located hospitals. Health care entered a new era in 1955 when the newly established Indian Public Health Service assumed responsibility, displacing the Bureau of Indian Affairs. With access to significant funding, new hospitals and health centers were constructed throughout the reservation. As Diné became more satisfied with the quality of their hospitals and health centers, they visited the hospitals and health centers more regularly, and as a result, tuberculosis and infant mortality rates dropped significantly (Iverson 2002a).

Cultural Changes

The Navajo world has always been characterized by rapid change, but a consistant value system has allowed for continuity through change. Navajos seemed uniquely able to incorporate new elements within their culture. At the same time, despite this remarkable capacity, many Diné feared the pace of change. They worried about children growing up in a world so decidedly different from the environment of their childhood. The full impact of technological change had only started to be felt within Diné' bikéyah at the conclusion of the 1950s. Enough had been altered to raise poignant and significant questions about the nature of Navajo identity. What does it mean to be Navajo? Iverson believes that the answer to this seemingly simple question can be somewhat complicated. Still, Navajos have realized numerous cultural successes and at the same time have retained their identity as well as their beloved Diné' bikéyah (Iverson 2002b).

CHAPTER 12

CHANGING ECONOMY

In the post-war years, Diné leadership faced a continuous challenge as it sought to expand the Navajo economy in directions beyond traditional shepherding, farming, and customary crafts. At the end of the war, thousands of unemployed veterans returned to a reservation in the midst of an economic crisis: the raising of livestock was on the decline, the result of the government's compulsory livestock-reduction program. Tribal leaders were confronted with the realization that it was no longer possible for their people to survive on a livestock-based economy.

In the 1950s, the vast majority of Navajos retained permanent residence on the reservation and many of the families in out-of-the-way locations continued to depend on shepherding and farming for their survival. Others earned money from jewelry, rugs, and other traditional crafts. Rug production by women was also of some importance. But subsistence for most families was moving in the direction of wages earned by some member of the extended family who was employed off the reservation. Most off-reservation wage employment came from the railroads. An ever increasing number of Navajos were going to work in seasonal employment: the beet fields of Colorado; the carrot fields near Grants, New Mexico, and Phoenix, Arizona; and in agricultural harvests elsewhere (Spicer, 1997).

Some on-reservation wage employment was available: the tribal government and federal government agencies offered employment to any who were capable of doing the work. Other on-reservation wage employment was provided by traders, who used Navajos as interpreters and handymen; by missionaries, with whom they served as interpreters and guides; and by some of the more prosperous Navajos, who employed their kinfolk during the lambing, shearing, and harvesting seasons (Kluckhohn and Leighton 1962). There were some well-paid jobs off the reservation, but they were out of reach to most Navajos, especially those with a limited command of the English language or a lack of education. Regardless, the majority of Navajos at the time did not want to leave their homeland to seek off-reservation employment.

Confronting the Challenges

It was clear to Navajo leadership that greater opportunities were necessary to meet the needs of an expanding population and to facilitate an orderly shift from shepherding and farming to a wage-employment economy and beyond. This called for prudent decisions from a succession of tribal councils to offset the challenges of the new era. The Diné, long known for their ability to adjust to cultural and environment changes, pressed ahead as a united people. With backing from the federal government, they embarked on a journey toward a more commercially viable economy, luring major industries to relocate on, or near the edge of, the reservation (Iverson 2002a).

Tribal Enterprises

One distinctive aspect of Native economics in the post-war era consisted of a special form of business enterprise known as "tribal enterprises." The Indian Reorganization Act of 1934 encouraged tribes to organize as business corporations and to pursue business activities that set tribal enterprises in motion. The Diné, in collaboration with representatives of the Indian Bureau, initiated the restructuring of a number of Navajo projects as tribal enterprises. In fact, the Navajo tribe itself became a large business enterprise with a considerable range of activities and interests. Thus, the Navajo Tribal Council was not only a political unit but also had a charter as a business corporation.

According to Spicer, these tribal enterprises were corporations with "collective division of proceeds like any other corporation, subject to the policies of the board of directors" (561–562). The tribal council hired or delegated the hiring and firing of employees for these enterprises and determined basic policy for management. What was different, writes Spicer, was the basis of membership in the corporation, specifically, genealogical descent or place of residence or a combination of these. This was in contrast with the usual basis of shareholding in a corporation—namely, investment in the enterprise with a coupled financial interest. Another difference, Spicer points out, was that tribal councils, which served as boards of directors, were composed of individuals elected as political representatives and did not necessarily have any kind of business experience. The basis of the Navajo corporation lay in the legal right of each individual Diné to the total natural resources of the reservation—a right embodied in the tribal title held in trust by the United States government (Spicer).

Industrial Development and Economic Progress

Spicer credits the Navajo tribe with leading the way in its collective enterprise approach with development of its business interests (ibid.). In an effort to bolster the Navajo economy, many construction projects were undertaken during the 1950s. Several of these projects were engaged with building the reservation's infrastructure: schools, roads, and hospital construction. Three major construction projects added substantially to Navajo employment rolls during their construction phases. The construction of Glen Canyon Dam, started in 1956 and finished in 1966, created Lake Powell, which in turn brought a significant number of tourists to the region. It managed to provide considerable employment during its construction phase, as did two major power plants at Page and at Fruitland, New Mexico. These projects not only aleviated, to some extent, unemployment on the reservation, but they gave many Navajos the training and skills necessary to acquire work on off-reservation projects (Link 1968).

The lumber industry became a more significant component in the overall economy in the early 1960s and inspired an interest in the potential for greater benefit from the reservation's natural resources. The Navajo Tribal Council appropriated $7.5 million for construction of a new modern sawmill in the late 1950s and created Navajo Forest Products Industries to manage the expanded operation. Navajo Forest Products

Industries represented Navajo control and management of the tribe's forests of nearly half a million acres. From there, thousands of board feet of lumber were milled annually. By the late 1970s, more than six hundred Navajos were on the Navajo Forest Products Industries payroll. Hundreds more were indirectly employed (Iverson 2002a).

Mineral resources are the Navajos' principal source of income. During World War II, Vanadium Corporation of America and Kerr-McGee began mining uranium on reservation lands. Interest in atomic energy grew rapidly after the war and uranium mining accelerated in the 1950s. Hundreds of Navajo men worked in these mines unguarded from the hazardous health effects of uranium exposure. There was plenty of work until the mines closed when knowledge of the deadly consequences of radiation contact began to surface. In the 1970s, a further effort was made to develop Navajo uranium resources. The Exxon Corporation, in a joint venture that would have made the Navajo partners rather than employees, agreed to pay the tribe $6 million for uranium exploration rights in northwestern New Mexico. The Navajo hoped to gain millions more from the actual operations, but local residents complained bitterly that they had not been consulted. Concerns escalated as reports spread about the poor health of Navajos who had worked in the earlier uranium mines. The highly publicized closing of the Three Mile Island nuclear power plant in 1997, the Church Rock, New Mexico, major radioactive dam spill that same year, and plummeting uranium ore market prices caused further anxiety, leaving the proposed joint venture in an indeterminate state.

Oil and gas revenues in the post-war years played a major role in the workings of the Navajo economy. The discovery of large oil and gas fields in 1956–57 on the reservation near the Four Corners was a great boon to the Navajo economy (Iverson 1990). Another oil field discovery near Aneth in southern Utah turned out to be a substantial find. Oil revenues increased remarkably during the latter half of the decade. In 1955, oil royalties received by the Navajo amounted to just under $50,000. From then until the end of the decade, income from oil exploration increased significantly, with 1957 and 1958 being the two most lucrative years, when the tribe netted $34.8 million and $28.7 million respectively (Iverson 2002a). From the early 1960s onward, oil and gas production went into decline, with corresponding declines in royalties.

Coal mining also became a major new source of income. In 1962, Utah Mining and Manufacturing signed a contract with the Navajo that allowed them to strip-mine coal from land south of the San Juan River in New Mexico. Adjacent to this land, the Arizona Public Service Company constructed an electricity-generating facility: the Four Corners Power Plant. In the mid-1960s, the tribal council also agreed to lease lands on Black Mesa for strip-mining by the Peabody Coal Company and to allow a power plant to be built at Page (ibid.). Besides creating income for the tribe, these industries provide work for many Navajo people.

The Birth of Navajoland Tourism

Tourism started to figure more prominently in the economic development strategies of the Diné after World War II. Driving conditions improved greatly in the 1950s with the paving of many roads. As a result, more tourists were heading to Navajo country. Canyon de Chelly and Monument Valley have become world-famous destination sites, the latter promoted through the films made by John Ford. Ford's films helped create international interest in the spectacular sandstone scenery on the Arizona-Utah boarder. People from around the world began to travel to Monument Valley, and visitors sought out Canyon de Chelly and other remarkable sites. The creation of a Navajo parks commission by the tribal council in 1957 helped produce information and materials about such destinations and led to the first Navajo Tribal Park being created at Monument Valley in 1960 (ibid.).

The Diné Today

Ruth M. Underhill (1985), anthropologist and an authority on the American Indian, writes:

> In the 1940s, the Navajos were reported starving. Their beautiful, arid land was too poor to support the population, and it was thought that half of the people must find a living elsewhere. Twenty years later, the population had almost doubled and the reservation was the richest in the United States. Oil had been discovered there. Between the years 1961 and 1964, the Navajo tribe had received in bonuses and exploration fees one hundred million dollars. (259)

The Navajo, having long been known for their ability to adjust to cultural and environment changes, did not squander their newfound wealth. With assistance from federal government agents, Navajo leaders decided against distributing the revenue windfall on a per capita basis, instead opting to spend it putting the reservation in order. To accomplish this, they developed programs for improving the lot of their tribal members. Millions of dollars were spent for land management, roads, health, education, and employment.

As a result, Navajoland is no longer a wilderness of rocks, brush, and piñon. Paved roads connect the main settlements. In the open country, where once the only moving objects were sheep and shepherds, one can see heavy machinery and truckloads of men engaged in digging and fencing. Lining ditches with concrete and digging rainwater reservoirs can now bring water to areas that looked hopeless before. Low-cost housing is being offered for rent by the tribe to its members. There are now several hospitals on the reservation and one in nearby Gallop. Schools that had been standing half empty are now filled beyond capacity (Underhill).

Navajos have come a long way in the last eighty or so years. Loosely united in clans and under headmen, they had no tribal organization until oil was discovered on their reservation in 1923. A meeting called then to discuss the disposal of the new wealth resulted in the permanent Navajo Tribal Council. In the years since World War II, the Navajo tribe has been gaining recognition in many ways. They have been American citizens, like other Indians, since 1924. Certain voting restrictions in Arizona, New Mexico, and Utah prevented them from exercising their voting privilege. These restrictions have since been removed and Navajos now vote with the other Americans on Election Day.

The Diné' bikéyah is presented proudly to visitors. The singular beauty of its landscapes, the richness of its history, and the warmth of its people are what make Navajoland uniquely Navajo, uniquely American, and an extremely worthwhile place to visit.

PART II

A VISITOR'S GUIDE THROUGH NAVAJOLAND

CHAPTER 13

INFORMATION FOR VISITORS

The Navajo reservation is a place of breathtaking beauty; it is also an arid country, stark and hard for those who live there. This high desert country has unique rock formations, such as those found in Monument Valley and Window Rock. Spectacular Antelope Canyon and Canyon de Chelly are important for their history as well as their beauty. The red cliffs of the Painted Desert are visible many places along US-89, and the rugged, pine covered Chuska Mountains take position in the east. It is a land of broad mesas, soaring buttes, and grand vistas shaped by millions of years of erosion. Glorious sunsets color the land and rocks as well as the sky.

Many peoples, from the earliest Basketmaker and the Anasazi to the Navajo, have called this area home. Ancient cultural traditions, religions, and ways of life survive to this day. Navajos have a uniquely different culture: traditional Navajos prefer to live in houses or hogans spread across the land, while Pueblo peoples, the Hopi in particular (whose land is completely enclosed within Navajoland), live in compact villages. Navajos live in accord with nature, adapting to the climate, plants, and animals of the land.

Navajoland has a long geological past; dinosaurs roamed the area. Ancient volcanoes and earthquakes stamped their marks on the land. The Painted Desert, Petrified Forest, and Beautiful Valley, a portion of Chinle Valley, expose all three periods of the Mesozoic age in the soft colorful shale, mudstones, and siltstones of their cliffs and mesas. The youngest cretaceous rocks, important for the extensive coal seams they contain, are found in Black Mesa and near Gallup. Evidence of human history going back to the hunter-gatherers is found in the artifacts left in the Petrified Forest, Canyon de Chelly, and Wupatki National Monument, among others.

The Navajo reservation, located on the Colorado Plateau, covers approximately 27,000 square miles, excluding the smaller Hopi reservation. Navajo reservation land covers about one-half of the traditional homeland of the Navajo; all of this land is sacred to Navajos (Linford 2000). There are national parks, monuments, and prehistoric sites within the Navajo traditional homeland and in many cases are where they made their homes. Many still live in these areas.

This road tour will cover most of the Navajo Nation and much of the extended homeland because Navajo influence extends beyond reservation borders (Goodman 1971, Linford). It will include side trips of historical, geological, and scenic interest along the way. Place names are given in Navajo as well as in English, thanks to the well-researched work of Laurance D. Linford in his book *Navajo Places: History, Legend, Landscapes.* Liberal use of his histories of local communities has added greatly to the research behind this book. You will find that Navajo names for places literally describe the place, or the people associated with the place, and/or a religious or historical event that took place there. Navajos complain that English names "don't tell you anything."

The Navajo Nation is unique because the people have achieved something rare: the ability of an indigenous people to blend both traditional and modern ways. This is in contrast to the Hopi and other Pueblo communities that struggle to keep their culture pure. Navajos have strong tribal religious beliefs; church associations are usually in addition to, not in place of, their own beliefs.

Navajos do not own their land; they hold traditional use rights under tribal customary law. Because of this, off-road hiking or camping requires permission and a local guide; otherwise, you are trespassing. This law respects property rights and the ancient archeological sites found on the property. The removal of, or tampering with, artifacts is prohibited by both federal and tribal law.

Time

The Navajo Reservation observes daylight savings time, while the rest of Arizona is on standard time all year. New Mexico, Utah, and Colorado also observe daylight savings time.

CLIMATE

The arid Colorado Plateau rainfall is less than ten inches per year, most of it occuring in December through March and in the summer monsoons from July through August. The mountains get more rain; a difference of two thousand feet or more can often mean over two inches of additional rain. Summer thunderstorms dump a major portion of annual rainfall. Temperatures are surprisingly diverse: average summer temperatures at an elevation of five thousand feet range from 95 to the 100s; at seven thousand feet it is in the 80s with cool nights. Layered clothes are a good choice for comfort. It can be cool in the spring and fall, and cold in the winter.

Weather for the Navajo Nation in particular, according to the Navajo Nation Hospitality Enterprise brochure, is "beautiful year round." Average summer daytime temperatures of 80 degrees give way to the 50s at night. During the winters expect highs in the 40s and lows in the teens. The rainy season takes place during August, September, and October, in the form of thunderstorms. This information is important if you plan to use dirt roads to visit places like Chaco Canyon; dirt roads are impassible when wet.

The Navajo Nation Hospitality Enterprise chart for average monthly temperatures and rainfall follows:

Month	Average High (°F)	Average Low (°F)	Average Precip. (inches)
January	44.0°	13.7°	0.93
February	48.9°	18.6°	0.68
March	55.4°	22.8°	0.92
April	64.2°	27.4°	0.41
May	73.3°	36.4°	0.67
June	84.4°	44.8°	0.51
July	87.0°	53.3°	1.72
August	84.8°	52.5°	2.11
September	78.7°	44.3°	1.04
October	67.8°	30.1°	1.06
November	54.3°	19.9°	1.00
December	45.2°	13.0°	0.76

Flash Floods

In mountain and canyon country, floods are a real danger to motorists and campers. Observing some commonsense rules will ensure a safe and happy trip, especially for travelers not familiar with mountain and canyon country.

1. Check the weather before starting out for the day, and always carry plenty of drinking water and some snacks.

2. Do not enter flooded areas on the road. The water may appear to be shallow but most often is deeper than you think. Sandy soil cannot absorb large amounts of rain, creating pooling in low areas. Runoffs from various elevated areas (that may be far away) rush down the washes, collecting large stones and debris that may spill over onto the road. Your engine can die in rushing water, and you may be unable to leave your vehicle. You could be washed downstream. Be aware: water on the road at night is hard to distinguish from tarmac.

3. The safe way to approach water on the road is to go back to higher ground and wait for the water to recede. Fast and furious, storms can hit or miss. You may be in an area where there is no rain; however, runoff from other areas can fill washes miles away. Dirt roads are often impassable when it rains.

4. Arizona Stupid Motorist Law allows local governments to fine motorists up to $2,000 for removing or driving around barricades at a wash and to recover the costs of their rescue from the victims.

Lightning

In high country, lightning is particularly dangerous. Find shelter and avoid areas next to cliff rims or in the open. Grounded metal objects, like a camera tripod or railings over steep overlooks, attract lightning. Remain in your car if no better shelter is available.

Information on Arizona and Adjoining States

Most of Navajoland is contained within the boundaries of Arizona. However, reservation lands extend into parts of Utah, New Mexico, and some disputed lands in Colorado.

1. Motorcycle helmets are required for operators under eighteen years of age in Arizona, New Mexico, and Utah. They are not required in Colorado.

2. You must be seventeen in Colorado and Utah to have an unrestricted driver's license. Arizona is age sixteen and New Mexico is sixteen years, six months.

3. It can be a long distance between gas stations, so it is a good idea to keep your tank full.

4. You may want to purchase the Navajo and Hopi Nations Map, published by North Star Mapping—it is the most detailed. The AAA map is also excellent.

5. As a general rule, you should always wear a seatbelt. Seatbelt laws are different in each state:

State	Seatbelt Required	Under Age 16	Under Age 5
Arizona	Driver and front seat passenger	Seatbelts required	Restraints required
New Mexico	Driver and all passengers	Seatbelts required	Restraints required under age 5 or less than 40 lbs.
Utah	Driver and front seat passengers over age 15	Seatbelts required for ages 6–15	Child restraints for children ages 4 and under
Colorado	All passengers over age 15	Seatbelts required for ages 6–15 and 55" tall	Child booster seats or restraints for children under age 4 or 40 lbs.

6. **America the Beautiful, National Parks and Federal Recreational Lands Pass** If you follow any of the side trips described in this Navajo tour, you will visit many national parks. Remember to check the National Park Service Web site for any special deals or park information if you are planning a trip. America the Beautiful passes are sold at any national park entrance. They will save many entrance fees:

   Annual Pass: You can purchase an annual pass honored at all Forest Service, Park Service, Bureau of Land Management, and U.S. Fish and Wildlife sites charging fees for entrance into federal recreation areas and national parks and monuments. As of 2007, the cost of this pass is $80 and admits the pass holder and up to three adult passengers in a noncommercial vehicle. Children under sixteen are admitted free of charge.

   Senior Pass: You can purchase a lifetime pass for U.S. citizens over 62 years of age. As of 2007, the cost of this pass is $10.

   Access Pass: A free, lifetime pass is available for anyone who is disabled. This pass admits all people in the car.

   Volunteer Pass: This pass is free for volunteers acquiring five hundred service hours on a cumulative basis and admits the pass holder and up to three adult passengers in a noncommercial vehicle. Children under sixteen are admitted free of charge.

Visitor Etiquette

While all Native Americans are U.S. citizens, tribal lands within the United States are recognized as sovereign nations with their own unique laws and customs. These may seem unusual or restrictive to outsiders; visitors should recognize that the laws and customs are simply part of the daily life of Native Americans. On tribal land, tribal rules are to be respected by all. Most of the rules are a matter of simple courtesy and common sense.

General exuberance that we see as friendliness can be misinterpreted and considered impolite. Navajos are taught from childhood not to talk too much, be loud, or be forward with strangers. You may not be successful in striking up a conversation, although Navajos are generally polite and soft spoken. Eye contact is considered to be impolite. A courteous group of Navajos may look down or away in conversation, even though you have their full attention. The only physical contact you will see is the handshake; a firm grip is considered overbearing, a soft handshake is preferred. Navajo women dress modestly, whether in modern or traditional clothes.

Navajo police ask that you obey all speed limits and watch for people or animals (especially at night) on the road. Much of Navajoland is open range, which means the onus is on the driver to watch for cattle; they do not have to be fenced in. It is best to get off the road before dark. It is illegal to drink or carry alcoholic beverages on the reservation.

There is no general photography fee. Sketching or photographing people requires their permission; a gratuity is usually expected. You may take all the scenery pictures you wish for your personal use, as long as you respect the privacy of people and their homes. A permit is required for commercial use. Contact the Navajo Nation Film Office at P.O. Box 2310, Window Rock, AZ 86515. Telephone 928-871-7351.

Suggested Short Trips and In-Depth Tours

Three-Day Trips

- Window Rock – Canyon de Chelly – Monument Valley
- Window Rock – Canyon de Chelly – Three Mesas
- Flagstaff – Navajo National Monument – Monument Valley
- Page – Navajo National Monument – Monument Valley – Canyon de Chelly
- Farmington – Shiprock – Monument Valley – Canyon de Chelly

Four-Day Trips

- Window Rock – Canyon de Chelly – Monument Valley – Navajo National Monument

- Flagstaff – Navajo National Monument – Monument Valley – Canyon de Chelly
- Page – Antelope Canyon – Navajo National Monument – Monument Valley – Canyon de Chelly
- Farmington – Shiprock – Monument Valley – Canyon de Chelly – Three Mesas

Five-Day Trips

- Window Rock – Three Mesas – Tuba City – Navajo National Monument – Monument Valley – Canyon de Chelly
- Flagstaff – Sunset Crater – Wupatki National Monument – Cameron Trading Post – Navajo National Monument – Monument Valley – Canyon de Chelly
- Page – Antelope Canyon – Navajo National Monument – Monument Valley – Canyon de Chelly – Three Mesas
- Farmington – Shiprock – Monument Valley – Canyon de Chelly – Navajo National Monument

One-Week Trips

- Window Rock – Three Mesas – Cameron Trading Post (include South Rim Grand Canyon) – Lees Ferry – Glen Canyon – Page – Antelope Canyon – Navajo National Monument – Monument Valley – Canyon de Chelly
- Window Rock – Canyon de Chelly – Monument Valley – Navajo National Monument – Shiprock – Farmington – Chaco Canyon
- Flagstaff – Sunset Crater – Wupatki National Monument – Cameron Trading Post (include South Rim Grand Canyon) – Lees Ferry – Glen Canyon – Page – Antelope Canyon – Navajo National Monument – Monument Valley – Canyon de Chelly – Three Mesas
- Page – Antelope Canyon – Navajo National Monument – Monument Valley – Shiprock – Farmington – Chaco Canyon – Window Rock – Canyon de Chelly

- Farmington – Chaco Canyon – Window Rock – Canyon de Chelly – Three Mesas – Cameron (include South Rim Grand Canyon) – Lees Ferry – Glen Canyon – Page – Antelope Canyon – Navajo National Monument – Monument Valley – Shiprock

Ten-Day Trips

- Window Rock – Three Mesas (include side trip to Homolovi Prehistoric Park, Petrified Forest, Painted Desert) – Tuba City – Cameron Trading Post (include side trip to South Rim Grand Canyon) – Lees Ferry – Glen Canyon – Page – Antelope Canyon – Navajo National Monument – Monument Valley – Canyon de Chelly – Shiprock – Chaco Canyon
- Flagstaff – Sunset Crater – Wupatki National Monument – Cameron Trading Post (include South Rim Grand Canyon) – Lees Ferry – Glen Canyon – Page – Antelope Canyon – Navajo National Monument – Monument Valley – Shiprock – Farmington – Chaco Canyon – Window Rock – Canyon de Chelly – Three Mesas
- Page – Antelope Canyon – Navajo National Monument – Monument Valley – Shiprock – Farmington – Chaco Canyon – Window Rock – Canyon de Chelly – Three Mesas (include Homolovi Prehistoric Park, Petrified Forest, and Painted Desert) – Tuba City – Cameron (include South Rim Grand Canyon) – Lees Ferry – Glen Canyon
- Farmington – Chaco Canyon – Window Rock – Canyon de Chelly – Three Mesas (including side trip to Homolovi Prehistoric Park, Petrified Forest, and Painted Desert) – Cameron (include South Rim Grand Canyon) – Lees Ferry – Page – Antelope Canyon – Navajo National Monument – Monument Valley – Shiprock

Two-Week Trips

You should be able to complete the entire trip through Navajoland, starting at any of the access towns: Window Rock, Flagstaff, Page, or Farmington.

CHAPTER 14

FROM ALBUQUERQUE TO WINDOW ROCK

Directions from Albuquerque to Gallup
Take I-40 west to Gallup, approximately 139 miles.

Gallup, New Mexico (elev. 6,506 ft.)

Navajo: *Na'nízhoozhí,* meaning "Spanned Across."

Gallup started out as a typical western town with saloons, trade, and houses of the night (brothels). Federal soldiers at Fort Wingate kept the peace. Gallup was the site of numerous clashes between Navajos and U.S. soldiers prior to the Great Walk in 1863–64. The Acheson, Topeka, and Santa Fe railroads established a presence in Gallup to take advantage of the area's coal deposits to fire its engines. The railroad station (built in 1882) was named "Gallup" after David Gallup, who was associated with the Atlantic and Pacific Railroad during the building of the transcontinental railroad (Linford 2005).

There are many Native American peoples in the Gallup region; in fact, Gallup calls itself the "Indian Capital of the World." Most numerous are the Navajo, famed for their Navajo rugs and blankets sought by collectors and museums around the world. The region also includes the Hopi, noted for their distinctive pottery; the Zuni, noted for their exceptionally fine jewelry; and the Acoma and Laguna people, with their own unique pottery. Gallup's economic well-being in large measure comes from the flow of dollars from the nearby reservations. Visitors will enjoy the wealth of diversity in this town.

Following are some places to see in town:

Downtown Gallup

Enjoy shopping in the trading posts and galleries, located along a twelve-block downtown area bordered by Route 66/Main Street (north), Hill Avenue (south), Fourth Street (west), and First Street (east). Main Street and Coal Avenue have the majority of galleries and trading posts. The downtown arts community hosts a monthly "Arts Crawl" with galleries holding extended hours and offering snacks for local arts browsers. Unique among towns, Gallup has no parking meters.

Gallup Cultural Center

(505) 863-4131. www.gallupnm.org.

The Cultural Center, in the restored railroad station at 201 E. Historic Route 66, houses the Tourist Information Center, the Greyhound lines bus station, Amtrak services, and a café. A project of the Southwest Indian Foundation, the Cultural Center offers a Storyteller Museum, Ceremonial Gallery, and the Kiva Cinema. Indian dances are held nightly, from Memorial Day through Labor Day, close to the Cultural Center. The Inter-Tribal Ceremonial Office holds monthly fine arts sales that attract buyers from across the nation. Admission is free.

Navajo Code Talkers Room

(505) 722-2228.

Photos and memorabilia commemorate the Navajo code talkers' World War II contributions. 103 W. Historic Rte. 66 in the Gallup/McKinley Chamber of Commerce Building.

Gallup Historical Museum

Located at Rte. 66 and Third Street in downtown Gallup, the museum it is operated by the Gallup Historical Society to showcase railroad and mining history.

Gallup Courthouse Square

The recently remodeled McKinley County Courthouse is a Work Projects Administration facility with beautiful artwork, murals, and furnishings produced during President Franklin Roosevelt's administration. 213 West Coal Avenue.

Red Rock State Park

Take I-40 four miles east from Gallup to Exit 33. The park features a Visitors and Conference Center, Trading Post, and rodeo grounds. The rodeo arena (6,800 seats) is situated at the base of picturesque red sandstone cliffs. A world famous event, the Inter-Tribal Indian Ceremonial, is held every August. Gallup has been a yearly gathering place for Native Americans from the United States, Canada, and Mexico since 1992. They come for four days and five nights of celebrations featuring traditional dancing, rodeos, parades, exhibits, and Native American food. Over fifty tribes participate. Events emphasize tradition and authenticity and offer unforgettable photo opportunities. Call 888-685-2564 for information. The Visitors Center (928-282-6907) offers restrooms and picnic areas and is handicapped accessible. Hiking and biking trails are situated in a scenic red rock area. There is also the opportunity for wildlife viewing.

Accommodations

A good resource for hotels in this area: http://www.gallupchamber.com/vacationplanner/accommodations.htm

Best Western Inn and Suites
3010 US-66 West (I-40, Exit 16)
(505) 722-2221, 1-800-722-6399
126 rooms, heated indoor pool, and restaurant

Best Western Red Rock Inn
3010 Route 66 East (I-40, Exit 26)
(505) 722-7600, 1-800-528-1234
77 rooms, heated indoor pool, sauna, whirlpool, and exercise room

Hampton Inn and Suites
1450 Maloney Avenue (I-40, 1 mile west of Exit 20)
(505) 722-4007
63 units, pool

Hampton Inn—West
111 Twin Buttes Road (I-40, Exit 16)
(505) 726-2700
60 units

Best Western Royal Holiday Motel
1903 Route 66 West (I-40, Exit 20)
(505) 722-4900, 1-800-528-1234
Heated indoor pool, sauna, and whirlpool

Comfort Inn—West
3208 Route 66 West (I-40, Exit 16)
(505) 722-0982, 1-888-722-0982
51 rooms and heated indoor pool

Days Inn—West
3201 Route 66 West (I-40, Exit 16)
(505) 863-6889, 1-800-DAYS-INN
Heated indoor pool and whirlpool

EconoLodge
3101 Route 66 West (I-40, Exit 16)
(505) 722-3800
51 rooms

Economy Inn
1709 Route 66 West (I-40, Exit 20)
(505) 863-9301
48 one-bedroom and 2 two-bedroom units

Gallup Travelodge
3275 Route 66 West (I-40, Exit 16)
(505) 722-2100
50 rooms, heated indoor pool, and whirlpool

Holiday Inn Express Gallup
1500 West Maloney Avenue (I-40, Exit 20)
(505) 726-1000
70 rooms, heated indoor pool, sauna, and whirlpool

Holiday Inn Holidome
2915 Route 66 West (I-40, Exit 16)
(505) 722-2201
212 rooms, heated indoor pool, sauna, whirlpool, and exercise room

Ramada Limited
1440 W. Maloney Avenue (I-40, Exit 20)
(505) 726-2700, 1-800-2-RAMADA
Heated indoor pool, whirlpool, conference room, and elevator

Sleep Inn
3820 Route 66 East (I-40, Exit 26)
(505) 863-3535, 1-800-753-3746
www.sleepinn.com
Heated indoor pool and whirlpool

Super 8 Motel
1715 Route 66 West (I-40, Exit 20)
(505) 722-5300
www.newmexico-lodging.com
Heated indoor pool, sauna, and whirlpool

RV and Campgrounds

USA RV Park
2925 Route 66 West
(505) 863-5021
www.usarvpark.com

Restaurants

Chelles Restaurant
2201 Route 66 West (I-40, Exit 16)
(505) 722-7698
Seafood and steaks. Desserts made in-house. Beer and wine only. Dinner only.

Earl's Family Restaurant
1400 Route 66 East (I-40, Exit 22)
(505) 863-4201
American and Mexican dishes

El Sombrero
1201 Route 66 West (I-40, Exit 20)
(505) 863-4554
Mostly Mexican food with some American. Beer and wine only.

King Dragon
828 North US-491 (I-40, Exit 20)
(505) 863-6300
Mandarin, Szechwan, and Hunan dishes

Olympic Kitchen
3200 Route 66 West (I-40, Exit 16)
(505) 863-2584
Specializing in steaks, Greek food, and pasta dishes. Beer and wine only.

Directions from Gallup to Window Rock

Go north on US-666 (note that US-666 used to be US-491) for five miles to Yah-Tah-Hey, where you meet NM-264. Proceed west on NM-264 for 19 miles to Window Rock, the Capital of the Navajo Nation.

Window Rock (elev. 6,755 ft.)

Navajo: *Tséghâhoodzání*, meaning "Perforated Rock" or "Natural Arch."

Window Rock is the seat of tribal government for the Navajo Nation; it is also a business and social center for the people. The Navajo Nation is lead by a tribal chairman and governed by representatives from various districts that make up the tribal council. The reservation is divided into chapters. You will see chapter houses in more populous areas; community meetings and social activities take place in these chapter houses. Navajos are traditionally a democratic society; there have never been hereditary chiefs.

Both Anasazi (dating to the earliest pueblo phases) and early Navajo archeological remains are found beneath Window Rock. The oldest rocks on the reservation—pre-Cambrian, Cambrian, Mississippian, and Pennsylvanian—are exposed in the eastern flank of the Defiance Plateau (just north of Window Rock) and in the "arch" near Window Rock. Prior to any white people setting foot in this area, Navajo medicine men used to collect herbs and used basketry bottles to collect water at the foot of Window Rock for the prayer ceremony for abundant rain (Linford). There are more than fifty different ceremonies that may be used in Navajo culture, all performed at various times for a specific reason. Some ceremonies last for several hours; others may last for nine days, with certain ceremonial dances open to the public.

Window Rock is home to Lieutenant Leaphorn (of Tony Hillerman fame). He is the major lead, along with his deputy, in *Dancehall of the Dead*, *A Thief of Time*, *Skinwalker*, *Sacred Clowns*, and *The Fallen Man*, among others. The Navajo Nation named Hillerman a "Special Friend of the Diné" for presenting Navajo people in a positive way in his books. These books are excellent reading before a trip to Navajoland.

Following are some in-town places to see:

Navajo Nation Museum and Visitor Center

To find your way around town, find the Navajo Nation Inn located on AZ-264 as you enter Window Rock. Next door to the inn is the Navajo Nation Museum, where you will find the visitor center (928-871-7941). The museum building is in the shape of a large hogan with the entrance facing east. You will see a traditional hogan near the entrance.

Diné Restaurant in the Navajo Nation Inn is a good place to eat. While there, if you listen closely, you will hear the soft Navajo language spoken. Most Navajos speak English as well, sometimes fractured English, but you will usually be able to communicate with Navajos.

The visitor center will provide you with a map that makes getting around town easy. You should be able to learn whether any ceremonial dances (open to the public) will be taking place in Window Rock or on the Hopi reservation. Hotels on the reservation are always good places to obtain information on activities in the area. Rodeos are a favorite sport of the Navajo. Ask if there is going to be one in Window Rock, or any other part of the reservation, during the time of your stay.

While in the museum, be sure to see the paintings on display in the gallery. Note the flat Navajo style. Works of different Navajo artists are displayed here each season and it is an excellent venue for reservation artists. Many excellent books on Navajo culture and history can be found in the museum bookstore. Open 8 a.m. to 5 p.m. Monday to Friday and from 9 a.m. to 5 p.m. Saturday.

Navajo Nation Council Chambers

Council chambers are housed in a structure much like a ceremonial hogan. Don't miss the murals inside depicting the history of the Navajo people. Visitors can observe the council on the third Monday of January, April, July, and October. When the council is in session, delegates conduct business in Navajo—a perfect example of Navajos retaining their cultural heritage while conducting business in a modern way. This building and other government offices are in close proximity to the mystical Window Rock formations.

Navajo Arts and Crafts Enterprises and Navajo Tribal Museum

Navajos are known for creating multifaceted art. Their silversmithing and turquoise art is exquisite. Turquoise is especially important to the Navajo because it represents well-being. Navajo rugs are valued throughout the world for their quality of workmanship and their unique styles. Distinctive styles of rugs identify designs woven in different areas of the reservation: Two Gray Hills, Ganado, Teec Nos Pos, and Crystal, among others. Sand-painting, a unique and symbolic art form, represents an array of ceremonies and sacred songs. Wedding baskets are used in certain ceremonies, and to decorate their homes.

Navajo Arts and Crafts Enterprises is across the street from the inn. Authentic rugs, silver, turquoise jewelry, and many other works of art will be found here. Exploring this store is well worth the effort, even if only for browsing.

The Navajo Tribal Museum is located in the same building as Navajo Arts and Crafts Enterprises. This museum has more than four thousand items that trace Navajo history from the 1600s. A replica of a dinosaur found near Tuba City is also on display.

Veterans' Memorial Park

The memorial to the WWII code talkers is located within Veteran's Memorial Park on Window Rock Monument grounds. The park features a circular path outlining the four cardinal directions. The names of Navajo war veterans are inscribed on sixteen angled steel pillars. There is a healing sanctuary that is used for reflection and solitude. Open daily 8 a.m. to 5 p.m. For more information, call 928-871-6647 or 928-871-6413. Information can also be found on the Web at http://navajonationparks.org.

Navajo Nation Zoological and Botanical Park

An abandoned bear was the impetus for building the zoo (opened in 1962) that today includes most native animals from Navajoland: bobcats, wolves, deer, elk, churro sheep, rabbits, wild turkeys, and snakes and lizards. Animals live in truly natural habitats surrounded by native vegetation and rock scenery. Open 8 a.m. to 5 p.m., Monday through Friday.

The Haystacks

Navajo: *Tséta' Ch'ééch'i*, meaning "Breeze Blows out from between the Rocks"; and *Tseyt'*, meaning "Between the Rocks."

The Haystacks, located immediately behind the Navajo Museum on the north side of AZ-264, are formations of abrupt sandstone monuments one hundred feet high in Tsé Bonito Tribal Park close to the New Mexico state line.

Flea Market

This event is held in the shopping center west of the Quality Inn on many Saturdays.

Major Rodeos and Celebrations

The annual 4th of July celebration, with a major professional cowboy and youth celebration, offers ceremonial dances, concerts, carnival, powwow, fine arts exhibits, and sports. The fireworks display, rodeo, ceremonial dances, and a parade are held in the Navajo Tribal Fairgrounds.

The Annual Navajo Nations Fair is held in September after Labor Day. This fair is a showcase event for the Navajo people. It is the largest Indian fair and rodeo in the United States with all-Indian contestants. There are twenty coordinated events extending over five days: powwow, Miss Navajo Nation pageant, wild horse race, fine arts/crafts exhibits, native cuisine, concerts, and contests. It is the most exciting event of the year.

If you plan to see any of these rodeos and competitions, book your hotel early; there are limited rooms in the Window Rock area. Otherwise, stay in Gallup a short distance away. For information on Gallup, see page 95.

Services

Hospital and medical facilities are available to travelers for emergency use. When stabilized, travelers will be transferred to non-native hospitals.

In Window Rock, medical services are available at Fort Defiance Indian Health Service (928-729-5741).

Bashas grocery stores are located in most of the larger towns, including Window Rock, Tuba City, Page (off the reservation), Kayenta, Farmington (off the reservation), and Chinle. They are the best places to stock up on water and snacks. Gas stations are in the same towns: do not count on finding gas stations elsewhere; they are few and far between. It might be a long way between restaurants or fast-food places, with the latter being more plentiful. Restaurants feature mutton stew (several kinds), fry bread, fry bread tacos, southwest and Mexican dishes, sometimes with a Navajo twist, and some serve chicken and steak. Chain hotels usually run by locals are very clean, with excellent and polite service. Hotels are somewhat pricey on the reservation; food is not overly expensive, even in hotel restaurants.

Accommodations

Quality Inn Navajo Nation
48 West AZ-264.
(928) 871-4108 or 800-662-6189
56 rooms, eight suites. Restaurant

Navajoland Days Inn
329 West AZ-264, St. Michael's, close to Window Rock.
(928) 871-5690 or 1-800-DAYS-INN
65 rooms, eight suites, heated indoor pool, sauna, whirlpool, and exercise room.

Restaurants

Diné Restaurant
Located in the Quality Inn Navajo Nation.
(928) 871-4108
Navajo mutton stew and fry bread. Navajo, American, and Mexican dishes.

Denny's Restaurant
Located next door to Days Inn
(928) 871-2067

Church's Fried Chicken
Located in the St. Michael's Shopping Center, AZ-264, St. Michael's
(928) 871-5780
Open 11 a.m. to 10 p.m.

RV and Campgrounds

JWJ RV Park and Campground
Ft. Defiance (seven miles north of AZ-264 on IR-12)
(928) 729-5917

Narbonna Pass Campground
(928) 777-2239
Located five miles east of Crystal, New Mexico on NM-134.

Instead of turning left off US-666 at Yah-Tah-Hey, continue on US-666 to NM-134, approximately 38 miles. Follow NM-134 for about 10 miles to the campground. Or, one can take IR-12 north out of Window Rock for 7 miles to where it joins NM-134 at Fort Defiance. Continue north on NM-134 to the campground.

This popular campground is in the Chuska Mountains near the recreation area. It is almost equal distance between Window Rock and Canyon de Chelly. Elevation is 8,150 feet.

General Information

- **Police:** (928) 871-6111
- **Hospital:** (928) 729-5741
- **Weekly newspaper:** *Navajo Times,* published for all of Navajoland
- **Radio stations:** KTNN 660 AM and KWRK 96.1 FM, both from Window Rock.

Recreation areas are open to the public only with the proper licenses and permits. Check with the proper department listed below before engaging in any of these activities:

- Permits for hiking, camping, and backcountry use: Navajo Parks and Recreation Department, P.O. Box 9000, Window Rock, AZ 86515; (928) 871-6647. Information can also be found on the web at http://navajonationparks.org.
- Licenses for hunting, fishing, trapping, and boating: Navajo Fish & Wildlife, P.O. Box 1480, Window Rock, AZ 86515. (928) 871-6451 or 6452. Or see www.navajofishandwildlife.org.

- Permits for commercial filming and photography: Navajo Nation Film Office (928) 871-7351

Window Rock and Canyon de Chelly Recreation Areas

Wonderful camping and fishing opportunities abound in the Chuska Mountain recreation areas, where it is much cooler on hot days. The scenery alone is worth the drive—an easy day trip from Window Rock. With the proper permit, you can fish from the shores of most lakes with good results. The highest peak is 8,795 feet. Be aware! Weather is very changeable in mountain areas. Roads can become impassable when it rains. Check the forecast on KTNN 660 AM before setting out.

Take IR-12 north from Window Rock for 7 miles to where it joins IR-134 at Fort Defiance.

Continue north on IR-134 to east on IR-31. Follow directions once you meet IR-30. Camp Asáάyi is a short distance north on IR-30 in the Bowl Canyon Recreation Area.

Lake Asáάyi (pronounced *Ah-Sy-Yeh*)

Camp Asáάyi is one of the Navajo Nation's major attractions in the Bowl Canyon recreation area. Camp Asáάyi provides hiking, fishing, picnicking, canoeing, and camping. Large groups can be accommodated. Facilities include a large dining hall with fully equipped kitchen and sixteen open cabins with bunk beds, showers, and restrooms. There is equipment for outdoor sports. Hikers on the two hiking trails within the recreation area are rewarded with beautiful panoramas. You will see wandering streams and towering pine trees. Camp Asáάyi is open from April through October, depending on weather conditions. Temperatures range from the mid-70s to the upper-90s.

The thirty-six-acre Lake Asáάyi is approximately one-half mile west of the camp. The view is breathtaking. Lake Asáάyi is open to the public; it is ideal for camping, canoeing, and trout fishing. Private boats or canoes are allowed on the lake with a boating permit; however, no motorboats are allowed. Canoes are available for rent to Camp Asáάyi participants only.

Whiskey Lake

This spot is well known by locals as a fantastic fishing hole for rainbow and cutthroat trout. Whiskey Lake is off IR-30 near Camp Asááyi; it is an ideal place for an all-day outing.

Todacheene Lake

Located just a mile or so north of IR-30 on NM-134, this lake is stocked with channel and warm-water catfish. Berland Lake is much higher on the same road. These lakes are more suited to the dedicated fisherman.

Berland Lake

This is the highest lake at 8,000 feet and is surrounded by grassy hills and tall mountain pines.

Red Lake

Located in the town of Navajo, off NM-134, near the junction of IR-31, channel and warm-water catfish patrol the lake. You can stock up on chicken livers and other bait in Navajo.

FORT DEFIANCE (elev. 6,892 ft.)

Navajo: *Tséhootzooí,* meaning "Meadow in between the Rocks."

Fort Defiance (7 miles north of Window Rock) is located at the mouth of Canyon Bonito. It was the site of repeated action in the Indian Wars of the 1850s and 1860s. U.S. soldiers nicknamed it "Hell's Gate," and no wonder: Navajos held the high ground. It was easy for Navajos to spy on U.S. troops camped at the bottom of the steep canyon; they could see everything that was happening (Linford). The army successfully repelled a series of attacks in 1860, before abandoning it during the Civil War.

The first Navajo Agency was located here after the Navajo returned from Bosque Redondo. The first trading post was opened in 1868. In accordance with the Treaty of 1868, in 1869 the Indian Agency at Fort Defiance gave out the first sheep and goats to Navajos as a base for rebuilding the herds decimated by Kit Carson.

Under the Treaty of 1868, Navajo children between the ages of six and sixteen were to be educated. The first school at Fort Defiance was built in 1880. Few Navajo children attended until mandatory attendance was enforced. Only one hundred students were enrolled in all reservation schools by 1892 (Linford). Indian boarding schools constituted a long, sad chapter in Navajo history. Teachers disregarded and often degraded the strong religious beliefs and cultural values of Navajo students; Anglo-American culture and values were taught instead.

Suggested Day Trips from Window Rock

Hubbell Trading Post National Historic Site

Take AZ-264 for 30 miles west of Window Rock.

One can easily visit the above and St. Michael's in one day. See page 116 (Hubbell) and page 113 (St. Michael's) for information on both places.

Canyon de Chelly National Monument

Take AZ-264 west to US-191 north just past Ganado, approximately 35 miles. Go north on US-191 for about 39 miles to Chinle. Turn right (east) at the light and continue until you arrive at Canyon de Chelly Visitor Center.

The interior of the canyon cannot be seen unless accompanied by a guide, and the canyon floor is the best view. It is best to arrange for a guide to descend into the canyon the evening before you leave on this trip. You can make arrangements there if a guide is available. You will visit ancient Anasazi sites and Navajo historical sites; Navajo guides will provide cultural and historical information. There is a map available at the visitor center for the road trip around the rims of Canyon de Chelly and Canyon de Muerte. The only place the canyon floor can be accessed without a guide is at White House Overlook. You can hike for about two miles across the canyon to the White House ruins. Unfortunately, cars have been broken into at some of the overlooks. Do not leave anything of value in your car.

This is one Navajo site where using a guide should be at the top of your list; the half-day and full-day tours from Thunderbird Lodge are your best value. Your car can be left at the Tourist Center or next door at Thunderbird Lodge; your guide will pick you up there. Bring lots of water. For further information on Canyon de Chelly, see page 107.

Hopi Cultural Center and the Three Mesas

(520) 737-2262

Take AZ-264 for 90 miles west of Window Rock.

A guide is necessary if you wish to see the old village of Walpi. Group tours are conducted Monday through Friday, 9:30 a.m. to 4:00 p.m. For further information, see page 123.

Zuni Pueblo (elev. 6,575 ft.)

Take NM-602 south from Gallup for about 30 miles to NM-53. Proceed west (right) on NM-53 for about 10 miles to the village of Zuni, where you will find the Visitors Center.

Navajo: *Naasht'ézhí,* meaning "Marked about with charcoal," refers to black paint around the eyes of Zuni warriors.

It can take most of a day to see Zuni Pueblo. You will be driving on good, paved state roads. A permit to take pictures can be purchased here; permits and tours are not overly expensive.

Two tours are available: a middle village tour, which is a walking tour through the "living past" of Zuni's Historic Original Pueblo Village, where you will also see the old mission; and an Artist's Workshop Tour that visits three known artists in their workshops. The tours take four visitors at a time. Call Zuni Tourism at (505) 782-7238 to schedule a tour and to find out what is open in the village the day you wish to visit. There is also an excellent nature, architecture, and archeological tour that is not always available—call ahead for reservations.

Be sure to visit the A:shiwi A:wan Museum and Heritage Center, where hundreds of artifacts are on display from the Zuni ancestral village of Hawikku. The museum is an eco-museum, in harmony with the cultural environmental values of the Zuni people. It is a community learning center that links the past with the present to deal with the future. Any traditional dances, ceremonies, and events should be observed from a distance and with quiet respect. These are expressions of religious beliefs. There are many aspects of Zuni life you may not understand or even recognize; these important practices enable Zunis to continue their way of life.

Zuni and El Morro areas were occupied as far back as 5000 B.C., when hunter-gatherers moved into the area. Farming started about A.D. 400, at which time they gathered into small villages, "the dawn of pueblo culture." At about A.D. 1000, construction methods changed. Evidence that Chaco Canyon construction methods influenced the Zunis is found in the changes in construction methods and the advent of *kivas,* underground chambers entered through an opening in the roof. The kiva could be used for meditation, prayer, and preparation for important ceremonies (Kosik 1996).

There may have been up to seven thousand people living in the area at this time. There were six villages at the time of Spanish contact in 1540: Hawikku, Kechiba:wa, Kyaki:ma, Mats'a:kya, Kwa'kina, and Halona:wa (present Zuni Pueblo) (Linford). Zuni Pueblo was one of the villages visited by Coronado in his quest for the "Seven Cities of Gold."

Zuni Pueblo, the largest of nineteen tribes of New Mexico Pueblos, is considered the most traditional. They have a unique language, culture, and history that, it is believed, resulted in part from their geographic isolation. Acoma, Zuni, and Hopi peoples are descendents of the Anasazi. Zunis developed their artistic skills in tight family settings; they honed their competitive edge through involvement in powwows and local fairs. Almost 80 percent of the population is involved with artistic endeavors, creating a vibrant atmosphere for a community of focused artists. Zuni products are recognized for their intricate beauty and quality workmanship, while remaining subtly individual in design. The economy of Zuni Pueblo is based on agriculture and livestock, as well as arts and crafts. Be sure to sample the sourdough bread made in their outdoor, rounded ovens. The Inn at Halona (800-752-4288) is a historic B&B located in the middle of Zuni Pueblo. There are eight guest rooms. A deli is located in the adjacent Halona Plaza; meals can be arranged.

One-Day Side Trip from Window Rock

Take NM-602 south from Gallup for about 30 miles to NM-53. Proceed east (left) on NM-53 for 12 miles to the village of Ramah.

Ramah Reservation (elev. approx. 7,000 ft.)

Ramah reservation—a Navajo chapter—is one of three chapters outside the main reservation; it has a representative on the tribal council in Window Rock. Ramah was settled in 1876. The Ramah Weavers Association has developed a local economy based on sheep and other land-based traditions. It is home to many fine weavers who raise and use the wool of churro sheep in their art. Visitor Center of Ramah: (505) 552-6654. Ramah Historical Society: (505) 783-4150. Ramah Stagecoach Café: (505) 783-4288.

Go east from Ramah on NM-53 for thirteen miles to El Morro National Monument.

El Morro National Monument (elev. 6,800–7,000 ft.)

Navajo: *Tsék' I na' asdzooí,* meaning "Rock Hat Has Marks [writing] on It."

El Morro, also known as Inscription Rock, is a massive sandstone bluff rising over two hundred feet from the valley floor. Two thousand historic petroglyphs and inscriptions are carved into the rock. It was a distinct landmark and a reliable source of water for travelers through the ages.

The Anasazi, ancestors of the Zuni, were the first to leave their mark on this giant bluff. About 1,500 people lived on top of the mesa in the early 1300s. The village of Atsina (which is a Zuni word meaning "writing on the rock") was abandoned by the late 1300s (ibid.). The Atsina people left behind petroglyphs—etched symbols depicting animals, handprints, and other designs. Their meanings have been lost to our world.

The Spanish were next to leave their mark on El Morro. Don Juan Oñate carved his name on Inscription Rock in 1605. As late as 1774, Spanish friars, soldiers, and travelers also entered their names. U.S. soldiers who surveyed the land in the mid-1880s were the last set of names etched on the rock.

A guidebook at the visitor center gives detailed information on Inscription Rock. The visitor center and museum are open 9 a.m. to 5 p.m.

Last admission for those wishing to hike is one hour before closing: (505) 783-4226. A gentle half-mile walk along a paved trail will take you to the inscriptions. Visitors in good shape can also take a two-mile strenuous hike to the top of the mesa to see the ruins of Atsina. There are picnic tables and a campground. The trailhead for the Zuni-Acoma Trail starts here.

Ice Caves (elev. 8,000 ft.)

Navajo: *Dibé Hooghan*, meaning "Sheep Hogan."

The ice cave at the foot of Bandera Volcano is in the El Malpais lava beds. The "temperature hovers just below freezing in the 'cave' (which is really a collapsed horizontal volcanic tube), preserving a wall of green-tinted ice" (Linford, 219–220).

Continue east on NM-53 for 16 miles to the Bandera Volcano and another 26 miles through El Malpaise National Momument to Grants, where you meet I-40.

Bandera Volcano and Malpaise National Monument

(505) 285-4641 or (505) 783-4774

Between El Morro and El Malpaise National Monument are the twenty-nine volcanoes of the Fire and Ice region that forms the backbone of the Continental Divide in this area. It is best to proceed to the Malpaise National Monument Visitors Center on NM-53, just past the ice caves, to obtain information on the geology, history, and the hiking trails. Adjacent to the ice fields is Bandera Crater, the largest of the twenty-nine extinct volcanoes, with a huge cone remaining from its last eruption some five thousand years ago. The cone is one thousand feet deep, and native trees grow in the cone area. Paths to the crater provide great views of the enormous amount of lava that flowed out in its last eruption. If you plan to hike, be sure to let someone at the visitor center, or at the trading post nearby, know where you are going and when you expect to return. Dried lava can be very sharp, so wear heavy boots to avoid injury. Locals run the trading post, and they are familiar with the trails and the history of the area.

Return to Window Rock on I-40 west to Gallup, then north on US-666 to Yah-Ta-Hey, and west on NM-264 to Window Rock.

CHAPTER 15

FROM WINDOW ROCK TO THE THREE MESAS

Directions from Window Rock to St. Michael's
To continue the tour of the Navajo Nation, take AZ-264 west from Window Rock to St. Michael's, approximately 3 miles.

St. Michael's (elev. 7,000 ft.)

Navajo: *Ts"íhooto*, meaning "Yellow Meadow" or "Area That Extends out Yellow and Green."

The Diné won a battle against Mexico at St. Michael's. Chách'oshnééz, an enemy Navajo (*Diné 'Ana'í*) who had sided with the Spanish, informed the Diné of the Mexican attack plans. He was then invited to join the main body of Navajo, and he accepted. He was later one of the signers of the Treaty of 1868, using the name Delgadito (Linford 2000).

Blessed Katherine Drexel, founder of the Sisters of the Blessed Sacrament, inherited a large fortune from her father. Determined to supply educational facilities for the Navajo people, she persuaded the Franciscan friars from Cincinnati to send missionaries to Navajoland. Father Juvenal Schnorbus and Father Anselem Weber answered the call. Over the years, a great friendship was established among the Franciscans, the Sisters of the Blessed Sacrament, and the Navajo.

Navajos first accepted the Ohio Franciscans because they had just returned from Bosque Redondo and needed the help of the Franciscans to protect themselves against the bureaucracy of the Indian Service and hostile neighbors. The Navajo trusted the Ohio Franciscans because these Franciscans were willing to learn the Navajo language and incorporate Navajo traditions and ceremonies into the Catholic service. Spanish Franciscans had failed in their dealings with the Navajo because of their disregard for the highly developed Navajo belief system and language (Kosik 1996).

Father O'Connor wrote in the *Padre's Trail* (a magazine published by St. Michael's Mission) of the friendship and respect between Catholics and Navajos. The reason this relationship worked so well, according to Navajo medicine men, is the great respect and honor the Navajo and the Catholics held for each other's beliefs. Many orders of sisters came to St. Michael's over the following years: they were teachers, social workers, and health service workers. There are presently eighteen missions serving the Navajo.

The Mission of St. Michael's claims that Father Weber wrote the first dictionary of the Navajo language in a romanized English alphabet. Father Weber spent years becoming fluent in Navajo and performed a tremendous linguistic service for the Navajo people. Father Weber was even better known and respected for his unceasing efforts to protect the rights of Indians and Indian lands.

The St. Michael's Visitor Center is the original mission building. Mary Mother of Mankind Church is on the east side of the road. It was built in 1937, replacing an earlier adobe structure. The staff is friendly, helpful, and has plenty of informational literature handy.

A small circular chapel is located close to the church, behind the parking area. In keeping with its hogan structure, it has an earthen floor. Of special interest is the sixteen-foot sculpture carved from a single 500-year-old juniper tree. The sculpture, completed in 1992, commemorates the 500th anniversary of European and Native American relations. Sculptor Ludwig Schumacher had Michelangelo's marble pieta in mind, but the shape of the tree dictated the vertical image. Schumacher describes his work as follows:

> The name of this work is "the redemption of humankind." This work has been created from a very old juniper tree. Maybe this tree was

growing up even before one shoe of a white man stepped on this continent. . . .

Five hundred years after the discovery of the American continent in 1492 by Christopher Columbus we bring this work to you.

Now we bring something to you, not just take away from you. . . .

This work show(s) a dead Indian man being lowered from a large teepee tarp, like the body of Jesus Christ down from the cross.

The teepee represents the lives of the Indian peoples.

Out of the teepee smoke-hole a cross-like shape breaks forth, but this can be the teepee sticks, and smoke too. Below the figure of the dead Indian man is a woman. She is mourning the great pain and suffering that has been brought to the lives of the Indians since the white men first appeared. Two helpers stay close too.

All our hopes for peace for you, and with you, are united in this work.

All our faults are associated in this work; please welcome it to you.

This work will help to unite all human beings of this world in peace, love and brotherhood. The hands of many peoples have helped to make the creation of this work possible. The hearts and minds of these people are as one with me. Now we will bring this work to you as a gift from us, please welcome it.

Maybe we are brothers after all. A wise Indian man said this and Jesus Christ too. (Source: St. Michael's Museum)

Ludwig Schumacher wanted this carving to have its home on Indian land: after a long search, he offered it to St. Michael's. Since then, from personal friendship, he made a companion carving of Mary from an apricot tree. The sculpture is located in the main church. The Prayer Chapel is dedicated to Jesus Savior of Mankind. It is a place of centering, prayer, and healing.

Directions from St. Michael's to Ganado and Hubbell Trading Post
Take AZ-264 west out of St. Michael's for 32 miles.

The drive between St. Michael's and Ganado goes through the beautiful Navajo Forest. You will see many homes and hogans hidden among the trees; Navajos like to live in family groups well set off from others. Small clusters of hogans, trailers, and a house usually implies more than one generation of a family. Small herds of goats and sheep, important to many Navajos, are often herded and watched by two dogs, one in the lead and one behind. The dogs can be mean; they are very protective of the herd if you come too close.

Ganado (elev. 6,400 ft.)

Navajo: *Lók'aahnteel*, meaning "Wide Band of Reeds up an Elevation."

Ganado, thirty-two miles west of Window Rock, was named after Ganado Mucho (Spanish meaning "much livestock"). He was the twelfth signer of the Treaty of 1868. Ganado was head chief of the western division of the Navajo. There are no reliable services in Ganado, but there is a grocery store.

Hubble Trading Post National Historic Site

Navaho: Possibly *Nák'ee Sinilí*, meaning "Eye Glasses," or *Naakaii Sáni'*, meaning "Old Mexican."

The trading post is well signed, but it is hard to see from AZ-264. Drive in a short way and you will see the visitor center on the right. Hubbell Trading Post is the oldest, continuously operating trading post on the reservation. Trading posts were often the only link the Navajo had with non-natives and the outside world. Hubbell was known for fair business dealings; he spoke Navajo and therefore traded with them in their own language. Hubbell settled quarrels, wrote and translated letters, explained government policy, and looked out for the welfare of his neighbors. Respected by the Navajo, Hubbell did more to popularize Navajo arts and crafts than any other person, and he was a leader in the revival of Navajo weaving in the late nineteenth century.

Hubbell took in over a quarter of a million dollars in wool and hides alone during the early days (Trimble 1997). He commissioned artists to develop rug designs as examples for the skilled Navajo weavers to follow. He was influential in helping to develop the Ganado Red design that local weavers are famous for. Navajos liked to linger after the trading was completed, socializing with their neighbors. Everyone at the trading post gathered at the house kitchen at noon each day for the bread prepared by the house cook, which was shared with everyone.

The trading post has changed very little; many of the same goods are still for sale. The rug room contains stacks of varicolored rugs, displaying the skill of Navajo weavers. Certificates of authenticity are available. There is also high-quality silver and turquoise jewelry and baskets for sale. The Hubbell Trading Post has rug auctions fairly often.

The visitor center is a good place to begin your visit: open 8 a.m. to 6 p.m. in the summer and 8 a.m. to 5 p.m. all other times; (928) 755-3475. The park provides public restrooms, a drinking fountain, and picnic tables. No overnight facilities are available. Navajo weavers frequently display their works in progress in the visitor center. Demonstrations of arts and crafts are often seen as well. Ask before photographing weavers; they usually expect a few dollars in return. You can take a self-guided tour of the grounds.

Rangers conduct a tour of Hubbell's house, which contains original period furniture, paintings, outstanding rugs, and an unusual basket collection. There are four bedrooms, a grand central room, and a formal dining room, furnished with beautiful handcrafted and carved quarter-sawn furniture. The tour is well worth the small fee.

Directions from Hubbell's Trading Post to Keams Canyon
Continue west on AZ-264 for 48 miles to Keams Canyon, which is on the Hopi reservation.

KEAMS CANYON (elev. 6,400 ft.)

Navajo: *Lók'a'deeshjin* can be interpreted as "Black Reeds in a Distance."

Keams Canyon was originally known as Peach Springs; the Hopi used to farm here. Billy Dodd, the brother of Indian agent Major Theodore Dodd, opened a trading post in this canyon in the 1860s. John Keams (an

Englishman who fought the Navajo under Kit Carson) was next to establish a trading post and ranch in 1880. He acted as agent and inspector until a separate Hopi agency was opened on his land. The agency later moved down the canyon to its present site. The government purchased Keam's old land and buildings for the BIA (Bureau of Indian Affairs) Boarding School. Keams rebuilt at his present site in 1887 (Linford).

Keams experienced trouble with BIA superintendent Charles Burton in 1899. Burton demanded that all Hopi ceremonial dances stop. He required that Hopi children have their long hair cut and attend boarding school, even if force had to be used. Keams publicly disagreed with this policy and was accused of defrauding the government. He had to go back to Washington to fight his case, and subsequently Burton was removed (Kosik 1996). The hospital here serves both Hopis and Navajos with 24-hour service. Emergency air transportation is available to Phoenix.

Restaurants

Keams Canyon Restaurant
Located in the Keams Canyon Shopping Center on AZ-264.
(928) 738-2296
Typical roadside family-style eating: Navajo tacos, lamb stew, and American food. Above the restaurant is an arts and crafts gallery, which offers high-quality Hopi crafts: jewelry, pottery, beautiful carvings, and baskets.

Services

Police: (928) 738-2233

HOPI RESERVATION (elev. 4,650–7,220 ft.)

Navajo: *'Ayahkiníí*, meaning "Underground People."

Hopis are a Pueblo tribe who live in thirteen villages on their 2.4-million-acre reservation, located entirely within the Navajo reservation. Anasazi pueblos of the classical style are still in evidence on the mesas. Hopi villages cluster on the top of mesas, but people are increasingly moving into scattered trailers and houses below the mesas. The tribe is divided into clans and kiva societies. Hopis are among the Southwest's most conservative (traditional) native people; they struggle to keep their old customs and culture (Brown 1996).

Hopis are the oldest continuous inhabitants of northern Arizona and may have lived there from A.D. 700. Hopis prefer their ancient ancestors be called "Hisatsinom," meaning "Peaceful People," instead of "Anasazi," a Navajo name that means "Enemy People." Tradition has it that some of their ancestors came from the Canyon de Chelly Anasazi ruins. Later groups are said to have come from Homolavi and Chaves Pass, and still later groups such as the Tewas and Keres were from the Rio Grande area of New Mexico (Linford).

Hopis are a collection of smaller Pueblo tribes or clans as described above. It is said that each new group had to demonstrate they had something to contribute to the tribe before they were accepted. In this manner, they have become a "melting pot" of different tribes. Hopi villages have a complicated social structure: each village is a completely separate unit, and each clan has designated duties to perform. Kivas—underground ceremonial chambers—are in all the villages. Religion is a daily aspect of their lives. Most of their ceremonies center on crops, with corn symbolically the most important (Trimble).

There are no permanent streams running through Hopiland, but there are many springs. Rainfall is less than twelve inches per year (mostly in the summer), necessitating a uniquely specialized form of agriculture. Farmland lies along the washes. Most farmers have several fields in different locations around the base of the mesa because of sporadic rainfall that occurs in localized showers. In Hopi traditional farming practices, fields are not usually plowed, but "wind breakers" are placed in the fields at intervals to retain soil, snow, and moisture. They build dams of stone, brush, and earth that dike the area so flood waters flow over the land. On the mesa tops, farmers construct brush barriers to accumulate the wind-blown sand for mulch. Indian corn and many varieties of beans and melons are grown. Peach trees, introduced by the Spanish, grow on sand and rocky slopes near springs in sub-irrigated places. Some farmers also have sheep and cattle (Linford).

Hopi religion is centered on agriculture and the harmony that comes from living as one with nature. Their sole economy used to center on farming; today they are as likely to live on the income from jobs in Winslow, Holbrook, and Flagstaff, or jobs with tribal government. The patterns of daily life are changing. Nevertheless, Hopis are still the most traditional among native cultures in the United States (Brown).

Hopi villages are located on the southwestern fingers of Black Mesa. Each village has its own plaza where ceremonies are held, much as they have for centuries. Hopiland includes part of Black Mesa in the north and much of the barren Painted Desert in the south. They believe their immediate ancestors came from the area of Homolovi Prehistoric Park, sixty-seven miles directly south on AZ-87, just before I-40 at Winslow. Homolovi Park and ruins serve as a research center for the late migration period of Hopi history in the 1200s and 1300s. Hopiland was unattractive to the white population, which kept it isolated from the settlers who poured into New Mexico and Arizona after the arrival of the railroad.

Hopi Kachinas

Kachinas, or Katsinas, are stylized religious icons meticulously carved from cottonwood root and painted to represent figures from Hopi mythology. Traditionally, kachina figures have been used to teach Hopi children about their religion. It takes years of practice and religious study to master Kachina carving. Only a small number of Hopi carvers have dedicated their lives to this art.

A kachina can take three forms: a powerful unseen spirit, a dancer filled with the spirit, or a wooden figure representing the spirit. Kachina dancers are always male, even when the spirit is female. The men may present gifts of kachina figures to women and chidren during the dances. Each village sponsors its own ceremonies.

Kachinas appear to the Hopi from the winter solstice on December 21 until mid-July. They dance and sing in unison, symbolizing the harmony of good thought and deed, harmony required for rain to fall and for a balanced life. The rest of the year the kachinas remain in their home in the San Francisco Peaks. (Read more at www.native-languages.org/kachinas.htm.)

Hopi Calendar

Wuwuchim and Soyala (November to December). These months symbolize the time of creation of the world. The villages tend to be quiet as the Hopi spend time in silence, prayer, and meditation.

Wuwuchuim, a tribal initiation ceremony, marks the start of the ceremonial calendar year. Young men are initiated into adulthood, joining one of four ceremonial societies. The society a man joins depends on his sponsor. Upon acceptance, the initiate receives instruction in Hopi creation beliefs. He is presented with a new name, and his childhood name is never used again.

Only Shungopavi village performs the entire Wuwuchuim ceremony, and not every year. Other villages engage in parts of the Wuwuchuim ceremony.

The Soyala Kachina appears from the west in the winter solstice ceremony, marking the beginning of the kachina season. As the days get longer, the Hopi begin planning the upcoming planting season; fertility is a major focus of the ceremony.

Buffalo Dances (January)

Men, women, and children perform these social dances in the plazas. They deal with fertility, especially the need for winter moisture in the form of snow.

Powamuya, the Bean Dance (February)

Bean sprouts are grown in a kiva as part of a sixteen-day ceremony. On the final day, kachina dancers form a long parade through the village. Children of about ten years are initiated into kachina societies during the Powamuya. Ogre kachinas appear on the First and Second mesas.

Kiva Dances (March)

A second set of nighttime kiva dances consists of *Anktioni*, or "repeat dances."

Plaza Dances (April, May, and June)

The kachina dancers perform in all-day ceremonies lasting from sunrise to sunset, with breaks between dances. The dancers, and the people watching the ceremony, concentrate in a community prayer. They call on the spirits to bring rain for the growing crops.

Niman, the "Home Dance" (July)

At the summer solstice on July 21, the plaza dances end and preparations begin for the Going Home Ceremony. In a sixteen-day rite, the last of the season, kachina dancers present the first green corn ears, then dance for rain to hasten growth of the remaining crops. Their spiritual work done, the kachinas return to their mountain home.

Snake, Flute, and Butterfly Dances (August)

The Snake and Flute ceremonies, held in alternate years, represent the clan groups who perform them in the interests of a good harvest and prosperity. The Snake Dance, usually closed to non-Hopi, takes place in even-numbered years at Shungopavi and Hotevilla and in odd-numbered years at Mishongnovi. The snakes, often poisonous rattlers, act as messengers to the spirits.

The Flute Ceremony takes place in odd-numbered years at Shungopavi and Walpi.

The Butterfly Dance, a social dance performed mainly by children, takes place in all villages. It also celebrates the harvest.

Women's Society Dances (September, October, and Early November)

Held in the plazas, these ceremonies celebrate the harvest with wishes for health and prosperity. Chaos reigns during the Basket Dances; female dancers throw out baskets and other valuables to the audience, who engage in a mad free-for-all to grab the prizes. They mark the end of the ceremonial year.

Visitor Etiquette

It is prohibited to photograph, record, or sketch villages and ceremonies. Alcoholic beverages and drugs are strictly prohibited. Overnight camping is allowed, with permission, for a maximum of two nights at specifically designated camping areas only. Each village is autonomous; therefore, to enter a village to visit or to watch a ceremony, it is necessary to get permission in the visitor center or from the village leader.

The Three Mesas

Directions to The Three Mesas

Continue west on AZ-264 through the Three Mesas. Drive slowly or you may miss some of the entrances to the villages. Be aware that permission must be obtained to enter a village. Information on entering a village can be obtained from any trading post or store on AZ-264.

The Three Mesas are high, dry sandy areas where it is often windy; blowing dust can be a problem. The only restaurant (and hotel) is located on Second Mesa at the Cultural Center. Carry snacks and plenty of water. Call Punsi Hall Visitor Center, 928-737-2262, before five o'clock the evening before your trip to Hopiland to arrange for a tour of the ancient town of Walpi. Call the Hopi Cultural Center at 928-734-2401 or the Cultural Preservation Office at 928-734-3613 to see if there are any ceremonial dances open to the public on the day you wish to visit. Old Walpi ruins, below the present town, date back to A.D. 900.

Several villages hold dances on Saturday and/or Sunday, continuing intermittently throughout the day with breaks for lunch and rest periods. The ceremonies usually end at dusk. Often, several villages will have dances on the same day, giving visitors the opportunity to witness parts of several dances by spending a few hours in each village. The dates of these ceremonial dances are determined by Hopi customs and traditions; exact dates are known only a few days in advance.

There is a small fee for the tour of Walpi, but it can be seen only with a guide. Be prepared to climb a fairly steep, uneven road. There are many weekend closures for private ceremonies; plan your trip accordingly. A guided tour of the village of Walpi consists of a forty-five-minute to one-hour walk through the old pueblo site. The guide will share the history, general life, and traditions of the Hopi people.

Personal Tours of the Hopi Reservation

Left Handed Hunter Tour Company
(928) 734-2567
Specialized tours to Walpi, Old Oraibi, and a petroglyph site. The studios of a Kachina carver, a potter, a silversmith, and goldsmith are also visited. All day tours include lunch, transportation, and entrance fees. These tours are less expensive if you have four people.

Ancient Pathways
(928) 306-7849
Specialized tours to Hopi petroglyph sites. These sites are not open to the public unless you are with a Hopi guide. Tours visit Old Oraibi as well.

First Mesa

Polacca (elev. 6,000 ft.)

Hopi: *Polakaka,* meaning "Butterfly."

This is the first village on your approach to First Mesa. The older, more interesting villages of Hano, Sichomovi, and Walpi are at the top of the mesa above Polacca. From Polacca, a 1.3-mile paved road winds steeply up to a parking lot near the village of Sichomovi, where you will find the Punsi Hall Visitor Center. This is where you will meet your tour if you have called ahead. You can sometimes join a tour without a reservation, but you may have to wait. If you have a trailer or large vehicle, you must park it in Polacca or at parking areas a half-mile and one mile up the road. Note: There is a signpost "First Mesa Village" near milepost 392 on AZ-264.

Hopi women on First Mesa used to make all the decorated pottery until the 1970s; now they make pottery on Second and Third Mesas as well. Men paint, create objects with silver, and carve wood kachina dolls, along with weaving blankets.

Hano (elev. 6,200 ft.)

Hopi: "*Hanie*" from the Hopi language, referring to the "ha" in the Tewa language that has come to mean "Tewa" in Hopi. The Tewa people (one of the Pueblo tribes) were accepted by the Hopis because they were fierce fighters and could help protect the Mesa. They lived in the village of Hano. They brought their own language and became known as the "Hanie" in the Hopi language.
Navaho: *Naashashí,* meaning "Bear People" or "Enemy Bear."

The Tewa refugees from the Spanish re-conquest of the Rio Grande pueblos were considered great warriors. The Hopi promised them attractive land in exchange for their help in fighting the Ute and Navajo. Although they live close to and even intermarry with the Hopi, they retain their own language. They guard the entrance to the Mesas and are the policemen for the Hopi reservation (Brown).

Nampeyo, a famous Hano potter born in 1860, developed her world-famous pottery designs from pottery shards dug up by anthropologists. She used ancient techniques in developing her pottery; it became known as Sikyatki Revival. Nampeyo was invited to the Grand Canyon and back east to demonstrate her pottery skills. She became blind in later years, but she had passed her skill on to her daughters, and that skill has been passed to succeeding generations. Traditional Hopi pottery is hand fired over an open fire of sheep dung or coal (Kosik 1996).

Sichomavi (elev. 6,200 ft.)

Hopi: "Place of the Wild Current Mound."
Navajo: *'Ayahkin*, meaning "Underground House."

Sichomavi lies between Hano and Walpi. Several clans from Walpi built this village around 1750. A Tanoan clan from the Rio Grande joined the village later, after being invited to help fight the Ute. There was a Jemez group (also fleeing the Rio Grande) that used Sichomavi as a stopping place. They joined the Navajo in Canyon de Chelly later and became the *Mą'ií 'Deeshgizhnii* ("Coyote Pass People" clan of the Navajo). Sichomavi was once decimated by smallpox; the survivors fled to Tsegi Canyon, Monument Valley, and Zuni. They returned later and rebuilt the village (Linford).

Walpi (elev. 6,225 ft.)

Hopi: "Place of the Gap."
Navajo: *Deez' áajį'*, meaning "Up to the Point" [of the Mesa].

Walpi was built prior to 1700 on the narrow, southernmost rocky tip of the mesa. Steep cliffs protect the village of Walpi; the only access is the narrow road. Only 150 feet across at the widest point and 15 feet at the most narrow point, its location may have protected it from the Spanish after the Pueblo Revolt of 1680. Anasazi ancestors of this village built the original pueblo on a ledge below the Mesa in 1300. Pit houses on the slopes of the mesa date back to the time of Christ. The Snake Dance is held here. The area below the ledge is off limits to tourists (ibid.).

Visitors may enter Walpi only with a Hopi guide; the walking tour lasts one hour. The view from Walpi is fabulous. The village lacks electricity and running water; residents have to walk back toward Sichomovi to get water or to wash. Frequently, the village holds ceremonial and social dances that are open to the public. Call Punsi Hall Visitor Center at 928-737-2262 to see if any dances open to the public are scheduled. When there are private ceremonies, the village may be closed, so remember to check ahead.

SECOND MESA (elev. 6,200–6,450 ft.)

Mishongnovi (elev. 5,750 ft.)

Hopi: "Place of the Black Man."
Navajo: *Tsétsohk'id,* meaning "Big Boulder Hill."

Mishongnovi is located on the eastern rim of Second Mesa, at the junction of AZ-264 and AZ-87 (AZ-87 takes you to Homolovi ruins). Mishongnovi and Walpi host the Snake Dance in odd years. Shungopovi, Hotevilla, and Shipaulovi have the Snake Dance in even years. The old village of Mishongnovi, dating back to 1300, was located on the first terrace below this town but was abandoned before the 1680 Pueblo Revolt. The old mission of San Buenaventura was destroyed during the uprising (ibid.). The people of this village are charged with protection of the Corn Rock Shrine. Hopi Fine Arts–Alph Secakuku Gallery sells arts and crafts. Honani Crafts Gallery is a half-mile west of the intersection of AZ-264 and AZ-87.

Shipaulovi (elev. 6,050 ft.)

Hopi: *Shung–o-hu Pas Ovi,* meaning "Place of the Mosquitos."
Navajo: *Tsésohk'id,* meaning "Big Boulder Hill," same as for Mishongnovi.

Shipaulovi had its beginnings around 1750. It is supposed to have used the beams from the old mission at Shungapovi, indicating some of the inhabitants must have come from there. Some residents came from Homolovi, which was abandoned around that time because of a plague of mosquitoes. Others are supposed to have come from old Shungapovi (Linford).

Shipaulovi and Shungopovi are close neighbors on an eastern projection of Second Mesa. Dances often take place here. You reach these villages by a short paved road that climbs steeply from AZ-264, one-half mile west of the AZ-87 intersection. Mishongnovi is east of Shipaulovi at the end of the mesa. (*Continued on page 132*)

Side Trip to Homolovi Ruins State Park, Petrified Forest, and Painted Desert

Directions from the junction of US-264 and AZ-87 to Homolovi Ruins State Park

Follow AZ-87 south for about 59 miles to the entrance of the Homolovi ruins. There is a paved road (about 4 miles) leading to the visitor center.

Homolovi Ruins State Park (elev. 4,900 ft.)

Hopis believe that several of their clans moved from this area in the fourteenth century because of the mosquito plague and water-logged soil during that century (ibid.). Archaeologists are still excavating some of the sites. Be sure to ask the rangers what areas are open to the public. You will want to see the Pueblo IV Ruin area that was occupied from A.D. 1300 to 1540. It is located on the east bank of the Little Colorado River in the park.

RV and Campgrounds

If you are interested in staying at Homolovi, there are more than fifty excellent campsites, and restrooms, showers, and picnic grills are all located at these sites. Several interpretive hiking trails wind through Pueblo ruins where you will find pictographs. RV vehicle sites are serviced with drinking water, partial hookups for electricity and water, and a water dump station.

Visitor Center

The visitor center is open 8 a.m. to 5 p.m.; 928-289-4106. A small museum displays Hopi pottery and artifacts. If you plan to spend time at Homolove Park, you can stay in either Winslow or Holbrook nearby.

Winslow (elev. 4,938 ft.)

Navajo: *Béésh Sinil,* "Iron Laying Down," referring to the stocks of rail stored here by the Atlantic and Pacific Railroad.

La Posado Winslow is one of the great railway hotels with the ambience of an eighteenth-century hacienda. Mary Coulter designed this hotel for the Fred Harvey Company. The general charm of the hotel is enhanced by the antique furniture and lush gardens. Even if you are not staying the night, La Posada is worth a look—walk the gardens and have lunch or dinner. The Amtrak train stops in Winslow.

Accommodations

La Posada Winslow
303 E. Second Street (I-40 to Route 66, Exit 252)
(928) 289-4366
Restaurant and gardens. Serving steak, seafood, and some Mexican food.

Days Inn
2035 West Highway 66 (I-40, Exit 252)
(928) 289-1010
Indoor heated pool, spa, and Jacuzzi

Best Western Adobe Inn
1701 N. Park Drive (I-40, Exit 253)
(928) 289-4638
Indoor heated pool, spa, and Jacuzzi

Holiday Inn Express
816 Transom Lane (I-40, Exit 252)
(928) 289-2960
Heated indoor pool and whirlpool

Super 8 Motel
520 West Desmond (I-40, Exit 252)
(928) 289-4606

Directions from Winslow to Holbrook
Go east on US-40 for 33 miles to Holbrook. To see the Painted Desert and the Petrified Forest, follow directions after Holbrook.

HOLBROOK (elev. 5,080 ft.)

Navajo: *T'iisyaa Kin,* "House under the Cottonwoods."

Holbrook is a good place to stay the night because of the close access to the south entrance of the Petrified Forest. Holbrook was named after H. R. Holbrook, first chief engineer of the Atlantic and Pacific Railroad. The Old Courthouse Museum has memorabilia from the old Rte. 66 days, and it also has railroad records.

Accommodations

Best Western Adobe Inn
615 West Hopi Drive (I-40, Exit 285)
(928) 524-3948
Heated outdoor pool and restaurant next door

Best Western Arizona Inn
2508 Navajo Blvd. (I-40, Exit 289)
(928) 524-2611
Denny's Restaurant and heated outdoor pool

Days Inn
2601 Navaho Boulevard (I-40, Exit 289)
(928) 524-6949
Heated indoor pool and whirlpool

Holbrook Holiday Inn Express
1308 E. Navajo Boulevard (I-40, Exit 286)
(928) 524-1466

Restaurants

Mesa Italiana Restaurant
2318 E. Navajo Boulevard (I-40, Exit 286)
(928) 524-6696
Authentic Italian food and salads.

Butterfield Stage Co. Steak House
609 W. Hopi Drive, (I-40, Exit 285)
(928) 524-3447
Steak, soup, and salads.

Directions from Holbrook to the Petrified Forest and Painted Desert

Proceed south from Holbrook on AZ-77 (which is Navajo Blvd. in Holbrook, and turn east (left) on AZ-180, just past the bridge. Follow AZ-180 for 18 miles to the south entrance of the Petrified Forest. The Painted Desert is at the north end of the Petrified Forest.

Note: Stores at the south entrance of the Petrified Forest are not connected to the park, and the petrified wood they sell does not come from the park. There is a fee to enter the Petrified Forest.

Petrified Forest and the Painted Desert

The largest collection of fossilized trees in the world is found in the Petrified Forest. Vast areas of petrified wood are becoming visible from the eroding clay in a semi-arid grassland landscape. Linford (2000) describes the process as follows:

> The region was once the center of a great basin overflowed by running water. Giant fallen trees gradually became waterlogged and were eventually covered by layer upon layer of sand and gravel that washed down from the surrounding elevations. Over the eons, the mineral-laden waters impregnated the trunks with silica, petrifying them for posterity. The earth's crust gradually rose to its present elevation, and wind and water eroded the many layers of stone, breaking them up and grinding them into the loose earth that now yields up the harder stone of the petrified wood. (119)

This region was once a tropical flood plain; the Petrified Forest sat on the equator. At the end of the Mesozoic period, the continents drifted due to tectonic movement of the earth's crust. This area moved north and west to its present position, and the climate shifted from tropical to semi-desert grassland.

The first to inhabit the area were hunter-gatherers who lived off the plants and the animals. Next came the Basketmaker people; they occupied the area mostly in the summers. Early Anasazi people appeared in the Petrified Forest area when farming became feasible around A.D. 700. These early people lived in pit houses. From the 1250s to 1400s they occupied the Puerco pueblo or Puerco ruins, which are near the north entrance of the park, close to the visitor center. Agate House, built of petrified wood, is at the south entrance, near the visitor center. (There are two main entrances. At the south entrance is the Petrified Forest, and you travel north [all Petrified Desert] until you reach the north entrance, where you find the Painted Desert.)

Take time to see the free half-hour film in the visitor center. The rangers conduct educational tours to the petrified wood area. From a hilly area nearby, you can see the erosion process and the uncovering of petrified wood in the buttes and hills. Painted Desert cliffs expose the old multicolored, but mostly pink silica layers, which visitors can see at various points in the park, but the north end is particularly vivid. The beauty of the Painted Desert is stunning and not to be missed.

The best way to see the park is to hike some of the trails. Stay on designated trails to protect the fragile grassland. Loose rocks and hidden cliffs are hazardous. At this altitude (4,400–6,000 feet) you can have symptoms of altitude sickness—nausea, dizziness, headache, rapid heartbeat, and shortness of breath. Keep hydrated, take rests, and eat lightly. If you are injured or ill, yellow emergency telephones are located at Puerco Pueblo, Blue Mesa, and at Crystal Forest. The park's emergency number is 928-524-9726. The visitor center's number is 928-524-6228.

The two-mile hike to Agate House is the longest trail. There are bathrooms at Agate House, at Puerco Pueblo, and at the visitor centers. Most restrooms, visitor centers, and picnic areas are accessible, or accessible with help, for wheelchair users. There is a restroom and a museum at the North Visitor Center.

Hiking and Camping

Wilderness hiking and camping are accessed at the park's north entrance at Kachina Point Lookout, where one can see the Painted Desert. Trailheads are behind the Painted Desert Inn Museum. A one-mile access trail leads into the wilderness. No permits are required for daylight hiking. There are no developed trails, no water, and little shade in the backcountry. Carry one gallon of water per person per day and enough snacks and food to last you for the length of time you will be gone. A free permit is required for overnight camping.

To return to Second Mesa on the Hopi reservation, go west on I-40 to AZ-87 and take AZ-87 north for 60 miles to US-264.

Second Mesa (continued from page 126)

Shungopovi (elev. 6,440 ft.)

Hopi: "Place by the Spring Where the Tall Reeds Grow."
Navajo: *Kin Názt'i'*, meaning "Houses Strung in a Circle."

Ancient Shungopovi ruins on the hills below this town are supposed to be the oldest of the Second Mesa villages. Tree ring data indicate a date in the 1300s, making it as old as Oraibi. In the uprising of 1680, the San Bartolome Mission was destroyed and the friars were killed. According to Shungopovi tradition, only seven village families escaped the Spanish reprisals in 1692 (ibid.).

In 1898, the military from Fort Wingate had to remove Hopi priests, tear down houses, and vaccinate the surviving villagers because of a smallpox outbreak. In 1941, a government day school was opened on the lower part of the mesa. Shungopovi is regarded as the most conservative (traditional) of all the villages (ibid.).

The villagers make exquisite silver overlay jewelry and coil plaques. The plaques are woven from galleta grass and yucca, with cultural designs of katsinas, animals, and corn. Dawa's Art and Crafts, on the road into the village, sells locally made work. More galleries lie between the village turnoff and the cultural center.

Hopi Cultural Center and Museum

This museum is dedicated to presenting accurate cultural and historical information on the Hopi people. It is a small museum packed with ancient pottery, wonderful baskets, and carved kachina dolls.

Hopi Cultural Center Gift Shop
The gift shop displays silver overlay jewelry of outstanding quality, guaranteed to be authentic. Talk with the staff and learn the fine points of their jewelry and other art. The gift shop is expensive; however, it represents the best of local work. Local artists also show their work at the west side of the parking area, mostly on the weekends; their prices are more affordable. The famous Namoki family potters from Walpi often show their work here.

Hopi Cultural Center Visitor Information, Restaurant, and Hotel
The Tourist Information Office is open Monday through Friday 8 a.m. to 5 p.m., for a short time on Saturday, and closed on Sunday; 928-734-2401.

The only hotel and restaurant on the Three Mesas is in the Hopi Cultural Center. The rooms are basic, clean, and quiet. The restaurant serves American and traditional Hopi dishes. They have a good salad bar and they serve piti bread, paper-thin bread made from blue corn. They make excellent blue corn pancakes and good Hopi, American, Mexican, and pizza dishes. Try their noqkwivi, traditional lamb stew, with hominy and lamb, Hopi tacos and a Hopi tostada (vegetarian). The surrounding landscape is parched. However, if you want to spend some time visiting the artists and learn about Hopi customs, this is the place to be.

Shopping

Hopi Arts and Crafts/Silvercrafts Cooperative Guild
Located west of the Cultural Center, the guild shows the works of all its members. Fred Kabotie, from Shungopovi, founded the guild, an ideal place to purchase authentic silver overlay jewelry, pottery, and kachina dolls. Kabotie painted the Hopi Room at the Watchtower (Desert View) in the Grand Canyon. He also painted three murals at the Painted Desert Inn.

Tsakurshovi Store
The store is located 1.5 miles east of the Cultural Center. This is where Hopis buy their supplies—items needed for their ceremonials. The store is a good place to learn about Hopi people and their culture. The proprietor is very knowledgeable and is responsible for the very large, unique collection of Hopi baskets. He will know if any dances will be held that are open to the public.

Third Mesa

This mesa is fifteen miles long and from one-half mile to five miles across. You should visit the Tribal Headquarters & Office of Public Relations in Kykotsmovi to get permission to visit Third Mesa villages. You may find vendors along AZ-264, but you will also want to visit the craft shops and art galleries. These villages are known for their wicker baskets, kachina dolls, silver overlay jewelry, textile weaving, and especially for their agricultural products.

Bacavi (elev. 6,583 ft.)

Hopi: *Baakavii,* meaning "Place of the Jointed Reed."
Navajo: *Tł'ohchintó Biyáázh,* meaning "Offspring of Wild Onion Spring" (referring to Hotevilla).

Founded in 1907, the people of early Bakavi in the easternmost village were forced out of Oraibi because of differences with the Bureau of Indian Affairs (BIA) presence in their village. The original people were "conservatives" or "hostiles," opposed to BIA interference in their lives (ibid.).

Hotevilla (elev. 6,000 ft.)

Hopi: *Hitaveli,* meaning "Skinned Back."
Navajo: *Tłochintó,* meaning "Wild Onion Spring."

Hotevilla, on the west side of Third Mesa, was a good site for a village as there was reliable spring water. Hotevilla was born out of the 1905–06 strife in Oraibi between the "progressives" or "friendlies" and the "conservatives" or "hostiles," who claimed government programs interfered with religious life. Their leader, Youkeoma, was jailed (along with a few others) after the fracas in Oraibi. The "hostiles" founded the village of Hotevilla. Hotevilla further split in 1907 and the "moderates" founded Bacavi. Hotevilla leaders refused to send village children to school for twenty years. They even refused to have their sheep dipped. This is one of the most conservative of all the villages. They produce high-quality baskets and textiles. The Snake Dance is performed here in even years (ibid.).

Hotevilla men plant gardens along the mesa slopes, known as terrace gardens. It is a very attractive site as you look down on the gardens from the mesa top.

Dinnebito Trading Post (elev. 5,923 ft.)

Navajo: *Diné Bito'*, meaning "Navajo's Spring."

Dinnebito, a Navajo village, is accessed from Third Mesa just past Hotevilla.

This town is not of interest to travelers except to note that Dinnebito Wash is a ninety-six-mile tributary of the Little Colorado River, one of four main drainages off Black Mesa. The other three drainages are the Moenkopi, Oraibi, and Polacca washes. Dams save water from these washes to irrigate land for farming. Hastiin Naat'aánii, a Navajo leader, constructed many diversion dams and ditches to control the down flow from Black Mesa. None survived the spring and summer flash floods. Finally, a reinforced concrete dam was built by the Indian Irrigation Service in 1937, which provides irrigation for 230 acres (ibid.).

Kykotsmovi (elev. 5,770 ft.)

Hopi: *Kiakochomovi*, meaning "Place of the Hills of Ruins."

Founded in 1906, Kykotsmovi is the seat of Hopi tribal government, located on AZ-264 at the east foot of Third Mesa. The first trading post opened here in the 1880s. This group of "progressives" from Old Oraibi settled around the trading post, school, and Evangelization Movement Mission. Kykotsmovi was also politically independent of Oraibi. A high school was built in 1937; previously, students went to Phoenix (ibid.).

The modern-day politics and bureaucracy of the BIA were a constant irritant among the villages. Hopis do not differentiate between life and religion; their whole purpose in life is found in adherence to ancient teachings and plan for life. Each village usually has a "father of the people" who makes decisions for his village based on prayer and meditation. However, when the Hopis decided in 1951 to fight for land, the federal government would work with only one representative of the Hopi people, the leader to which they all agreed (it was very difficult to pick such a leader since each village was fiercely independent) (Kosik 1996).

The Cultural Preservation Office (928-734-3613) provides information for visitors to the Hopi reservation at its office in the tribal headquarters building, one mile south of AZ-264.

Quotskuyva Fine Arts and Crafts is on Leupp Road, 1.2 miles south of AZ-264 between mileposts 46 and 47.

Oraibi (elev. 6,050 ft.)

Hopi: *Oraive,* meaning "Place of a Rock Called Orai."
Navajo: *'Oozéí Biyashi* from 'Odzai, meaning "Many Eagle Nests."

Oraibi is located on the southeast tip of Third Mesa. It shares with Acamo Pueblo the distinction of being the oldest, continuously occupied community in the United States. Tree ring data, from beams used in the town's buildings, date back to 1260 and 1344. Hopi tradition claims these timbers came from the San Francisco Peaks some hundred miles away. The attitudes of the "friendlies" and "hostiles" regarding government programs caused much unrest in this village. In 1906, Chief Tewaquaptewa forced out all villagers who were Christian, or were going to become Christian. Then he forced out the "hostiles" who went on to establish Hotevilla (Linford).

Loololma was the Hopi most vehemently against BIA and missionary encroachment in Oraibi. He was also against Hopi children attending BIA schools. Thomas Keam, the Indian agent at the time, encouraged Loololma to come back to Washington as his guest. When Loololma returned from Washington, his opinion had changed. He said there were so many white people it was like "disturbing an ant hill." He believed they had no choice but to cooperate (Kosik, 132).

The population in this town numbered in the thousands in the 1700s but had declined to fewer than one hundred by the middle of the twentieth century. Smallpox and alternate floods and droughts between 1890 and 1904 decimated the population. Utes were their biggest enemy, but Navajos also raided them. Navajo medicine men used to visit a Hopi priest named Na'ashja' for certain medicines. Navajos regarded Oraibi as their favorite place to obtain *ló K'aatsoh ba'ádí,* which is a large cane used to make Navajo prayer sticks (*k'eet'áán*). Oraibi reeds were used to make arrows for the Navajo Male Branch of Shootingway. Despite the Navajo and Hopi tribal councils' disagreement over land, there has been a lot of intermarriage between the two tribes (Linford).

Old Oraibi lies two miles west of Kykotsmovi. Avoid driving through the village and stirring up dust; park outside—or next to Hamana So-o's Arts and Crafts—and walk. You can shop for Hopi arts and crafts here and at galleries nearby on the highway.

CHAPTER 16

FROM HOPI RESERVATION TO CAMERON

Directions from Hopi Reservation to Tuba City

Continuing northwest on AZ-264, it is 50 miles from the end of Third Mesa to Tuba City, a good place to spend the night. Along the way, do not miss the views at Coal Mine Canyon.

Water is a precious commodity. The San Juan River (flowing through the Navajo reservation in Utah and New Mexico) and the Colorado River (which borders the northwestern part of the reservation) flow through steep-walled gorges, which means there are no floodplains from these river sources useable for irrigation. Some of the most important ceremonies for both Navajo and Hopi are rain prayers for their crops. It was not unusual for families to go two to ten miles or much farther in times of drought to obtain drinking and household water. Today, many isolated areas are serviced with water trucks.

Traveling throughout the Navajo reservation, you will notice that many hogans and trailers (many people live in the trailers and use hogans for religious ceremonies) sit well back off the road. Often, you will think there is no one around for miles. Off the main road there are many dirt roads and lanes where traditional Navajos live close to their grazing areas. It is too expensive to bring electric lines to homes miles apart. Even though Navajo coal mines and power plants supply electricity for millions of people, only about one half of Navajo households have electricity (Sherry 2002).

It is common for women in traditional households to keep some of the wool from their sheep, which is then hand spun to make blankets and rugs. Navajo men make silver jewelry, buckles, and belts. You will see many roadside stands with handmade goods for sale. Increasingly, men and women are working in tourism, native government jobs, and as teachers in Navajo and state schools. For needed cash they work off the reservation in nearby towns as well.

Coal Mine Canyon (elev. 6,500–5,000 ft.)

Navajo: *Honoojí,* meaning "Jagged Area."

Continuing west on AZ-264, you soon reenter the Navajo reservation. There is an overlook off the road for Coal Canyon. This canyon was preserved because the coal was of poor quality (coal in other areas of Black Mesa is very high in quality). Hoodoos and crenulated cliffs of red, white, and gray rocks present a striking sight from the overlook.

Coal Canyon is a deep, jagged, multicolored canyon cut into Mesa Verde and Mancos shale of Coal Mine Mesa. Navajo medicine men use the fine sands and shale, which come in many colors and hues, for sand paintings (Linford 2000).

The scenery is a striking combination of red mudstone and bleached white rock with coal streaks. The sun creates photographic wonders as it catches the different colors in the rock. Hiking is allowed with valid permits. Contact the Cameron Visitor Center at 928-679-2303 or 928-871-6647 for more information.

Moenkopi, a Hopi Village (elev. 4,750 ft.)

Hopi: *Moncapi,* meaning "Place of Running Water."
Navajo: *'Oozéí Hayázhí,* meaning "Little Oraibi."

Chief Tuvi from Oraibi founded Moenkopi as a farming community in the 1870s. It is situated on the north terrace of Moenkopi Wash, two miles southeast of Tuba City. Navajos call this wash *Naak'a' K'éédílyéhé,* "Where Cotton Is Cultivated" (ibid.). Hopis used to run from Oraibi to Moenkopi several times a week to tend their crops.

Since the village was not established under a traditional form of government, it created some problems. As a result, a division occurred, thereby creating two villages—Upper Moenkopi and Lower Moenkopi. The residents of Upper Moenkopi adopted a village constitution in 1958, while those choosing to live the traditional way of life occupied the lower village of Moenkopi.

Tuba City (elev. 4,950 ft.)

Navajo: *Tó Naneesdizí*, meaning "Place of Water Rivulets," referring to the irrigation ditches the Mormons used to irrigate their fields.

Tuba City is named after Chief Tuvi, who became a friend of the early Mormon settlers. In 1903, the Mormons were forced to relocate when the boundaries of the Navajo reservation were expanded. Tuba City is the administrative center for the western section of the Navajo Nation. It is known for the Western Navajo Fair, which takes place in October. There are music, songs, dances, a parade, and a rodeo.

In 1928, while developing a spring area for the BIA, the construction crew found fossils of extinct mammals. Among the skeletons recovered were the camelops (similar to a llama), a bison larger than those of today, an equis (an extinct type of horse), and an *Elephas columbi* (a mammoth similar to an African elephant) (Kosik 1996). During the twelfth to thirteenth centuries, Anasazi people built communal pueblos on the Moenkopi sandstone ledges west of Tuba City.

The arts and crafts exhibits are excellent. Storm-pattern rugs developed in this area are justly famous: zigzag lines represent lightning bolts evident in the local weather; triangles in the four corners represent the four sacred mountains; and the center of the rug is a representation of the center of the universe. Tuba City Trading Post on Main Street is well worth a visit to see its unusual architecture and to view some of these incredible rugs. The Babbitt family bought this trading post in 1902 and developed ten other trading posts throughout Northern Arizona.

The wonderful colors of the Painted Desert near Tuba City come from the exposed siltstones and shales of the 150–250-million-year-old Chinle formation. You will find great views of the Painted Desert at the junction of US-89 and AZ-160. Navajos call the Painted Desert *halchííitaah*, meaning "Among the Red Areas."

Linford states that "Tuba City became a major agriculture center for both Navajo and Hopi farmers. Early United States Indian Service (USIS) irrigation projects of the 1930s included the lower Moenkopi Project (400 acres), Reservoir Canyon (225 acres), Moenkopi Wash Project (305 acres), and Moenkopi Spring Project (32 acres)" (141).

You can have great fun at the swap meet that takes place on Friday mornings starting at 8 a.m. There can be surprising buys on jewelry, pottery, and other handmade items, plus some interesting food and herbs.

Accommodations

Quality Inn Navajo Nation
Main St. at Moenave Road
(928) 283-4545 or (800) 644-8383
Clean, comfortable rooms; coin laundry.

Grey Hills High School Inn and Hostel
Located off US-160, one-half mile north of AZ-264
(928) 283-6271, extension 142, or (928) 283-4450 for after-school hours and weekends
Hotel management students run this dormitory-style inn. Bathrooms and showers are down the hall. Basic, clean, inexpensive accommodations.

Restaurants

Kate's Café
On Edwater, east of Main Street
(928) 283-6773
Open 6 a.m. to 10 p.m. every day. Good choices, extensive menu, including local favorites. This is considered the best restaurant in Tuba City.

Tuba City Truck Café
(928) 283-4975
Fast service of local favorites—Indian Tacos and mutton stew

Quality Inn Restaurant
(928) 283-4144
Basic meals

Fast Food Restaurants

Kentucky Fried Chicken, Dairy Queen, and Taco Bell (all located on Main Street).

(*Continued on page 142*)

Alternate Route from Tuba City to Kayenta on US-160

If you do not wish to see Page, Lake Powell, Glen Canyon Dam, or Antelope Canyon (a slot canyon that is a must-see for photographers), you can take this shortcut to Kayenta, a stopping point for Monument Valley.

US-160 crosses AZ-264 at Tuba City. Take US-160 northeast to the junction of US-160 and AZ-98, almost 40 miles. Continue northeast on US-160 to Kayenta, almost 32 miles.

There is little for tourists to see except Red Lake Trading Post. Two tall sandstone towers are nearby; the base of these towers looks like elephant feet. Black Mesa Plateau runs along the east side of the road for about fifteen miles. Above these buttes is Black Mesa, where there is more than 20 billion tons of coal, a major resource of the Navajo Nation.

Be sure to stop at Navajo National Monument, located just beyond the junction of US-160 and AZ-98, on US-160. Within this park are the Betatakin and Keet Siel ruins. Betatakin is a 135-room ruin, the most accessible of the group of ruins found near this site. Keet Siel is the largest cliff dwelling in Arizona, with 160 rooms and five or six kivas. See page 184 for complete information on this site.

Continue northeast on US-160 to Kayenta. Information on Kayenta and Goulding (which is just across the road from Monument Valley) is on page 185 (Kayenta) and page 188 (Goulding).

Tuba City (continued)

RV and Campgrounds

Quality Inn Campgrounds
On Main Street at the back of the Quality Inn
(928) 283-4144
The facility is structured toward RVs. This campground provides a safe place to park under shade trees and close to restaurants. Flush toilets, full hookups, dump station, drinking water, coin laundry, showers, grills, and picnic tables.

Services

Shopping: Bashas grocery store in the Toh Nanees Dizi Shopping Center on US-160, about one-half mile north of where AZ-264 (which becomes Main Street) crosses US-160.
Navajo Police: (928) 283-3111
Hospital: (928) 283-2501

Directions from Tuba City to Cameron
Take US-160 west at Tuba City to US-89. At the junction of US-89, you can choose to take US-89 north to Page, about 68 miles, or continue south to Cameron Trading Post, the East Rim of the Grand Canyon, and Wupatki National Monument. Cameron Trading Post is 16 miles south on US-89.

On the way, take time for a short visit to see the Dinosaur Tracks. There will be signs that lead to roadside stands. A guide will approach the car and, for a small gratuity, will lead you to the tracks. You can find the paths on your own—look for stone-lined paths. These tracks, found in 1942, along with similar tracks found in China in the 1980s, are the only examples in the world of "running dinosaurs." The tracks are about 200 million years old.

Cameron (elev. 4,200 ft.)

Navajo: *Na'ní a Hayázhí*, meaning "Little Span Across."

Bill Kona Sani (Bilagáana Sani, "Old Anglo") was the first to trade here with his pack train as early as 1850. S. S. Preston, a Navajo, built the first trading post during the construction of "Government Bridge," the swaying bridge over the Little Colorado River Gorge. Hubert Richardson built a longer-lived trading post in 1914 (Linford). Only Hopi and Navajo visited the post at that time to barter wool, blankets, and livestock for flour, sugar, and canned goods. The trip to the post could take days, as they traveled by horse-drawn wagon. Guests were treated as family and were fed and housed by the trading post.

Once roads improved, Cameron Trading Post provided easy access to the Grand Canyon, and it became popular with visitors. Employees from around the area own the post today. The president of the company is a direct descendent of the original owners.

R. H. Cameron was the Sheriff of Coconino County in 1893. He and some range-hungry stockmen enforced a questionable cancellation of Navajo allotments on the west side of the Little Colorado. According to Linford, "he forcibly ejected Béêsh Łigai Atsidii and his people from their hogans, forcing them to cross over to the eastern bank of the Little Colorado. The river was carrying a great amount of ice. Many sheep were lost and the Navajos suffered greatly from exposure" (38–39). Navajos were unable to regain their property because the Navajo Superintendent at Tuba City had failed to notify interested Navajos in time to act on acquiring the land.

The community was named for Senator Cameron, the last territorial delegate from Arizona to the U.S. Congress. Before Government Bridge was built, the only crossing of the Little Colorado was at Tanner's Crossing, which was dangerous because of quicksand. The bridge was purportedly built at Senator Cameron's urging, with money taken from Navajo Tribe Trust Funds without tribal consent (ibid.).

Cameron Visitor Center

This visitor center is located at the junction of US-89 and AZ-64. You will pass Cameron Trading Post on the way to the visitor center—you might like more information on the area than what is provided at the trading post (928-679-2303). Open 7 a.m. to 6 p.m. daily, May through September; 8 a.m. to 5 p.m. Monday through Friday the rest of the year. Recreation and hunting permits can be purchased here.

Cameron Trading Post

This is a good place to break your journey for a night or two. There is a gas station, hotel, and restaurant and a large gift shop.

Accommodations

Cameron Trading Post Lodge and Restaurant
Fifty-four miles north of Flagstaff on US-89
(928) 679-2231 or 800-338-7385
AAA and AARP discount of 10 percent. The buildings are sometimes as high as three stories, and there are no elevators. Book several months in advance in the summer, as this lodge fills quickly. The rooms and suites are well furnished, pleasant, and some have a view of the Little Colorado River Gorge. There is a small, well-maintained garden. Cost is moderately higher than in Tuba City.

The gift shop is huge, carrying everything from souvenirs and trinkets to pottery, sand paintings, and rugs. You may see a weaver at work in the Navajo rug section. Ask to see the upstairs rooms as well. If you wish to purchase museum-quality work, be sure to visit the separate gallery in a stone building out front. Navajo Arts and Crafts sells beautifully crafted, authentic Navajo handmade items. They are expensive but well worth a look. Educate yourself about authentic Navajo art here, as everything is guaranteed to be what it claims to be.

The restaurant is part of the old Cameron Trading Post. A huge stone fireplace is the focal point in the room, and local art decorates the walls. American, Mexican, and local Indian dishes such as the "Navajo taco" are served.

RV and Campgrounds

Cameron RV Park
Adjacent to Cameron Trading Post
(928) 679-2231 or 800-338-7385
There are sixty spaces with full hookups for water, electric, and waste disposal. There are no public restrooms or showers. No reservations accepted. Recreation and hiking permits can be obtained at the Cameron Visitor Center.

Suggested Day Trips from Cameron Trading Post

Wupatki National Monument and Sunset Crater National Monument

Travel south from Cameron on US-89 to Wupatki National Monument, approximately 25 miles.

To see all of this site, which eventually leads to Sunset Crater on the Wupatki/Sunset Crater Loop, will take a full day. Bring lots of water, a lunch, and snacks; no food is available at either site. There is some hiking, so wear appropriate closed shoes. See page 145 for information on both of these sites.

Grand Canyon South Rim

The best way to see the Grand Canyon is to stay at one of the lodges in Grand Canyon Village. You can see the canyon in one day, but you must limit what you see. The Grand Canyon trip will take a full day, so plan to leave early in the morning; the best views are at sunrise and sunset. You might want Cameron Lodge to pack a picnic lunch. It will take nearly two hours, with viewing stops along the way, to get to Grand Canyon Visitor Center. The tour of the South Rim will take a minimum of two hours; four hours is more usual. If you are planning to return to Cameron Lodge, the South Rim is about all you have time to see along with stopping for a meal. It will take in all the major views.

The trail along the South Rim is a good place to see how well you do with high altitude hiking. The air is thin at this altitude (around 7,000 ft.), and it is not unusual to feel lightheaded. You will tire easily; plan to take a short rest every forty-five minutes or so, drink some water, and eat a salty, high-energy snack at each of these breaks. The beauty of hiking in this area is that if you do become tired, you can hop on the free bus at the next stop (they do not pick up between stops) and see the rest of the South Rim the easy way. There is no food on the South Rim Drive. Pack a substantial lunch, snacks, and water if you plan to do any hiking.

Just south of Cameron, take AZ-64 west along the Little Colorado Gorge to the east side of Grand Canyon National Park.

There are numerous viewpoints of the Little Colorado River gorge along the way—some with incredible views. Once you reach Grand Canyon National Park, there will be paved areas where you can stop and enjoy breathtaking canyon views. Continue on this road, carefully following the signs, until you arrive at the visitor center, where there are clean restrooms. Pick up a map of Grand Canyon South Rim. If you plan to do some hiking, check with the rangers regarding weather conditions and information on the trails. They will have detailed maps of the trails and can provide any registration that may be necessary. Overnight camping requires a permit, and there is a fee. It is strongly recommended that hikers do not plan to hike to the North Rim and back in one day. A combination of high altitude and extreme heat down in the canyon during the day can cause many problems. It is a strenuous two-day hike for experienced hikers, and it will cost the hiker $2,000 for helicopter evacuation.

Grand Canyon Village has very little parking. If you have a handicapped passenger, you can drive along the South Rim. Pick up the special accessibility permit to display on the window of your car at the visitor center. A Grand Canyon Accessibility Guide is available at any of the entrance stations or the Visitor Information Center. Otherwise, everyone must park and ride the courtesy shuttle, which stops at ten designated viewing places along the rim.

Leave your car at the visitor center (free parking) and take the courtesy shuttle to Grand Canyon Village, where you will pick up the South Rim shuttle. There may be some parking along the railroad tracks, but your best bet is to park at the visitor center and take the free shuttle.

Note: Views are a short, easy walk from the bus stops on developed paths. There are usually Jiffy Johns at two of the stops (the bus driver will tell you where) and a restroom at Hermits Rest. It takes seventy-five minutes to ride the bus round-trip; it takes about four hours to see all the overlooks. There are ten overlooks with each view more spectacular than the last. Take plenty of water.

Roads are very dark in this area at night, which can make finding your way back to Cameron Lodge difficult. Try to get back to the lodge before dark. Information on Grand Canyon lodges and restaurants follow.

Accommodations

If you are going to stay at the Grand Canyon, accommodations inside the park are best. All lodges are within walking distance of the rim. Call 303-297-2757 for central booking for all the lodges.

El Tovar Hotel at Grand Canyon Village
(303) 297-2757 / Direct hotel line: (928) 638-2631 (not for reservations)
The hotel has three floors (no elevators) and interior corridors. It is a Registered National Historic Monument, built in 1904. The hotel has a native Arizona stone base with Oregon pine exterior and exposed beam interior. A wonderful stone fireplace takes center stage in a rustic lobby. Close to all activities. No smoking rooms, room service, eight suites, cable TV, bar, hotel parking. This hotel can be booked up to a year in advance. Book the dining room at the same time you book your room; it is hard to get reservations. It has a well-deserved reputation. Sometimes, there are dining room cancellations, and you may be lucky to get one. In any case, be sure to visit El Tovar, take in the view, and have a drink on the back porch of the cocktail lounge.

Bright Angel Lodge at Grand Canyon Village
(303) 297-2757 / Direct hotel line: (928) 638-2631 (not for reservations)
There are thirty rooms, mostly cabins, some with views and fireplaces. Rooms inside the lodge share bathrooms, and cabins are spread throughout the trees, some with fireplaces and views. Lots of charm, little luxury. Mary Jane Colter designed this native stone and timber lodge in 1935, preserving some of the handmade cabins of the older Red Horse Station and Cameron Hotel. Of special interest is the geological fireplace in the main lobby. It incorporates rock from each geological layer in the canyon in its construction, each stone coming out of the canyon by mule (Kosik).

Kachina Lodge at Grand Canyon Village
(303) 297-2757 / Direct hotel line: (928) 638-2631
Modern rooms with refrigerators and cable TV. No smoking rooms. Some rooms have a canyon view. Recently updated. Two stories, no elevators, inside corridors.

Maswick Lodge at Grand Canyon Village
(303) 297-2757
Regular, modern rooms are heated. Rustic cabins have neither heat nor air conditioning. 250 rooms, 28 cabins, cafeteria, sports bar, shop. No smoking rooms. Two stories, no elevators.

Thunderbird Lodge in Grand Canyon Village
Located next to Bright Angel Lodge
(303) 279-2757 / Direct hotel line: (928) 638-2631
All rooms have two queen beds. No overnight reservations at direct number. No

smoking rooms. Data ports and refrigerators. Two stories, no elevators, inside corridors.

Yavapai Lodge at Grand Canyon Village
Located near the RV Park and General Store
303-297-2757 / Direct hotel line: (928) 638-2631 (not for reservations)
358 rooms, cafeteria, and shop. No smoking rooms. Basic rooms and standard cafeteria fare.

RV and Campgrounds

Mather Campground
Off Village Loop Drive
(800) 365-2267
No reservations accepted from December to March, but they are recommended for the rest of the year, especially in the summer. 97 RV and 190 tent sites. Flush toilets, drinking water, showers, laundry, fire grates, and picnic tables. Open year round. No hookups.

Trailer Village
In Grand Canyon Village
(303) 297-2757 or (888) 297-2757 / Direct hotel line (928) 638-2631
RV sites with full hookups and bathroom facilities. Dump station, drinking water, laundry, showers, and fire grates. Spaces on a first-come basis.

Desert View Campground
On Desert View Drive, 23 miles east of Grand Canyon Village off AZ-64
(928) 638-7875
Great canyon views at nearby Watchtower at Desert View. First come, first served. No reservations, no hookups. 50 RV and 50 campsites. Drinking water, flush toilets, grills, and picnic tables. Books up fast in the summer.

Restaurants

El Tovar Dining Room
(928) 638-2631
Reservations are hard to get. Call months ahead or try for a cancellation. Lovely dining room with hand-hewn logs and beamed ceiling. Southwestern cuisine. Fish, steak, and chicken are served with imagination and flare.

Yavapai Lodge Cafeteria
(928) 638-2631
Serves inexpensive fast food: burgers, pizza, pasta, fish, and fried chicken. Open for breakfast, lunch, and dinner.

Arizona Room at the Bright Angel Lodge
(928) 638-2631
Open 4:30 p.m. to 10:00 p.m. Specializing in steak, barbeque, chicken, and seafood. This restaurant is very popular, one of the best places to eat on the rim. Windows overlook the canyon.

Hiking

Recommended guidelines for hiking: Stay hydrated (drink plenty of water and electrolyte drinks). Avoid hiking in the heat of the day (10 a.m. to 4 p.m.). Eat carbohydrates and salty foods often. Rest often (sit in the shade). A good rule is to eat and drink a little every time you stop to rest. Get wet: wet your shirt and hat, and wear a wet bandana around your neck. Do not attempt to hike down to the river and back in one day.

Rim Trail. Begin your hike from any viewpoint in the village or along Hermit Road. You can customize the hike to meet your needs by utilizing the shuttle buses. Part of the trail is paved and accessible.

Bright Angel Trail (Steep). Round-trip, the trail can range up to twelve miles. It begins just west of Bright Angel Lodge. There is some water on the trail in the summer, subject to pipeline breaks. Check at the visitor center or Backcountry Information for water status.

South Kaibab Trail (Steep). Access to the trailhead is by shuttle bus. The trail begins south of Yaki Point on Yaki Point Road.

Hermit Trail. Trail conditions are tougher than the Bright Angel and South Kaibab trails. Hikes go to Santa Maria Springs (4.5 miles round-trip) and Dripping Springs (6.5 miles round-trip). This trail is not maintained. It begins five hundred feet west of Hermits Rest. Water from springs must be treated before drinking. Experienced hikers only; heavy boots recommended.

Grandview Trail (Very Steep). The hike begins on the canyon side of the retaining wall at Grandview Point on Desert View Drive, twelve miles east of Grand Canyon Village. The trail is not maintained and is very steep. Hikes go to Horseshoe Mesa (6.4 miles round-trip). Experienced hikers only; a hiking permit is required.

Mule Rides

If you wish to book a mule ride down into the canyon, call 888-297-2757. You need to make reservations at least eight months in advance.

CHAPTER 17

FROM CAMERON (OR FLAGSTAFF) TO PAGE

Flagstaff is where travelers from Tucson and Phoenix will meet this tour. It is about 100 miles from Tucson to Phoenix and it is 146 miles from Phoenix to Flagstaff.

Take I-10 from Tucson, through Phoenix, until you meet AZ-17. Proceed north on AZ-17 until you reach Flagstaff, where you connect with I-40. Flagstaff is a good place to stay for a night or two.

Travelers from Las Vegas can travel north on I-15 and east to Page (see page 176), or they can travel south, then east to Flagstaff. Take I-95 south from Las Vegas to I-93. Proceed south on I-93 to Kingman. Take I-40 from Kingman to Flagstaff, approximately 241 miles.

FLAGSTAFF (elev. 6,905 ft.)

Navajo: *Kin Łání Dook'o'oosłíid Biyaagí,* meaning "Many Houses Below San Francisco Peaks."

Flagstaff is northern Arizona's largest city. It has been a wholesale trade center for the Hopi and western Navajo reservations for many years. Stock and lumber are shipped from here. Northern Arizona University and the world-class Museum of Northern Arizona are in Flagstaff.

Edward Whipple, owner of the Texas Star Saloon, was the first to settle near Flagstaff in the spring in 1871. Some eastern settlers known as the "Boston Party" tried to settle near the Mormon town of Joseph City, east of Flagstaff. However, they were suspicious of the Mormons and discouraged with the area, so they moved west to Prescott. On July 4, a party of them camped near Flagstaff and celebrated by hoisting a flag on a pole made by stripping the boughs from a large pine tree. The pine was still standing when the Atlantic and Pacific Railroad reached Flagstaff, and this natural flagpole gave the name to the city. Some facts of the story alter with different sources, but this is the gist of it (Linford 2000).

The Museum of Northern Arizona

3101 North Fort Valley Road, Flagstaff. (928) 774-5213.

This museum is a must-see for those wanting to understand the native peoples in this area: the Navajo, Hopi, and Zuni in particular. The museum hosts individual annual exhibitions of the work of all three groups. Everyone can benefit and will have a greater understanding of these complicated cultures from a docent-led tour. All group tours must be arranged in advance by calling 928-774-5211, ext. 275. Space in docent-led tours needs to be reserved up to four weeks in advance.

Navajo Festival of Arts and Culture

This festival is sponsored by the museum at the end of July each year. Artists, musicians, dancers, and food preparers gather at the museum. Hozho, the central philosophy in Navajo life (meaning everything Navajos think of as good—harmony, beauty, blessedness, and balance), is explored. Navajos believe that creating art is one way to maintain this perfect state.

There are over fifty booths displaying juried fine arts and crafts. Rug weaving is the most recognized art form. Navajo baskets, which tell stories in their patterns, are found here. You will also find clothes made by various Navajo designers.

This festival is broadened and enriched every year by Navajos who specialize in Navajo philosophy and linguistics. The ideas and concepts behind Navajo art are explored, and there is always a rich sampling of music and dance.

The Venture Program, run by the education department of the museum, sponsors excellent tours of the area led by scientists, historians, and artists. They offer bus tours into the Navajo reservation to visit with Navajo artists.

The Hopi Festival

This festival is held each year during the first week in July.

Arboretum at Flagstaff

(928) 774-1442

The arboretum is located 3.8 miles south of Route 66 on scenic Woody Mountain Road, on the west side of Flagstaff. The last portion of Woody Mountain Road is unpaved but is suitable for all vehicles.

The arboretum is a botanical garden, research station, and environmental education center. Their center of interest is the plants and flowers of the Colorado Plateau. They have a collection of 2,500 species of plants. There are one-hour guided tours of this spectacular mountain, meadow, and forest setting offered at 11 a.m. and 1 p.m. Persons with limited mobility may ride in a golf cart during the tour, but it needs to be reserved in advance.

Accommodations

Amerisuites Flagstaff
2455 Beulah Boulevard
(928) 774-8042
117 suites, five stories with inside corridors. Small heated indoor pool, whirlpool, and exercise room. Coin laundry.

Best Western Kings House
1560 E. Route 66
(928) 774-7186 or (888) 577-7186
57 rooms. Small, heated indoor pool and spa.

Hampton Inn East
3501 E. Lockett Road (off I-40 Business Loop)
(928) 526-1885
50 rooms. Small, heated indoor pool and whirlpool.

Hilton Garden Inn
350 W. Forest Meadows Street (I-40, Exit 195)
(928) 226-8888
90 rooms. Small, heated indoor pool, whirlpool, sauna, and exercise room.

Best Western Pony Soldier Inn and Suites
3030 E. Route 66
(928) 526-2388
75 rooms (59 one-bedroom and 16 one- and two-bedroom suites).

Budget Host Saga Motel
820 W. Route 66 (near the university)
(928) 779-3631
29 rooms

Comfort Inn
2355 S. Beulah Boulevard
(928) 774-2225
65 rooms and 20 suites. Small, heated outdoor pool and whirlpool. Coin laundry.

Days Inn East
3601 E. Lockett Road (off I-40 Business Loop)
(928) 527-1477
54 Rooms. Small, indoor heated pool and whirlpool. Coin laundry.

Embassy Suites Flagstaff
706 S. Milton Road (adjacent to the university)
(928) 774-4333
119 Suites. Heated outdoor pool, whirlpool, and exercise room.

Hampton Inn and Suites
2400 S. Beaulah Boulevard (off I-40, Exit 195)
(928) 913-0900
126 units. Heated indoor pool, whirlpool, and exercise room.

Holiday Inn Flagstaff
2320 E. Lucky Lane (I-40, Exit 198)
(928) 714-1000
Heated indoor pool, whirlpool, exercise room.

Quality Inn Flagstaff
2000 S. Milton Road (I-40, Exit 195)
(928) 774-8771
96 rooms. Heated outdoor pool.

Radisson Woodlands Hotel
1175 W. Route 66 (I-40, Exit 195)
(928) 773-8888
183 rooms. Heated outdoor pool, sauna, whirlpool, exercise room. Restaurant.

Ramada Limited West
2755 Woodlands Village Boulevard (I-40, Exit 195)
(928) 773-1111
89 rooms. Heated outdoor pool, sauna, whirlpool, and exercise room. Coin laundry.

Residence Inn by Marriott
3440 Country Club Drive (I-40, Exit 201)
(928) 526-5555
102 rooms. Heated outdoor pool, whirlpool, exercise room, and sports court.

Restaurants

Black Bart's Steakhouse Saloon
2760 East Butler Avenue
(928) 779-3142
Hours: 5 p.m.–9 p.m. Friday and Saturday in summer, open to 10 p.m. Fresh fish is also served.

Buster's
1800 S. Milton Road
(928) 774-5155
Hours: 11:30 a.m. to 10:00 p.m. Lively restaurant serving steak, chicken, and fresh fish.

Cottage Place Restaurant
126 W. Cottage Avenue
(928) 774-8431
Hours 5:00 p.m. to 9:30 p.m. Closed Monday. Reservations suggested. International menu. Wine and beer only.

Lupo Horsemen Lodge and Restaurant
8500 N. US-89
(928) 526-2655
Old West-style casual steakhouse. Opens for dinner at 5 p.m. Closed on major holidays.

Josephine's
503 N. Humphrey Street
(928) 779-3400
Reservations suggested. Extensive menu: pork, chicken, lamb, steak, and seafood. Open 11:00 a.m. to 2:30 p.m. and from 5:30 p.m. to 9:00 p.m.

Mountain Oasis International Restaurant
11 E. Aspen Avenue
(928) 214-9270
Hours: 11 a.m. to 9 p.m. Open to 10 p.m. Friday and Saturday. Varied international menu: Asian, Middle Eastern, Mediterranean, and American dishes.

Western Gold Dining Room
2515 E. Butler Avenue
(928) 779-2741
Open 11 a.m. to 2 p.m. and 5 p.m. to 10 p.m. Reservations suggested. American and Continental menu.

Note: There are many fast food and casual restaurants.

Before leaving Flagstaff, you might want to pack a picnic lunch, snacks, and lots of water. This leg of the tour will take in Sunset Crater National Monument and Wupatki National Monument. It will take a minimum of four hours to see everything in both parks. There are restrooms in both visitor centers; however, there are no gas stations and there is no food available until close to Cameron. Cameron Trading Post Lodge is fully booked in the summer months, and with good reason; it is recommened that you spend a night or two there. If you wish to stay there, book several months in advance. (See page 144 for further information.) Otherwise, stay at the Quality Inn in Tuba City. (See page 140 for information.)

Directions from Flagstaff to Wupatki National Monument
Travel north from Flagstaff on US-89 for 17 miles to the entrance for Sunset Crater. Follow the Wupatki/Sunset Crater Loop to the Wupatki National Monument. Along the way you will see the San Francisco Peaks.

San Francisco Peaks (elev. 6,000–12,633 ft.)

Navajo: *Dook'o'oslííd,* meaning "Never Thaws on Top."
Hopi name: *Nuvatekiaqui,* meaning "Place of Snow on the Very Top."

The San Francisco Peaks are the highest mountains in Arizona. There is Humphrey's Peak (12,633 ft.), Agassiz Peak (12,340 ft.), and Fremont Peak (11,940 ft.) These mountains could have been up to 15,000 feet high before collapsing into an empty magma chamber 500,000 years ago. These peaks, and Blanco Peak (Colorado), Mount Taylor (New Mexico), and Hesperus Peak (Colorado), mark the rightful boundaries of Navajoland according to the Creation Myth (Linford 2000).

Hopis claim the San Francisco Peaks are the home of the Kachina People. Havasupai Indians used to live on the western slope.

Sunset Crater National Monument (elev. 8,000 ft.)

Follow Sunset Crater–Wupatki Loop Road for about 2 miles to the crater. This road runs for 35 miles between the two national monuments.

Navajo: *Dził Bílátah Łitsooí,* meaning "Yellow Topped Mountain."

Hiking is not allowed around the rim of the crater, but there is a self-guided tour through Bonita lava flows. If you wish to do some hiking, Lennox Crater is only one mile away, east of the visitor center. The climb is 280 feet to the top, so bring sturdy shoes.

The visitor center has exhibits on volcanic explosions, cinder cones, and lava flows. Sunset Crater (the youngest of four hundred craters in the area) rises 1,070 feet from the foot of the crater to an elevation of 8,030 feet.

Wupatki National Monument (elev. 4,861 ft.)

Navajo: *Anaásází Bikin*, meaning "Anasazi House" or "Alien Ancestor's Home."
Hopi name: *Wapatkikuh*, meaning "Tall House Ruins."

Wupatki Monument, located between US-89 and the Little Colorado River, protects the prehistoric ruins of the Sinagua culture. They were a farming people, blending the traits of southern Hohokam, the western Anasazi, and the Mogollon cultures. The earliest evidence of this culture is a "widely dispersed hunter/gatherer/farmer population of pithouse dwellers" around Flagstaff (ibid.).

Sinagua farmed around the perimeters of lava cones, which were plentiful in the area. After Sunset Crater's eruption in 1064–1065, they moved to the Wupatki Basin, where they were joined by the Cohonina and Kayenta Anasazi cultures, from the west and the northeast. A more settled group of Hohokam and Cibola cultures added to the mix. The Sinagua quickly adapted to the masonry—above-ground structures that became Wupatki Pueblo (ibid.).

Sinaguas took their culture to other locations, such as Walnut Canyon twenty-five miles south. After about a hundred years, they abandoned the settlement, moving a few at a time to Verde Valley. Hopis may have attempted to settle here about fifty years later, but the whole area was largely uninhabited for six hundred years. Navajos have inhabited the area since about 1825 (ibid.).

There was continued strife between Anglos and Wupatki Navajos; whites considered Navajos intruders in the area. County officials placed a tax of five dollars per one hundred head on Navajo sheep and moved any family unable to pay the tax. Peshlakai Etsidi and the Reverend Philip Johnson convinced Teddy Roosevelt to extend Navajo reservation boundaries, which put an end to the strife (ibid.).

The largest and most impressive site is *Wupatki*, or "long-cut house," containing about one hundred rooms. It was originally three stories high. There is an open ball court (common in Mexico, but rare this far north), ceremonial amphitheater, and a blowhole. A blowhole is a geologic phenomenon where air is forced upward by underground pressure. The blowhole may have had some religious significance to the Hopi. Citadel, Lomaki, and the three-story Wukoki ruins can be reached by short, self-guided trails and are well worth the effort. For the more agile, there is a fourteen-mile, in-depth overnight hike to Crack-in-Rock Ruin. It covers areas marked by ancient petroglyphs and well-preserved ruins. These ranger-led treks are conducted in April and October. Space is limited, so you need to book several months in advance. Call 928-556-7040.

Doney Mountain is an ideal site for a picnic. It is located between Wupatki and Citadel ruins. A half-hour climb to the picnic area will reward you with 360-degree views of the San Francisco Peaks Volcanic Field and the spectacular Painted Desert. It can be windy!

Wupatki Visitor Center is open daily from 9 a.m. to 5 p.m. The park, however, is open daily from sunrise to sunset. Restrooms and picnic areas are available. Call the visitor center at 928-679-2365 for information on ranger-led hikes.

Directions from Wupatki National Monument to Cameron
Return to US-89 north for approximately 25 miles to Cameron. You will pass the Babbitt Brothers ranch and Gray Mountain.

The Babbitt Brothers Ranch

Dave and Billy Babbitt were the first of the brothers to head west. They bought a small ranching outfit and started raising cattle in the area between Flagstaff and Winslow in 1886. Their brand was "CO" with a bar underneath in memory of Cincinnati, Ohio, the brothers' former home. They shipped their first herd east the next year.

Charles, or C. J., and George sold the family business and joined Dave and Billy. They were strongly advised to diversify their holdings, so Dave opened a mercantile store and George got involved in real estate in Flagstaff. Dave and Billy continued to run the cattle operation. During the heyday of the CO Bar Ranch (1909–1919), they branded a "CO" bar on the hides of some one thousand cows. Within a few years they diversified their cattle operation into a variety of other businesses. By the end of World War I, Babbitt Brothers was one of the most prominent enterprises in the entire Southwest (Trimble 1990).

Flagstaff was the cultural and mercantile center of northern Arizona. The Babbitt brothers were involved in everything that went on, becoming a very influential power in northern Arizona. They did not live in pretentious houses, and they did not abuse their power. They operated numerous trading posts on the Navajo and Hopi reservations. Their holdings included a garage, an opera house, and a mortuary. It is said that Babbitts "fed, clothed, equipped, transported, entertained and buried Arizonians, doing it more efficiently and more profitably than anyone else" (ibid., 234).

The CO Bar Ranch, run by the Babbitt brothers, is located off US-89 and covers most of the grazing land on both sides of US-89 to Gray Mountain. It is still one of the largest ranches running cattle in Arizona.

Gray Mountain (elev. 7,000 ft.)

Navajo: *Dził Łibáí*, meaning "Gray Mountain."

Gray Mountain includes the mountainous area two to four miles south of AZ-64 (the road to the Grand Canyon) and six miles west of US-89. Navajos named the whole Cocinino Plateau *Dził Łibáí*. The area was important in several of their religious myths.

There are some motels, the better one being the Anasazi Inn at Gray Mountain. Gray Mountain Trading Post serves three meals a day. Because the town of Gray Mountain is off the reservation, it is legal to buy liquor here. You enter the Navajo Nation a few miles north of here.

Cameron Trading Post (elev. 4,200 ft.)

Refer to page 144 for information on the hotel, restaurant, and surrounding area, including the Grand Canyon. This is the recommended place to stay for a night or two.

Directions from Cameron to Page

Travel north on US-89 for 68.7 miles to the junction of US-89A where you can opt for a side trip to the North Rim of the Grand Canyon (see page 161). To continue on US-89 north to Page is a little more than 22 miles. Between Cameron and US-160 there are views of the Painted Desert to the east. Shortly after passing US-160 you will see a sign for Moenave. Cedar Ridge is halfway between Moenave and US-89A.

MOENAVE (elev. 5,000 ft.)

Navajo: *Kin Łigaaí,* meaning "White House."

This area is a green oasis with springs fed from the Kaibab Plateau. Havasupai and Hopis farmed here before any white men appeared in the area. Mormon leader Jacob Hamblin founded the community in 1879. By 1903, only three farmers remained here, and the Mormons sold the land to the BIA. John D. Lee is supposed to have hidden here after he was accused of being a participant in the Mountain Meadows Massacre (Linford 2000).

Continuing on US-89 north, Echo Cliffs take up position to the east, adding color to the landscape. Some widely scattered trailers and hogans dot the countryside, and where there are small villages, roadside stands appear beside the highway.

You may notice some of the hogans are in a general state of decay. If someone dies inside a hogan, the body is taken out through a hole that is broken through the north wall. The spirit of the dead person is believed to remain in the hogan, so it is never occupied again; the hogan is left to gradually decay and go back to the earth.

CEDAR RIDGE (elev. 6,200 ft.)

Navajo: *Yaaniilk'id,* meaning "Hill Slopes Down and Ends."

Cedar Ridge is at the eastern end of Budaway Mesa, where the beginning of Hamblin Wash cuts through the soft Chinle Formation. Strip Pauites (Pauites from west of the Colorado River) used to favor this site for a camping place in the early 1900s. Water from Hamblin Wash drains down to the Little Colorado River, and the beginning of Tanner Wash starts here and drains water there as well.

There is a spring at the foot of Echo Cliffs, one mile east of US-89, approximately five miles southeast of Navajo Bridge. Jacob Hamblin, and those that followed him on the Mormon Trail, used this site as a watering hole and campsite in the 1850s. Navajos use this site today (ibid.).

If you wish to take the side trip to Lees Ferry, Vermillion Cliffs, Jacob Lake, and the North Rim of the Grand Canyon, see page 161. If you do not want to take the side trip continue on US-89 to Page, a good place to spend a night or two.

(Continued on page 174)

Side Trip to Lees Ferry, Vermillion Cliffs, Jacob Lake, and the North Rim of the Grand Canyon

From the junction of US-89 and US-89A it is approximately 99 miles to Grand Canyon North. Arizona west of the Colorado River is considered wilderness area, with a few pockets of habitation. It is possible to make the trip to Jacob Lake and Grand Canyon North in one day. The North Rim of the Grand Canyon is a remote wilderness area; it is not as accessible as the South Rim, and there are few services if you lack reservations. If you wish to do some walking and hiking in the pristine old-growth ponderosa pine forest, you should consider staying at the North Rim for at least one day. There are paths near Grand Canyon Lodge that are wheelchair accessible, but Grand Canyon South is the far better choice for those in wheelchairs. There are short or long hikes or you can take a jeep tour of the area (not for people with bad backs).

Some of the more exciting drives at the North Rim require high clearance, four-wheel-drive vehicles. Dirt roads are often impassable in wet weather. The lookouts are fantastic, but you should check with a park ranger to be certain you have all the backcountry gear necessary for the trip. As with all arid country, bring at least one gallon of water per person, per day. Dirt roads are often impassable in wet weather.

There are gas stations at Lees Ferry, Jacob Lake, and Grand Canyon North; keep your tank full. Jacob Lake RV campgrounds have room for campers over thirty feet in length. You will need a car to get to Grand Canyon North from there. It is hard to get reservations on the North Rim in the summer, so plan your trip well ahead. There are nice cabins on the rim with a canyon view, and some cabins are among ponderosa pine trees. There are also more traditional accommodations. The North Rim Lodge dining room is often fully booked once the season gets busy; keep this in mind when traveling to the rim. Carry lunches, snacks, and water. If the dining room is accepting reservations, there can still be a long wait. There is a deli in the lodge that is quite good, and a small general store has supplies for campers and a gas station.

Plan to visit Navajo Bridge Visitor Center and Lees Ferry on the return trip. Otherwise, you will have little time at Grand Canyon North before dark. It is forty-two miles to Page from Lees Ferry. Food and lodging is plentiful in Page; however, reservations are a must in the summer. (See page 176 for information on Page.)

Directions from Junction of US-89 and US-89A to Navajo Bridge and Lees Ferry

Navajo Bridge (on US-89A) is about 10 miles west of the junction of US-89 and US-89A. One mile after Navajo Bridge, and before Marble Canyon Lodge, there is a turnoff north for historic Lees Ferry. The road winds for about five miles down to the Colorado River. There are interpretive sites along the road describing the geology of the area. Lees Ferry is 85 miles from the North Rim of the Grand Canyon and 42 miles from Page.

Navajo Bridge

The Visitor Information and Interpretive Center on the west side of Navajo Bridge provides information on the building and maintenance of the bridge. Displays are informative, and the talk given by a ranger every hour is well worth the time. There are clean restrooms, but no food. Open 9 a.m. to 5 p.m., May to October.

Lees Ferry

Lees Ferry is located at the confluence of the Colorado and Paria rivers. The Colorado River was a barrier to all settlers until Mormon frontiersman Jacob Hamblin made the first crossing by raft. Mormon settlers utilized this crossing and rapidly spread out into northern Arizona from the 1870s through the 1890s. It became a vital link for Honeymoon Trail couples on their way to the Mormon temple in St. George, Utah, to have their civil marriages sanctified. Lees Ferry opened the country to traders, settlers, and travelers between Utah and Arizona. They would pick up supplies and information here.

The most famous ferryman was John Doyle Lee, who had attained some status in the church working under Brigham Young. He lived near one of the trails that immigrants from Missouri passed on their way to California. Taunting by members of the wagon trains left the Mormons in fear that federal troops would uproot them again. This fear led to the Mountain Meadows Massacre.

However it happened, Lee, his followers, and a group of Paiute Indians attacked a wagon train on September 11, 1857. The siege lasted for four days, after which the Mormons offered the immigrants refuge if they put down their guns. As soon as the immigrants disarmed, a signal was given and 140 immigrants were slaughtered in cold blood. Only seventeen children too young to talk about what had happened survived. Lee became the scapegoat for the massacre, and he had to hide from federal authorities. Jacob Hamblin then put Lee in charge of the ferry operation, thinking it was a safe place for him.

Lee and his wife, Emma, established a trading post and ranch, trading with Indians and whites alike. He was later captured and sentenced to death for his part in the massacre. He was shot while standing in his coffin on March 23, 1877, at the Mountain Meadows site of the massacre.

Warren Johnson and his two wives operated the ferry between 1875 and 1895. The dugway (a path dug out of the steep canyon wall) was built in 1898 so travelers would not have to climb the forbidding "Lee's Backbone." The Grand Canyon Cattle Company bought Lees Ferry in 1909. Later, Coconino County purchased and ran the ferry until 1929, when Navajo Bridge was opened.

There is a walking guide to the Lonely Dell Ranch available at the ranger station. The complete tour is about one mile, and there are picnic tables and shade trees at the ranch. Bring lots of water; the canyon can heat up during the day to 115 degrees in the summer. The only services available at Lees Ferry are a national park campground, ranger station, and public launch ramp. There is a gas station, store, post office, motel, and restaurant at Marble Canyon next to the park entrance. Lees Ferry Lodge and Cliff Dwellers Lodge are west of the park entrance.

Fishing at Lees Ferry is probably the best in the southwest. Visitors can enjoy world-class trout fishing in the Colorado River upstream to Glen Canyon Dam. The area is known for good-size German brown and rainbow trout. No live bait is allowed; artificial flies and lures only. The limit is two fish in your possession. There are campgrounds above the river with toilets and raised fireplaces. Camping is limited to fourteen days, and campers must bring in their own firewood and carry out their ashes and any other garbage they produce.

Fishing Guides

Ambassador Guide Service
William McBurney
P.O. Box 545, Page, AZ 86040
(800) 256-7596

Arizona Reel Time
Frederick Smith
P.O. Box 6169, Marble Canyon, AZ 86036
(928) 355-2222

Bubba's Guide Service
Jim Cliburn
P.O. Box 3471, Page, AZ 86040
(928) 645-3506

Cannon Guides and Supplies
Ron Cannon
P.O. Box 2583, Page, AZ 86040
(928) 608-0273

Lees Ferry Anglers
Terry Gunn
P.O. Box 30, Marble Canyon, AZ 86036
(928) 355-2261

Marble Canyon Outfitters
Dave Foster
P.O. Box 32, Marble Canyon, AZ 86036
(800) 533-7339

Rafting

Lees Ferry is considered ground zero for any rafting trips down the Colorado River. There are many companies providing rafting experiences, including the following:

Hatch River Expeditions
P.O. Box 1200, Vernal, UT 844078
(800) 433-8966; fax (435) 789-4126

Arizona Raft Adventures
4040-XE Huntington Drive, Flagstaff, AZ 86604
(800) 786-7238 or (928) 526-8200
This company will accommodate all skill levels in six- to fourteen-day combination paddle and motor trips from May through October.

Canyoneers
Box 2997, Flagstaff, AZ 86003
(800) 525-0924
www.canyoneers.com
This company conducts trips of three to thirteen days, April through September.

Diamond River Adventures
Box 1300, Page, AZ 86040
(800) 343-3121 or (928) 645-8866
Long-established company offering oar-powered and motorized trips from May through September.

Grand Canyon Expeditions Company
P.O. Box 0, Kanab, UT 84741
(800) 544-2691 or (435) 644-2691
www.gcex.com
Excellent reputation. Trips from April through October.

Hiking

Temperatures in this rugged country range from zero in the winter to 115 degrees in the summer. This area is subject to flash floods, so be sure to let someone know where you are going and when you plan to return. Carry at least one gallon of water per person per day. Be sure to check in with the ranger station for information on current hiking conditions.

River Trail: Starts at the launch ramp and follows the old wagon road past the fort to the upper ferry-crossing site. A "Walking Tour Guide" is available. It takes about one hour to complete the two-mile round-trip walk.

Paria Canyon Trail: This trail starts at the Lonely Dell Ranch parking area and continues for forty-five miles upstream to US-89 in Utah. Permits from the Bureau of Land Management are required for overnight hikes. Day hikers can enjoy the unique geology of the area.

The Paria River flows from the Paunsaugunt Plateau near Brice Canyon in Utah to Lees Ferry in Arizona. The lower end is now within Vermillion Cliffs National Monument. It is famous for its tributary "Buckskin Gulch," the longest slot canyon in the world. Near the confluence, the river flows through a deep long section. The multi-day hike through here to Lees Ferry is (together with Zion Canyon Narrows) one of the two premier canyon hikes in the Southwest. Experienced hikers only.

Cathedral Canyon: Parking for this hike is at the Geology Wayside pullout from Lees Ferry Road. This two-mile round-trip hike is not along a defined trail. You must find your own way down the intermittent stream bed, or wash, inside a narrow slot canyon with interesting rock formations. Be alert for flash floods. There is a rapid and beach along the Colorado River at the mouth of the canyon.

Spencer Trail: This historic trail climbs 1,700 feet up the cliff behind Lees Ferry Fort. It is not regularly maintained, but it is passable to careful hikers. Views down Marble Canyon are memorable.

Accommodations

Marble Canyon Lodge
On US-89A, a quarter-mile west of Navajo Bridge
(928) 355-2225 or (800) 726-1789
This lodge is a central base access for a wide variety of activities: fishing, hiking, river rafting, and sightseeing. There are great views of the Vermillion Cliffs. Fifty-two units, TV, laundry, meeting room, and an airstrip. A restaurant in the lodge serves steaks, pasta, and seafood, plus sandwiches and vegetarian meals. Salad bar.

Lees Ferry Lodge
On US-89A, nine miles west of Navajo Bridge
(928) 355-2231 or (800) 451-2231
There are no in-room telephones and some rooms lack TV. This rustic native stone lodge caters to the fishing trade in an authentic western

setting. Vermillion Cliffs Bar and Grill is popular with river rafters and fishermen alike. The bar serves over one hundred different kinds of beer as well as wine. The restaurant serves good hearty fare—steaks and ribs.

Cliff Dwellers Lodge
On US-89A, nine miles west of Navajo Bridge
(928) 355-2228 or (800) 433-2543
Built in 1949, this lodge is the most modern of the three. The rooms are attractive. Cable TV, bar, shop, and a restaurant. Lees Ferry Anglers has its headquarters at this lodge. You can buy fishing licenses here.

Directions from Lees Ferry to Jacob Lake
Driving west on US-89-A, it is 44.5 miles from Lees Ferry to Jacob Lake. Vermillion Cliffs, San Bartholome Historic Site, House Rock Buffalo Ranch, and Jacob Lake are points of interest along the way.

Vermillion Cliffs

Vermillion Cliffs to the north are spectacular in their dominance of the area; they rise to more than three thousand feet in some areas. Condors were reintroduced to the area (and Grand Canyon South) several years ago. You can often see them flying around the cliffs.

San Bartholome Historic Site

About eighteen miles west of Navajo Bridge is an interpretive site that explains the plight of the near starving Dominques-Escalante Expedition of 1776. This isolated "Arizona Strip" area is separated from the rest of Arizona by the Grand Canyon.

House Rock Buffalo Ranch

Access is via a twenty-three-mile dirt road, impassable when wet. The Arizona Game and Fish Department oversees one of the largest herd of buffalo in the Southwest here. You are welcome to enter and try to see some buffalo; however, they have a huge roaming area, and you do not have much chance of seeing them.

The road ascends the Kaibab Plateau with some sharp switchbacks and beautiful outlooks. You will be leaving behind the part of Arizona dominated by sharp, blunt scenery (rocks, mountains, and cliffs) and entering the heavily forested land of ponderosa pine and aspen. The high country is peaceful and cool, even the summer.

Jacob Lake

Jacob Lake has a grocery store, gas station, motel, and the Kaibab Plateau Visitor Center, (928) 643-7298. Jacob Lake is at the intersection of US-89A and AZ-67, the access road to Grand Canyon North. **Note:** AZ-67 to the Grand Canyon closes from late November to early May. Heavy snow often closes the road earlier.

Accommodations

Jacob Lake Inn
Located at the junction of AZ-67 and US-89A
(928) 643-7232
www.jacoblake.com
Location is everything here. The accommodations are basic (no telephones or TV in the rooms).

Note: Whether you stay at the motel or in one of the campgrounds, pack a substantial lunch, snacks, and water for the trip to the North Rim of the Grand Canyon. It is almost impossible to get reservations in the restaurant in the summer, but it is one of the best picnic areas you will find.

RV and Campgrounds

Jacob Lake Campground
(928) 643-7395
Run by the U.S. Forest Service, spaces are on a first come basis, no reservations. RV and tent sites are available, but no hookups. There are

flush toilets, picnic tables, fire grills, and fire pits. Open May through October.

Kiabab Camper Village
Located one-half mile south of Jacob Lake on AZ-67
(928) 643-7804 in season; (928) 526-0924 or (800) 525-0924 out of season
Reservations are accepted by the trip outfitter (Canyoneers, Inc., www.canyoneers.com) and are recommended, especially in July and August. There are eighty RV and trailer sites with full hookups, and fifty tent sites. Drinking water, showers, portable toilets, picnic tables, and fire pits. Open mid-May through mid-October. This campsite is located in a nicely wooded area near a gas station, store, and restaurant.

Demotte Campground
Located twenty-five miles south of Jacob Lake on AZ-67
(928) 643-7395
The U.S. Forest Service runs this campground. Only RVs under thirty feet can be accommodated at this site. This is a quiet spot deep in Ponderosa Pine country. There are twenty-three RV or tent sites, but no hookups. Flush toilets, picnic tables, fire pits, and grill. No reservations accepted. Open mid-May to mid-October.

Directions from Jacob Lake to the North Rim of the Grand Canyon
Travel south on AZ-67 for 44 miles to the entrance of the Grand Canyon. **Note:** *AZ-67 to the Grand Canyon closes from late November to early May. Heavy snow often closes the road earlier.*

Ponderosa pines dominate this scenic wilderness highway. In the lower areas you will see aspen and, less frequently, maple trees. Watch for the Kaibob squirrels, identified by their all-white tails, charcoal body, and long tufts of white hair on their ears. Mule deer, elk, and black bear can be seen mostly in the early morning or late evening. This area and the North Rim gets buried in an average of twelve to fourteen feet of snow (and it can get up to twenty feet) in the winter. Precipitation is equally divided between snow in winter and the dramatic thunderstorms of the summer monsoons.

Few people will intrude on your enjoyment of true wilderness. The road climbs slowly to the North Rim of the Grand Canyon, where you reach 8,800 feet. During the summer, the air is very dry, so carry lots of water with you to any activity and on any trail hikes. One can sunburn quickly at this altitude, so sunscreen, a hat, and sunglasses are strongly recommended.

Grand Canyon North Rim (elev. 8,300 ft.)

Navajo: *Bikooh Ntsaa Ahkee,* meaning "Deep Canyon."

There is an entrance fee. Go to the visitor center near Grand Canyon Lodge, which is open 8 a.m. to 6 p.m. A ranger will advise what you can reasonably do in the amount of time you have.

Thunderstorms are extremely dangerous at this altitude! Stay away from exposed rim areas during thunderstorms. Avoid touching anything metal, like a railing or a camera tripod, if thunderstorms are even near the area, as they attract lightning. The safest place to be during a storm is inside a vehicle. Pets, except signal and guide dogs, are not allowed on trails other than Bridge Trail, which connects Grand Canyon Lodge with North Kaibab Trail. Pets must be on a leash.

A gas station that does repairs is located on the access road leading to the North Rim campground; there is no diesel fuel on the North Rim. A small store sells camping supplies and food near the campground.

How did the Grand Canyon form? About 70 million years ago, large sections of the American Southwest began rising because of a collision of tectonic plates. It pushed the Colorado Plateau from near sea level to more than ten thousand feet in height; there was little tilting or deforming of the layers. The North Rim cuts through a bulge in the southwestern part of the Colorado Plateau called the Kaibab Uplift. Erosion over 5 to 6 million years carved out the canyons.

There is evidence that Navajos crossed the Colorado River at the Crossing of the Fathers upstream from Navajo Canyon, hunting deer and wild horses along the North Rim of the canyon on the Kaibab Plateau. While this area was considered to be Havasupai territory, at times Navajos occupied the area right up to Grand Canyon Village on the South Rim. Many Navajos fled to the canyon when Kit Carson attacked them in his effort to move all Navajos to Bosque Redondo (Linford 2000).

The Grand Canyon National Park brochure describes the canyon experience as follows: "It is the visual impact of the landscape that impresses most people. The world seems larger here, with sunrises, sunsets, and storms taking on an added dimension to match the landscape. It is a land to humble the soul."

The difference between the South Rim and the North Rim is in the easy accessibility of the South Rim views and in the untouched wilderness experience of the North Rim. The South Rim goes on for miles with multiple outlooks relatively close to each other. A courtesy bus goes from outlook to outlook all along the South Rim. The North Rim has few outlooks (awe inspiring as they are) close to the lodge; however, the outlooks in remote areas are spectacular. If time is limited, the South Rim is your best choice, as you can accomplish more in one day. For a prolonged stay, either rim will keep you busy. However, the hiking and wilderness experience of the North Rim, along with the quietness, makes it a very special place to be.

Developed Scenic Viewpoints

Bright Angel Point. The trail starts at the southern end of the entrance road. Take a short walk to Grand Canyon Lodge and enjoy an awesome view of the canyon; this area is wheelchair accessible. A paved (one-mile round-trip) trail leads from the lodge to the point. The trail begins at the log shelter in the parking area by the visitor center or at the corner of the back porch behind the lodge; self-guiding nature trail pamphlets are available from a box along the trail. The trail is steep in places, with sheer drop-offs and stairs, but the dramatic view of Roaring Springs and Bright Angel Canyon is worth it. **Note:** Do not climb out to the edge, as several people die here from doing so every year. More hiking trails start near the lodge. No permits or fees are required for day hikes.

Point Imperial (elev. 8,803 ft.). This is the highest point on the North Rim; it overlooks the Painted Desert and the eastern end of the Grand Canyon. The trail is four miles round-trip and will take approximately two hours hiking time. Layers of red and black pre-Cambrian rocks add unique color and contrast to this view. Part of this viewpoint is accessible.

Cape Royal. This viewpoint is popular at sunrise and sunset because of its breathtaking panorama up, down, and across the canyon. The sweeping turn of the Colorado River is framed through the natural arch of Angels Window. You may be able to see the Desert View Watchtower on the South Rim (0.6 miles from Cape Royal).

Transept Trail. This popular trail winds around the canyon rim for three miles, round-trip. It goes as far as the North Rim Campground and General Store before going back.

Widforss Trail. Hiking time is approximately six hours on this ten-mile trail; it features a blend of forest and canyon scenery. There is an elevation change of two hundred feet. A self-guiding trail brochure is available at the trailhead. Numerous aspens, along with pine and spruce, make this trail ideal for fall colors.

Point Sublime. This westernmost point of the North Rim (17 miles) is accessible only by four-wheel-drive vehicles; it takes two hours each way. The view lives up to its name. Inquire about road conditions and closures at the visitor center before starting out.

Accommodations

Grand Canyon Lodge

(303) 297-2757 (reservations only); direct hotel line (928) 638-2611
www.grandcanyonnorthrim.com
The lodge is the best place to stay, but you will need to make reservations months in advance. At the same time, make dining room reservations; the dining room is always fully booked in the summer. The dining room is a huge sunroom with high, beamed ceilings. The menu is a little pricey,

but there is something for everyone. There are one-bedroom and two-bedroom rustic cabins, some with a view, right on the rim. Modern hotel rooms are also available. There is a cafeteria, dining room, laundry, bar, and shop; no A/C or TV. No smoking rooms. Closed mid-October to mid-May.

Kaibab Lodge
(928) 638-2389, or (928) 526-0924 in the winter
Kaibab Lodge was built in the 1920s and is located five miles north of the North Rim entrance. The cabins are rustic with basic furnishings. There is a restaurant; no A/C or TV. Closed mid-October to mid-May.

RV and Campgrounds

North Rim Campground
(800) 365-2267
Located two miles north of the rim and close to a general store for supplies. There are more than eighty RV and tent sites with no hookups. Flush toilets, guest laundry, drinking water, showers, fire grates, picnic tables, and dump station. Closed mid-October to mid-May. For information write National Park Reservation Service, Box 1100, Cumberland, MD 21501.

Directions from Grand Canyon North Rim to Page
Retrace your route, AZ-67 to east on US-89A. Follow US-89A to the junction of US-89. Take US-89 north to Page, about 108 miles. Enjoy a few days in Page; the hotels are comfortable, the food is varied, and there is plenty to see and do.

Cedar Ridge (continued from page 160)

Directions for Travelers from Utah and Nevada to Page
Most travelers will come via US-15, either from Las Vegas, Nevada, or from Salt Lake City, Utah, in the north. It is 142 miles from Las Vegas to the junction of UT-9. It is almost 227 miles from Salt Lake City to the junction of UT-17. Both UT-9 and UT-17 run into UT-59, which becomes AZ-389 as you travel east. Follow UT-59/AZ-389 east for 64 miles to Fredonia, Arizona. From Fredonia, there are two routes to Page. You can continue on US-89A to the junction of US-89, then north to Page, about 80 miles. Or, you can take US-89 north, then east to Page, about 112 miles.

It is shorter for travelers north of I-70 in Utah to take I-15 to east on I-70 to the junction of US-89. Follow US-89 south. You will pass by the access road to Bryce Canyon on the way. Continue south on US-89, then east all the way to Page.

Directions from Fredonia to Page *(Option 1)*
Travel via US-89A north to US-89 at Kanab. Continue north then east on US-89 all the way to Page. You will pass through parts of the Grand Staircase Escalente National Monument on the way.

Directions from Fredonia to Page via US-89A *(Option 2)*
Travel east on US-89A; it is 30 miles from Fredonia to Jacob Lake. From Jacob Lake to junction of US-89 is 55.5 miles. Turn north (left) on US-89 to Page, about 23 miles. Information on this route is under "US-89A Side Trip to Lees Ferry, Vermillion Cliffs, Jacob Lake, and the North Rim of the Grand Canyon" on page 161.

Kanab

Kanab has a history going back to the 1880s. Church of Latter-day Saints' president Brigham Young planned the town site. Mormon missionaries and settlers were among the first whites here. Show-business people found the town in the 1940s and historic Perry Lodge housed visitors such as John Wayne, Frank Sinatra, Glen Ford, and Charlton Heston. *Gunsmoke* was filmed at the Paria movie set nearby, and *The Outlaw Josie Wales* features buildings that are now part of Frontier Movie Town.

Kanab Information Center—Grand Staircase Escalente National Monument

There are no services inside the Grand Staircase Escalente Park. One can stay in Kanab or Page. Grand Staircase Escalente Park is 1.9 million acres of wilderness: cliffs, terraces, and the Kaiparowitz Plateau. It extends across the rugged Kaiparowitz Plateau to the wonders of the Escalante river canyons. All of the park's interior roads are dirt roads, impassable in wet weather. Four-wheel-drive, high-clearance vehicles are required. There are day hiking, backpacking, mountain biking, and off-highway vehicle use allowed in the park. The visitor center at Kanab, UT (435-644-4600) has information on the weather and road conditions.

Accommodations

Clarion-Victorian Charm Inn
190 North US-89
(435) 644-8660
Two stories, 20 units, bath combo or shower only, coin laundry.

Four Seasons Motel and Restaurant
36 North 300 W
(435) 644-2635
41 units, no elevator, two stories, restaurant.

Holiday Inn Express
815 East US-89
(435) 644-8888
71 units, heated outdoor pool, whirlpool, gift shop, and coin laundry. Free nine-hole golf course.

Aikens Lodge
79 West Center Street on US-89
(435) 644-2625
22 one-bedroom and 9 two-bedroom units, no elevator, heated pool, coin laundry.

Page (elev. 4,310 ft.)

Navajo: *Da'deesł'in Hótsaa*, meaning "Big Dam."

Page started out as a construction camp for crews working on Glen Canyon Dam. Today, Page is the gateway city for Utah residents and visitors from Las Vegas to access the Navajo reservation. The city was named for John C. Page, a commissioner of the Bureau of Reclamation from 1937 to 1943. It is the destination city for recreation on Lake Powell.

Lake Powell is the primary source of water for approximately 27 million people in Arizona, California, Colorado, Nevada, New Mexico, Utah, and Wyoming. The availability of water has led to rapid development within these states; Lake Powell at full capacity stores 27 million acre-feet of water. Lake Powell is insurance against drought for states depending on it for water.

Page is the city to visit for outdoor recreation: boating, water sports, fishing, hiking, and sightseeing. Lake Powell offers 250 square miles of cool water to explore on houseboats. Wide-open bays lead to a maze of waterways where you glide past up to four-hundred-foot walls of colorful sandstone. Page is on the border of the Navajo reservation and is a gateway for destinations like Navajo National Monument, Keet Siel, Monument Valley, and Canyon de Chelly.

Accommodations

Note: Hotel rates are well discounted in March, April, May, September, and October.

Best Western Arizona Inn
716 Rimview Drive (7 miles east of US-89 via SR-89L)
(928) 645-2466
103 units, outdoor heated pool, Jacuzzi, fitness center, TV, coin laundry. Ample parking for boats and RVs. It overlooks Lake Powell and Glen Canyon Dam.

Best Western at Lake Powell
208 N. Lake Powell Blvd. (0.8 mile east of US-89 via SR-89L)
(928) 645-5988 or (888) 794-2888
132 rooms (some three-bed family rooms), microwaves and refrigerators in some rooms, no smoking rooms, TV, laundry facilities, heated outdoor pool, whirlpool, and exercise room. Ample parking for boats and RVs. AAA discount of 15 percent. It overlooks Glen Canyon Dam, with views of the Vermillion Cliffs.

Courtyard by Marriott
600 Clubhouse Drive (on the grounds of Lake Powell National Golf Course)
(928) 645-5000; www.courtyard.com
153 rooms, fitness center, restaurant, heated outdoor pool, sauna, TV. No smoking rooms.

Days Inn & Suites
961 Hwy 89
(877) 525-3769; www.daysinn.net
Continental breakfast, pool, guest laundry, and ample boat parking with AC power. Jacuzzi suites available. Refrigerators in every room.

Lake Powell Resort
100 Lakeshore Drive (5 miles north of Page in the Glen Canyon National Recreation Area on Lake Powell)
(928) 645-2433, 1-800-528-6154
Formerly known as Wahweap Lodge. Spectacular lake views. Airport shuttle service and spacious parking for boats, motor coaches, and RVs. 350 units decorated in a southwestern theme. No elevator. The hotel offers a marina, water-skiing, boat trips, river rafting, houseboats, gift shop, coin laundry, and a pizzeria. **Note:** Trips to Rainbow Bridge are especially popular. Aramark's Lake Powell Resorts & Marinas have houseboats of various sizes for rent.

Quality Inn at Lake Powell
287 N. Lake Powell Blvd. (0.8 mile east of US-89/SR 89L)
(928) 645-8851 or (866) 645-8851
Outdoor pool and coin laundry.

Holiday Inn Express
751 Navajo Drive (SR 89L, 1.5 miles east of US-89)
(928) 645-9000
There are three one-bedroom units with kitchens and 71 regular units. Coin laundry and heated outdoor pool.

Motel 6 – Page/Lake Powell
637 S. Lake Powell Blvd. (on Business Loop SR 89-L, east of US-89)
(928) 645-5888
Outdoor pool and coin laundry.

Super 8 Gateways
649 S. Lake Powell Blvd. (on SR 89L, east of US-89)
(928) 645-5858
101 units. Outdoor pool, exercise room, and coin laundry.

RV and Campgrounds

Page/Lake Powell Campground
849 S. Coppermine Street
(928) 645-3374

Coming from Flagstaff on US-89 north, turn right at Texaco station on Haul Road; follow Haul Road for 3 miles to the intersection of Coppermine Road. The campground is directly across the street. Coming from Utah on US-89 south, turn left on Haul Road and follow for 3 miles to Coppermine Road.

Open year round. Convenience store, full hookups, information kiosk with maps, and local weather forecast. Heated pool, therapy pool, laundry, dump station, restrooms, and partitioned showers.

Wahweap Trailer Village
100 Lakeshore Drive (5 miles north of Page on US-89)
(928) 645-1004
Open year round. Reservations accepted. 120 full-service hookups, drinking water, guest laundry, showers, picnic tables, and flush toilets.

Wahweap Campground
100 Lakeshore Drive (5 miles north of Page on US-89)
(928) 645-1004
Located in the marina complex. Lake views. Serves RV and tent campers. 94 full hookups and 112 tent sites. Drinking water, guest laundry, showers, picnic tables, flush toilets, and a dump station.

Houseboats

Aramark's Lake Powell Resort and Marina
100 Lakeshore Drive (5 miles north of Page on US-89)
(800) 528-6154
Houseboats of various sizes for rent with accommodations for six to twelve people. Be sure to book early for the summer months or you will be disappointed.

Restaurants

Bella Napoli
810 N. Navajo Drive
(928) 645-2706
Italian dishes: pizza, pasta, and fresh fish and seafood. Reservations accepted. Hours 11 a.m. to 2 p.m. and from 5 p.m. to 9 p.m. Beer and wine only.

The Dam Bar and Grille
644 N. Navajo Drive
(928) 645-2161
Sports bar serving chicken, steak, pasta, and seafood. Open 3 p.m.

Ken's Old West Restaurant and Lounge
718 Vista Avenue
(928) 645-5160
Upbeat western atmosphere with live country and western music. Serves steak, prime rib, barbecued chicken, and seafood. Open 3:00 p.m. to 11:30 p.m.

Rainbow Room Lake Powell Resort
100 Lakeshore Drive (5 miles north of Page)
(928) 645-2433
Serves a luncheon buffet and dinner favorites like steak, chops, pasta, and trout.

Zapatas
614 N. Navajo Drive
(928) 645-9006
Great margaritas. Good selection of Mexican dishes, all made from scratch.

M Bar H Café
819 N. Navajo Drive
(928) 645-1420
Great breakfasts with large servings.

Strombolli's Pizza
711 N. Navajo Drive
(928) 645-2605
Italian food, outdoor seating.

Airlines

Scenic Airlines
(928) 645-2494

Great Lakes Aviation
(800) 554-5111.
This is the only airline that will take you from Phoenix to Page. No large airlines serve this area.

Museums

John Wesley Powell Museum and Visitor Center
6 N. Lake Powell Blvd.
(928) 645-9496
Powell was the first white man to ride the rapids all the way down the river to where the Grand Canyon ends; he named many places in the area. The museum is well done for its size. You can book tours from here; no additional fees are charged for booking through the museum and the museum benefits from this service.

Navajo Village Heritage Center
531 Haul Road
(928) 660-0304
The three-hour "Evening with the Navajo Grand Tour" includes two hours of cultural entertainment and a Navajo taco dinner around a campfire. Open April through October.

Tours

Lake Powell Jeep Tours
108 S. Lake Powell Blvd.
(928) 645-5505
www.jeeptour.com

Grand Circle Tours
(928) 645-5088
www.grandcircleshuttle.com
Part of Grand Circle Shuttle. They also run a taxi service: (928) 645-6806

Antelope Canyon Adventures
22 S. Lake Powell Blvd.
(928) 645-5501 or 1-866-645-5501

Navajo Tours
(928) 698-3384

Overland Canyon Tours
695 Navajo Drive (behind the Circle K)
(928) 608-4072
www.overlandtours.com
Group rates, senior discounts, and children under seven are free. Specializing in photo adventures. Offers Waterholes Canyon and the Finns alternative to Antelope Canyon.

Emergency Information

Police: 547 Vista Avenue, (928) 645-2463
Page Hospital: Located at the corner of Vista Avenue and Navajo Drive, (928) 645-2424
Arizona Game and Fish: (801) 596-8660

Canyon de Chelly, Arizona

Majestic Monument Valley

Monument Valley in the evening

MARBLE CANYON, ARIZONA

Window Rock
Veteran's Memorial, Arizona

San Juan River, Gooseneck State Park, Utah

Grand Canyon North Rim, Arizona

The Left Mitten, Monument Valley

John Ford Point, Monument Valley

View of Monument Valley

Left and Right Mittens, Monument Valley

Sandal Trail, Navajo National Monument, Arizona

Betatakin Ruins, Navajo National Monument, Arizona

Petrified Forest National Park, Arizona
(inset) Puerco Pueblo ruins

Sandstone formation, Monument Valley

Sun's Eye, Monument Valley

Painted Desert, Arizona

Multi-sided Log Hogan

Old-Style Hogan

Hubbell Trading Post, Arizona

Lee's Ferry, Colorado River, Arizona

St. Michaels Historical Museum (above) and Indian School (below), Arizona

Code Talkers Memorial, Arizona

Navajo Museum, Library and Visitor's Center, Arizona

CHAPTER 18

PAGE TO MONUMENT VALLEY

Directions from Page to Antelope Canyon
Take Lake Powell Boulevard (Business 89) southwest to Coppermine Rd. Follow Coppermine Road south to where it ends at AZ-98. Proceed east on AZ-98 to Antelope Canyon, across the road from the Navajo Power Plant.

You are back on the Navajo reservation. Upper Antelope Canyon (also known as Corkscrew Canyon) has been gated; only authorized tour guides are permitted to enter. Tours last for two hours, and there is a charge for every hour beyond this. Antelope Canyon is a photographers' dream, but it is expensive. Lower Antelope Canyon is more challenging, requiring ropes or ladders in some places to descend sheer drops. One needs to be in good physical condition, but it is well worth the effort.

Note: You cannot see both Upper and Lower Antelope Canyon unless you go with a tour.

Antelope Canyon

Antelope Canyon is a favorite spot for pro and amateur photographers, tourists, and movie producers. Slow-speed film, time exposures, and tripods are recommended to get the best pictures. The most dramatic pictures are taken from 11:30 a.m. to 2:00 p.m. There are special tours for photographers. The canyon is cool, even in the summer, so bring a sweater.

Antelope Canyon is famous for its corkscrew rock formations. This narrow slot canyon of red sandstone is the most visited canyon in the Southwest because of its easy accessibility. Once inside the entrance, the temperature drops 20 degrees. You enter one of the most beautiful of all natural formations. Sunlight filters through curved sandstone walls, making constantly changing patterns and shadows in many shades of color. These colorful rocks are petrified sand dunes of the prehistoric inland sea that once covered the area.

Sections of the canyon are wide and bright; others are narrow, almost cavelike, with no light reaching the sandy floor. After approximately 150 meters, the canyon becomes suddenly much shallower near the top of the plateau. Although it may take only three minutes to walk through this area of the canyon, it is well worth the effort. Pictures from here adorn camera shops and professional photographic magazines and manuals throughout the world. Usually, there are several people with light meters and tripods trying to compose the perfect shot, and they grumble if anyone walks in front of their two-minute exposure. Extra care and consideration is necessary here.

Directions from Antelope Canyon to Navajo National Monument

AZ-98 east from Antelope Canyon to US-160 is a pleasant 66-mile trip. Proceed east on US-160 for 15 miles to AZ-564. Navajo National Monument is 9 miles north on AZ-564. Betatakin and the Keet Siel ruins here are fascinating to visit. It is almost 16 miles from the junction of US-160 and AZ-564 to Kayenta.

The landscape is less red. You will notice the absence of debris on the roadsides; this is either respect for the land or from the efforts of a scrupulous cleanup crew. Navajoland is clean, pleasant, and often a spectacular place to visit. Sometimes, small herds of sheep and goats (watch out for guard dogs) become visible.

Navajo National Monument (elev. 7,286–5,800 ft.)

Navajo: *Bitát'ahkin*, meaning "House on a Ledge," refers to Betatakin ruin.

Navajo Monument is a "series of isolated islands of territory around three major ruin complexes" (Linford 2000: 115). Anasazi (Kayenta branch) are believed to have inhabited this area since the Basketmaker II period, around the time of Christ (ibid.). Hopi are among the descendents of these early people. Ancient stone villages in Navajo National Monument are believed to have been stops along the sacred migration paths of at least eight Hopi clans. Two of the largest villages are Betatakin and Keet Siel. The alcoves in the cliffs offered safe shelter; the canyons offered springs and fields.

Navajos followed the Pueblo people into the Southwest in the late 1500s (some may have come earlier). They hunted and lived among the Pueblo people, who were more settled farmers. Navajos learned to grow corn. Relationships with their neighbors were characterized by times of peace and trading and times of raiding and counter-raiding. When Navajos acquired the horse and sheep from the Spanish, they became more powerful.

Visitor Center

(928) 672-2700

The center has a small museum, Indian craft shop, and restrooms. Free campgrounds are available on a first-come basis, and picnic areas are nearby. Be sure to pick up a brochure, map, and list of flowering plants and shrubs. The half-mile walk to the overlook of Betatakin ruin is signed with the names of these plants and shrubs and their uses by native peoples. There is an excellent twenty-five-minute video on the Hisatsinom (Hopi name for ancient Pueblo people), and a twenty-minute Betatakin tour video, which is shown on request. A gift shop sells Navajo work. Mosquitoes can be pesky here, so campers and hikers need to carry repellant.

The park radio station, AM 1810, broadcasts 24 hours a day with the latest park information regarding weather and hiking conditions. Metal railings, tripods, and open cliffs and mesas attract lightning; plan your day accordingly.

Betatakin Overlook

The paved path from the visitor center to the overlook goes slowly downhill all the way. The return trip, for people not used to physical exercise, is quite a climb. There are too many steps for wheelchairs.

Betatakin Ruin (elev. 7,000 ft.)

Navajo: *Bitát'ahkin,* meaning "House on a Rocky Ledge."
Hopi: *Kawestima*

Betatakin ruin is the second largest cliff dwelling in the Tesgi region, and the most accessible of the Navajo Monument group. Richard Wetherill and Charlie Mason discovered it during the winter of 1895. The overhanging red sandstone cliff is five hundred feet above the 135-room ruin. You can visit this ruin only with a ranger. Ranger guided tours are conducted from May through September. Check with the visitor center for times and schedules.

The strenuous, round-trip hike takes about five hours. The elevation is 7,300 feet and, according to the park brochure, the climb out of the canyon is equivalent to walking up the stairs of a seventy-story building. Carry a gallon of water and wear sturdy shoes. Not suitable for people with heart or respiratory problems.

Keet Siel (elev. 7,200 ft.)

Navajo: *Kits'iil,* meaning "Shattered House."
Hopi: *Talastima*

Tree ring dating and pottery found below the cliff indicate that some people were settled here by A.D. 950. Richard Wetherill discovered Keet Siel when he was searching for his wayward mule. It is the largest cliff dwelling in Arizona. Both Betatakin and Keet Siel were occupied for only about fifty years. Whether the Anasazi (Kayenta branch) left because of drought, erosion of arable land, deforestation, social pressures, or religious dictates, they joined other peoples in the Southwest in regional migrations. This isolated cliff dwelling of 160 rooms is one of the best preserved in the Southwest.

You will need a backcountry permit to visit Keet Siel. Call the visitor center at 928-672-2700 at least two months in advance if you want to be sure of a space. To pick up your permit, you must attend a scheduled trail orientation; the afternoon before your hike is best, so you can get an early start the next morning. Daily visits are limited to twenty people from Memorial Day weekend to Labor Day only. The hike to Keet Siel is an arduous trek of 8.5 miles one way. The trail is primitive and takes at least a full day. You need to be an experienced hiker. Carry plenty of water; canyons become very hot—up to 110 degrees in the summer. There is a primitive campground (free, one night limit) near Keet Siel. Spring water, which needs treating, may be available.

Sunset Valley Campground

Both campground and picnic areas are in a pinyon-juniper woodland. They are offered on a first-come basis. The nearest food and fuel are at Black Mesa Trading Post at the junction of AZ-564 and US-160. Wood fires are not allowed. Pets must be kept on a leash and are not allowed in buildings or on trails. There are thirty sites, flush toilets, and drinking water. On the way back to US-160, stop at Tsegi Overlook for the view!

Accommodations—Tsegi Canyon

Anasazi Inn
Located on US-160, 10 miles east of Black Mesa
(928) 697-3793
Basic and clean, with great Tsegi Canyon views. There is a restaurant. **Note:** It is only 9 miles from Anasazi Inn to Kayenta.

Kayenta (elev. 5,800 ft.)

Navajo: *Tó Dínéeshzhee'*, meaning "Fringed Water" or "Fingers of Water."

John and Louisa Wetherill were the first traders to settle in Kayenta, in 1910; the Babbit Trading Company opened in 1915. The Wetherills also operated a large ranch in the area. John Wetherill was known for his explorations of Keet Siel, Inscription House, Betatakin ruin, and Mesa

Verde. Louisa Wetherill, who spoke fluent Navajo, accompanied her husband on most of his travels. She had been brought up among Navajos and Pauites, and she knew their habits, religion, and life (Kosik 1996). There were shallow lakes and bogs here at one time.

Hashké Neiniihí led his people into deep canyons in the area during the Kit Carson Campaign of 1863–64. He waited in the canyons for the bulk of the Navajos to return from Bosque Redondo. An early day school was established here, along with a USIS tuberculosis sanitarium (now a Public Health Hospital). There were 150 acres of land under irrigation by 1941, served by an Indian Irrigation Service concrete dam on Laguna Creek (Linford 2000).

Kayenta is a small town in a bleak windswept valley with several good motels, a Bashas grocery store, and easy access to Monument Valley. Be sure to see the excellent memorial to the code talkers in Burger King, near the Hampton Inn. The Navajo Culture Center is next door to Burger King; traditional and forked stick hogans, a sweathouse, and a shade-house are on the site. Ceremonial dances take place at various times. Artists weave their rugs, and sometimes you will see sand paintings completed.

Tours

Kayenta Geoscience Tours – Geologic Tours of America
e-mail: info@kayentasci.com
This is an inquiry-based tour company that takes visitors off the beaten track and offers an opportunity to learn about the geology that formed this amazing landscape. They offer both standard and student tours by the University of Delaware Professional and Continuing Studies.

Rowland's Navajo Tours
(928) 697-3524
Hour-long to overnight tours and photography guided tours. Craft demonstrations.

Accommodations

Note: All hotels in this area are pricey during tourist season. They fill early, so book in advance.

Best Western Wetherill Inn
On US-163, 1.5 miles north of the junction of US-160 and US-163
(928) 697-3231
A/C, TV, gift shop, and small indoor heated pool.

Hampton Inn of Kayenta
On US-160, west side of town
(928) 697-3170
This is an adobe-style hotel with Native American décor. Great dining room and gift shop, high-speed Internet, dual phone lines, and small heated outdoor pool.

Holiday Inn Monument Valley
At the junction of US-160 and US-163
(928) 697-3221
Heated outdoor pool, exercise room, gift shop, and restaurant.

Goulding Lodge
Off US-163, one mile west of Monument Valley Navajo Tribal Park, on IR-42
(435) 727-3231
There is a museum with Indian artifacts and Goulding family memorabilia. Restaurant, laundry, in-room movies, and indoor pool. This is an excellent choice if you can get a reservation. Fantastic views of Monument Valley sunsets and sunrises. Tours leave directly from the hotel; access to certain parts of Monument Valley is only possible with an authorized tour guide, so it is convenient to leave with a tour from the hotel. There are also many tour guides within Monument Valley Park.

Restaurants

Golden Sands
Next door to the Best Western Wetherill Inn
(928) 697-3684
Basic décor. Serves hamburgers, Navajo tacos, and local specialties. Closed Monday.

Hampton Inn Restaurant
(928) 697-3170
American and local specialties. Tasteful native Indian décor. Pleasant service by Navajo staff. Patio dining.

Amigo Café
On US-163
(928) 697-8448
Clean, basic, well-prepared local food.

Stagecoach Dining Room
Located in Goulding Lodge
(435) 727-3231 or (800) 874-0902
Serves steak, chicken, pork chops, fish, pasta, stir-fry dishes, sandwiches, salad bar, and local specialties.

Emergency Numbers

Navajo Police: (928) 697-5600
Hospital: (928) 697-3211

Directions from Kayenta to Goulding and Monument Valley
Take US-163 north from Kayenta to Goulding and then Monument Valley.

The valley is dotted with sheer-walled, red buttes. Shifting shadows and changing colors across rock faces and rippling sand in an otherworldly landscape create feelings of awe and enchantment. This land is sacred to both Navajos and Hopis (many Anasazi ruins are found here).

Goulding (elev. 5,192 ft.)

Navajo: *Tségiizh*, meaning "Rock Gap."

Harry Goulding founded the Goulding Trading Post in October of 1925 and built the existing stone building (which is now the museum) in 1928. Built on a "school section" of land set aside from the Paiute Strip of land that was added to the Navajo reservation in 1933, it was 1937 before Goulding was able to officially acquire the land (Linford 2000). His museum is full of prehistoric and modern Native American artifacts, movie photos, period rooms, and Goulding family memorabilia. There is a major hotel, trading post, museum, and a hospital on the site. Goulding donated the land for the hospital. Nearby, a cabin built for John Wayne in *She Wore a Yellow Ribbon* has exhibits from the movie. Also nearby, the multimedia show "Earth Spirit" describes the region.

Harry Goulding enticed the movie industry to make movies in Monument Valley, and the landscape of Monument Valley is familiar because of all the movies made in this area. Monument Valley Navajos were especially hard hit when the U.S. government ordered stock reductions to combat overgrazing on the reservation. Movie industry jobs helped to ease their dire situation at that time (Bryant 2005).

John Ford (who made eight movies in Monument Valley) made Goulding his headquarters, and many film stars stayed there. There is a rocky ledge called "Ford's Seat," as it was his favorite place from which to view the valley when making a movie.

Movies made in Monument Valley include 1939, *Stagecoach* (John Ford); 1941, *Billy the Kid*; 1946, *My Darling Clementine* (John Ford); 1948, *Fort Apache* (John Ford); 1949, *She Wore a Yellow Ribbon* (John Ford); 1950, *Rio Grande* (John Ford); 1950, *The Wagon Master* (John Ford); 1956, *The Searchers* (John Ford); 1964, *Cheyenne Autumn* (John Ford); 1968, *2001: A Space Odyssey* (Stanley Kubrick); 1969, *Easy Rider* (Dennis Hopper); and 1993, *Forest Gump* (Robert Zemeckis).

Certain parts of Monument Valley Tribal Park can only be seen with a Navajo guide, so it is convenient to go with a tour from the hotel. Many tour guides are also in Monument Valley Park. There is little negotiation of price. You can do your own tour and drive the scenic seventeen-mile dirt road in your car. Check the weather before you start, as the road is impassible when it rains. The worst part of this very rough road is near the visitor center where you access the road. No low-clearance vehicles or RVs should attempt this drive. Blowing sand accumulates on the road at times, so avoid getting stuck by driving slowly and steadily through these areas—do not stop! No hiking or driving off the signed route is permitted; overlooks provide fantastic sweeping vistas. Be sure to take the short walk around the end of Cly Butte for the view. Allow 1.5 hours for the drive.

RV and Campgrounds

Goulding's Good Sam Campground
On IR-42 past Goulding's Lodge
(435) 727-3231
Stunning views. This modern campground can be windy. 66 RV sites and 50 tent sites. There are flush toilets, full hookups, guest laundry, showers, grills, general store, and indoor pool. Campers have access at no additional cost to the 17-mile loop drive around Monument Valley. Free shuttle vans to Goulding's Restaurant and Museum. Open year round.

Mitten View Campground
Located within Monument Valley Navajo Tribal Park
(435) 727-3287
Although crowded together, sites offer spectacular views. Flush toilets, dump station, coin-operated showers, drinking water, and picnic tables. Open May through October. This location is exposed, so be prepared for wind.

Monument Valley Navajo Tribal Park (elev. 4,800–5,700 ft.)

Navajo: *Tsé Bii' Ndzisgaii,* meaning "Stretches of Treeless Areas" or "Clearing among the Rocks."

Monument Valley straddles the Arizona and Utah state lines, twenty miles north of Kayenta on US-163. Navajo Tribal Park contains about one hundred square miles of some of the "most astonishing . . . natural geological formations in the world. These include Mitchell and the Mittens Buttes, and Mystery Valley—sheer, isolated mesas, and sandstone pillars of various sizes and shapes" (Bryant, 295–6).

When you enter the Monument Valley parking area at the visitor center, there is a confusion of buses, and the guides are off to the side. There are various tour vehicles, mostly trucks with benches and jeeps available for a tour. It is a very dusty and bumpy ride, definitely not for anyone with back trouble. Having an Indian guide is the only way to get close to many interesting sites. Be sure your guide speaks fluent English. A tour can be expensive unless you have a group. You can drive the seventeen-mile scenic loop; four-wheel-drive vehicles are best, but you can make it in a regular car with good clearance if you travel slowly.

Monument Valley was formed during the Cenozoic era, 25 million years ago. This entire region was under the vast inland sea that covered all the area. When the sea receded, "beds of sand compacted into stone some hundreds of feet thick" (Linford 2000: 296). Receding waters (and rain since then) may have affected some of the general topography, but the awe-inspiring monuments that we see today were "formed by wind driving minuscule grains of sand in a relentless sculpting of the landscape" (ibid., 296).

Monument Valley is one of the world's most recognized landscapes. Red sandstones push skyward from the vast desert floor, and it is so vast that it makes one feel insignificant. It is one of the most photographed sites in America, and it has become synonymous with how the western United States is perceived by the rest of the world. Unpreserved ruins give evidence of occupation by Anasazi people hundreds of years ago.

According to Linford (2000), Navajos view the whole of Monument Valley as a giant hogan. Grey Whiskers Butte (*Dághaa' Łibáí*) is a doorpost of the hogan; Sentinel Mesa (*Tsé Awéé Yałtélí,* meaning "Rock Holding a Baby") is the other doorpost. The two Mitten Buttes (*Álá Tseh,* meaning

"Big Hands"), according to tradition, are the "hands the deities left behind as a sign that the Gods will return some day" (ibid., 296). Eagle Mesa, according to Navajo mythology, is where spirits go after death.

Visitor Center

(435) 727-3353; www.navanonationparks.org
Park hours are 7 a.m. to 7 p.m. from April through September. Winter hours are 8 a.m. to 5 p.m. Restaurant, gift shop, restrooms, and campground on site.

Tours

Roland's Navajoland Tours
(928) 697-3524
Offers many backcountry drives, photography tours, and hiking trips.

Simpson's Trailhandler Tours
(435) 727-3362; www.trailhandlertours.com
Offers driving, photography, and hiking tours, plus a Hogan overnight cultural experience.

Totem Pole Tours
800-345-8687 or (435) 727-3313

Homeland Tours/Monument Valley Horseback Trail Rides
(435) 727-3466; www.cas-biz.com/homelandtours
Will take you on a variety of back road drives, trail rides, or hikes.

Dineh Trail Rides
(435) 678-2960
Trips from one-half hour to overnight.

Sacred Monument Tours
(435) 727-3218; www.monumentvalley.net
Driving, horseback riding, hiking, and photography tours from a booth on the right side of US-163 just before Gouldings.

CHAPTER 19

MONUMENT VALLEY TO CANYON DE CHELLY

Directions from Monument Valley to Mexican Water

There are two routes from Monument Valley to Mexican Water:

Option 1: From Monument Valley to Mexican Water.

Retrace your steps to Kayenta via US-163. Follow US-160 northeast to Mexican Water at the junction of US-160 and US-191, approximately 66 miles. You will pass the village of Dinnehotso on the way.

Option 2: From Monument Valley via Goosenecks State Park and Mexican Hat in Utah, to Mexican Water back in Arizona.

Continue north on US-163 from Monument Valley to where it joins US-191 and follow US-191 to US-160. Continue south on US-160 to Mexican Water, about 69 miles.

DINNEHOTSO (elev. 5,000 ft.)

Navajo: *Dinnehotso*, meaning "Upper Ending of the Meadows."

This small town is noteworthy for the agriculture in the area. Dinnehotso Canyon, covered by growth of chico or black greasewood trees, is drained by Laguna Creek. To the south is 793 acres of excellent agricultural land irrigated by a modern reinforced concrete diversion dam built in 1941 (Linford 2000).

The landscape from Monument Valley north continues to be dominated by red buttes and spires in vivid earth tones for a pleasant and scenic 20 or so miles north of the Monument Valley Park entrance.

The road from Mexican Hat to the junction of US-191 is interesting with unusual rock formations and ridges. Follow US-191 south to US-160. The only recommendation for the 22-mile south stretch of US-191 is that it gets you to US-160. US-191 continues south about one-quarter mile west of US-160 at Mexican Water. **Note:** US-191 is another access route from Utah to the Navajo reservation.

Goosenecks (elev. 5,000 ft.)

Navajo: uncertain, but translates to "The One Who Crawls with Her Body," referring to Big Snake (a powerful supernatural being), who created the deep twisting canyons.

The thirty-mile stretch of tortuous twists, turns, and switchbacks of the San Juan River (with its steep eroded canyons) runs between Mexican Hat and Johns Canyon. It takes six river miles to travel one mile in this area (Linford 2000). The spectacular 360-degree turn in the river can be seen at the overlook in Goosenecks Park. A signed, paved, five-mile, mostly twisting road leads to the overlook. There are no restrooms, and there is no water available at this site. Access to the river is impossible because of the sheer canyon walls; the San Juan River can be accessed at Mexican Hat.

Mexican Hat (elev. 4,150 ft.)

Navajo: *Ch'ah Łizhin*, meaning "Black Hat."

The name "Mexican Hat" refers to a rock formation a few miles north of the San Juan River that resembles an upside-down sombrero on top of a sandstone spire. Rubber rafts float down the San Juan River from Mexican Hat. A gold rush in 1892–93 brought nearly two thousand prospectors to Mexican Hat. Uranium was milled here between WWII and the 1980s (ibid.).

Directions from Mexican Water South to Chinle and Canyon de Chelly
Take US-191 south to Chinle and Canyon de Chelly (about 62 miles). Along the way visit Rock Point, Round Rock, and Many Farms.

Rock Point (elev. 5,000 ft.)

Navajo: *Tsé Łichíí Deez'áhí*, meaning "Red Rock Extending out to a Point."

Rock Point is a small day school community with new government housing. A large diversion dam on the Chinle Wash irrigates some seven hundred acres of agricultural land at Rock Point. When Chinle Wash is running, waters are diverted into large checks or rectangles with two-foot dikes. Water soaks deeply into the soil, and farmers can rely on adequate moisture for their crops in the dry season (ibid.).

Continue south on US-191 to Round Rock.

Round Rock (elev. 6,020 ft.)

Navajo: *Tsé Nikání*

Round Rock is a six-hundred-foot rounded sandstone butte. Traditional Navajos "will not climb the precipitous sides of this rock for fear of punishment by lightning, snakes, whirlwinds, or bears" (ibid., 125).

Continue south on US-191 to Many Farms.

Many Farms (elev. 5,304 ft.)

Navajo: *Dá'ák'eh Halání*, meaning "Many Fields."

This is a farming community with about 650 acres of irrigated land. Many Farms Lake is not far from Canyon de Chelly; channel catfish can be caught here. There are no restrooms.

Accommodations

Many Farms Inn
Located at the intersection of US-191 and IR-59, approximately seventeen miles north of Chinle.
(928) 781-6362 or (928) 781-6226
Dormitory-style living; clean, comfortable, and basic. Shared baths and TV room. The inn is a learning lab for Navajo students who seek experience and training in hotel management.

Continue south on US-191 to Chinle.

Chinle (elev. 5,058 ft.)

Navajo: *Ch'ínílį*, meaning "Water Outlet," referring to the mouth of Canyon de Chelly.

Chinle is one of the fastest growing towns on the reservation. It is a tourist and major trading center with many trading posts, galleries, and a major Arizona public school complex. Diversion dams irrigate land that is suitable for farming.

Franciscan fathers established their mission here in 1904. Navajo agent Ruben Perry and his followers were held captive by Doo Yáłti'í (Silent One) in 1906 for trying to force Navajo children into the boarding school at Fort Defiance. Doo Yáłti'í was sent to Alcatraz prison (later transferred to Fort Huachuca) for his stand against boarding schools. The fifth boarding school on the reservation was established in Chinle in 1910 (ibid.).

Accommodations

Best Western Canyon de Chelly Inn
One block east of US-191 on IR-7, Chinle; only three miles from Canyon de Chelly
800-327-0354
TV, indoor heated pool, hot tub, and sauna. Family-style restaurant with helpful, pleasant service is open for breakfast, lunch, and dinner. Wild, homeless dogs sometimes gather around the back of the restaurant.

Holiday Inn Canyon de Chelly
Located at the entrance to Canyon de Chelly on IR-7 (two miles east of US-191)
1-800-Holiday or (928) 674-5000
TV and outdoor heated pool. Junction Restaurant, part of what was Garcia's Trading Post, serves well-prepared beef, chicken, and pork dishes plus local specialties. Good ambience, pleasant service. Open for breakfast, lunch, and dinner.

Thunderbird Lodge
Located within Canyon de Chelly National Monument, one-half mile from the visitor center
(928) 674-5841 or 800-679-2473; www.tbirdlodge.com
In 1896, Sam Day built a trading post on this site, which later became Thunderbird Lodge. Units match the architecture of the old trading post. The restaurant is located in the old trading post; a wide variety of meals are served, from salads to steaks. The Lodge offers four-wheel drive jeep and six-wheel drive truck tours into the canyon. The truck tours into the canyon are the best value—private tours are very expensive. Sometimes a small group will get a better rate.

Note: Both Holiday Inn and Thunderbird Lodge will pack lunches. If you want to make your own lunches, there is a Bashas grocery store on US-191 near the junction of IR-7.

RV and Campgrounds

Cottonwood Campgrounds
Located close to Thunderbird Lodge
(928) 674-5501; for groups from 15 to 50 call (928) 674-8261
RVs and tents welcome; first-come basis. Flush toilets, drinking water, picnic tables, and grills. This is a popular national park service–maintained campground; it can be very crowded.

Spider Rock RV Park
(928) 674-8261
Camping and hiking. Comfortable campground with partial hookups, dump station, showers, drinking water, picnic tables, and fire pits. Owned and run by Navajo Howard Smith, who will customize hikes into the canyon.

Tsaile Lake Campground
Located two miles off IR-12 south of Diné College in Tsaile at the eastern tip of Canyon de Chelly
(928) 871-6645 or (928) 871-7307
RVs welcome, but site may be inaccessible in wet weather. As you loop around the Diné College campus, you can branch off the road at the southern end to the

lake. Tsaile Lake is ideal for launching boats or canoes. Overnight camping is allowed with a permit. There are portable toilets on the grounds. See page 105 for information on other lakes and recreation areas between Canyon de Chelly and Window Rock.

Wheatfields Lake

Located between mileposts 64 and 65 on IR-12, ten miles south of Tsaile. Trout swim in these waters; you can cast in your line just a few feet off the road, or you can drive around to the opposite side of the lake and launch a boat near the base of the Chuska Mountains. There is a bait shop with tackle, snacks, and drinks. Restroom facilities are also available. Bring your own water.

Canyon de Chelly National Monument (rim elev. 6,000–7,000 ft.; floor elev. 5,800–6,400 ft.)

Navajo: *Tséyi*, "Canyon" or *Tséyi' Etso*, meaning "Big Canyon." *Tséyi* is a Navajo word combining *tsé*, "rock," and *yi'*, "inside."

Canyon de Chelly National Monument covers 130 square miles. The visitor center is at an elevation of 5,500 feet, while the elevation is 7,000 feet at the end of the canyon. The canyon depth ranges from 30 feet at the mouth to over 1,000 feet just 15 miles away. The 26-mile-long Canyon de Chelly and adjoining 35-mile-long Canyon del Muerto join a few miles upstream from the visitor center. During summer afternoons thunderstorms arrive almost daily, creating thousands of waterfalls that cascade over the rims.

The geology of these canyons is fascinating; they cut through or into three layers of sandstone. At the bottom of the canyon is the Supai Formation, exposed only intermittently beneath sandy river beds. It dates to the Permain Age, making it about 250 to 280 million years old. There have been fossil plants found in the mud, silt, and sandstone of the Supai layer that tell us the climate was hot and moist at that time. Above the Supai Foundation is De Chelly sandstone, which makes up the bulk of the canyon walls. Approximately 230–250 million years ago, the climate changed from subtropical to arid desert and De Chelly Sandstone was formed from desert sand dunes. The Chinle Formation was deposited on top of De Chelle Sandstone approximately 200 million years ago. For the most part only the Shinarump Conglomerate remains.

According to archeological and historical evidence, people have lived in Canyon de Chelly for nearly five thousand years. The first were hunter-gatherers, and the area provided an abundance of food for them. They built no lasting homes, but remains of their campsites and etchings or paintings on the canyon walls tell us their stories. Later, people known as the Basketmakers built household compounds, storage facilities, and social and ceremonial complexes high on ledges in the walls of the canyons. They lived in small groups, hunted game, and grew corn and beans. The Basketmakers were followed by the Anasazi, an ancient Puebloan people who are the predecessors of today's Pueblo and Hopi Indians. These Puebloan people built the multistoried villages and kivas with decorated walls that dot the canyon alcoves and talus slopes. About A.D. 1300, the Anasazi abandoned the site. Later, migrating Hopi Indians and other tribes spent the summers hunting and farming here. After a long journey, Navajos entered the canyon in the eighteenth century, bringing domesticated animals acquired from the Spanish and a culture tempered by centuries of migration and adaptation.

The canyon became known for its corn and its peach orchards, which were introduced by Spanish missionaries. Small groups of hogans dotted the canyon floor. However, this idyllic life was shattered when lengthy warfare erupted between Navajos, other American Indians, and the Spanish.

Navajos used the canyon as a fortress, stockpiling food and water at strategic points. Nevertheless, Spanish, Ute, and later the U.S. military penetrated the canyon, leaving death and uncertainty in their wake. Evidence of these times is found in the traditional histories of the Navajo people, in the archeological remnants of the canyon's fortified areas, and in graphic rock paintings.

In 1864, Colonel Kit Carson entered the canyon at the far eastern end and pushed the Navajos toward the canyon mouth. All resistance proved futile and most of the Navajos were killed or captured. Carson's troops returned later that spring and destroyed the hogans, orchards, and sheep, leaving nothing for any Navajos that had managed to escape to survive on. The Long Walk followed; Navajos did not return to the canyon until 1868. They faced mass starvation. Food distribution centers, such as the one at Fort Defiance, helped to alleviate the suffering.

The National Park Service brochure describes the association between Navajos and the canyon:

> To the Diné the canyon means more than a summer home or a place to raise sheep and corn. The Navajo culture emerged from this land. The language often refers to the landscape, and the people identify themselves by this . . . deriving meaning, culture, and spirituality from the natural features that surround them. The land nourishes the people and is intrinsic to the activities of daily life. The elders are especially close to the land. From their stewardship comes a set of ethics based on experience and tradition. Through their teachings, stories, and songs, traditional information is sustained through the generations.

Visitor Center

(928) 674-5500
Be sure to pick up the two main park brochures. One describes the history of the canyon and the other outlines the seventeen-mile road trip of both Canyon de Chelly and Canyon del Muerto and their outlooks. "Canyon Voices," a twenty-two-minute video, provides insight into the cultural significance of the canyon. Open every day from 8 a.m. to 6 p.m. during the summer. **Note:** There have been problems with vandals breaking into vehicles parked at the lookouts. Check with the visitor center and leave no valuables in your vehicle.

Ranger Activities

Hogan talks are offered several days a week through Labor Day. Campfire programs are offered several nights a week. Call for information on special programs (three- and four-hour ranger-led hikes).

Emergency Numbers

Police: (928) 674-2111
Hospital: (928) 674-7001
Ambulance: (928) 674-7098

Guided Tours

Note: Access to the floor of the canyon is by guided tour only. Quicksand, dry deep sand, and flash floods make the canyon hazardous. In winter and during wet weather the canyons can be impassable. A guide is necessary.

On Horseback

Justin's Horse Rental
(928) 674-5678
Located at the mouth of the canyon, down a dirt road opposite Thunderbird Lodge. Prior reservations are suggested.

Tohsonii Ranch
(928) 755-6209; www.tohsoniiranch.com
Located 1.25 miles beyond the end of pavement on South Rim Drive.

By Vehicle

Thunderbird Lodge Canyon Tours
(928) 674-5841 or (800) 679-2473
Half-day and all-day tours in six-wheel-drive vehicles.

Private Four-Wheel-Drive Tours

Tsegi Guide Association
(928) 674-5500
Guides are available for hire at the visitor center using your own vehicle (four-wheel-drive only). Minimum of three hours—up to five vehicles per guide.

De Chelly Tours
(928) 674-3772; www.dechellytours.com
Four-wheel drive vehicles.

Tsiyi Tours
(928) 674-3262
Four-wheel drive vehicles.

Sandstone Tours
(928) 674-3134
Four-wheel drive vehicles.

Canyon de Chelly Tours
(928) 674-5433; www.canyondechellytours.com
Four-wheel drive vehicles.

Hiking

White House Ruin. The only hike that can be done without a guide is from White House Overlook to White House ruin. The trail is narrow and strenuous; take lots of water and some snacks. Anasazi people occupied White House ruin between A.D. 1060 and 1275. It is comprised of about sixty rooms and four kivas. In the cave above, a twenty-room complex was accessed from the multistory building below.

Tsegi Guide Association
(928) 674-5500
Guides can be hired at the visitor center for a minimum of three hours. All-day and overnight camping is available. You can wait until you arrive to discuss a short hike; however, you need to make arrangements ahead for groups or overnight hikes. One guide is needed for every fifteen people. A park ranger will assist with obtaining the necessary permit.

Canyon Hiking Service
(928) 674-5326
For further information write to P.O. Box 2832, Chinle, AZ 86503.

Completing the Trip through Navajoland
There are two travel options from Canyon de Chelly to complete the trip through Navajoland, a distance of 146 miles:

Option 1: *Follow US-191 south to I-40 and from there return home.*

Option 2: *Retrace your steps north on US-191 to US-160, then go east on US-160 to visit Teec Nos Pos, Shiprock, Farmington, and the Chaco Culture National Park, all in New Mexico.*

Side Trip from Canyon de Chelly to Diné College (Tsaile Campus)

Take IR-64, the road along Canyon Del Muerto, to south on IR-12 to Diné College at Tsaile.

Diné College (Tsaile Campus)

This campus was opened in 1973. Prior to the opening, students had to leave the reservation to pursue their education, and the cultural gap between Navajos and the outside world proved so great that many students dropped out. Students can choose from courses in many Navajo and Native American subjects: crafts, language, politics, music, dance, herbology, and holistic healing. The college also offers vocational training and adult education.

The unusual campus layout resulted from Navajo elders and healers working together with architects. The campus grounds and many of the buildings were built in a circle; it is in the Navajo tradition for all important Navajo activities to take place within a circle.

Hatathli Museum claims to be the first "true Native American museum." The collection occupies the third and fourth floors of the Hatathli Center. It is actually two museums in one: one museum specializing in Navajo culture and the other containing intertribal exhibits from across the United States. The library, bookstore, and cafeteria are on the first floor of this center. Ned Hatathli, a tribal council member, was the first Navajo manager of the tribal Arts and Crafts Guild.

CHAPTER 20

FROM CANYON DE CHELLY TO FARMINGTON

Directions from Canyon de Chelly to Teec Nos Pos
Retrace your steps north on US-191 to US-160, 62 miles. Proceed east on US-160 for about 30 miles to Teec Nos Pos. About halfway between the junction of US-191 and US-160 and Teec Nos Pos is Red Mesa.

RED MESA (elev. 5,500 ft.)

Navajo: *Tsé Łichii Dah' 'Azkání*, meaning "Red Rock."

Red Mesa is about three miles north of US-160. According to Navajo mythology, the sand was stained red when Monster Slayer killed Déégééd here (Linford 2000). In Navajo mythology, Monster Slayer was one of the twins born to Changing Woman. See page 9 for the full story.

Continue north on US-160 for 15 miles to Teec Nos Pos.

TEEC NOS POS (elev. 5,450 ft.)

Navajo: *T'iis Nászbas*, meaning "Cottonwoods in a Circle."

Teec Nos Pos is a very small trading, chapter, and school community located at the junction of US-160 and US-64. Concrete diversion dams built in the 1930s irrigate some five hundred acres (ibid.). Peter MacDonald, former chairman of the Navajo Nation, spent his childhood here. His great-grandparents were prisoners at Bosque Redondo. Their son, Deshna Chiseillige, was the second chairman of the Navajo tribe in 1928. Peter MacDonald was convicted of fraud but was later pardoned (Kosik 1996).

This community is rightly famous for their Teec Nos Pos design carpets. The design is very intricate, and making these rugs is long and labor intensive, so they are very expensive.

Directions from Teec Nos Pos to Shiprock

Continue east on US-64 for 34 miles to the town of Shiprock. Off to the right, just before the town of Shiprock, you will see Shiprock Pinnacle, a 1,800-foot volcanic plug. To reach Shiprock Pinnacle, take US-666 south from the town of Shiprock, go west on IR-13 and follow the signs. There are no facilities but there is a rest area and picnic tables near the volcanic pressure ridge.

Shiprock Pinnacle (elev. 7,178 ft.)

Navajo: *Tsé Bit'a'í*, meaning "Winged Rock."

Shiprock Pinnacle can be seen for miles from all directions, and it is easily visible from US-64 before reaching the town of Shiprock. This volcanic plug is at the center of three volcanic pressure ridges that pushed the rock skyward over five million years ago.

The pinnacle is the scene of Monster Slayer legends and a number of other Navajo ceremonies, including the Bead Chant and the Naayee'ee Ceremony for dispelling evil monsters (ibid.).

Shiprock (elev. 4,965 ft.)

Navajo: *Naat'áani Nééz*, meaning "Tall Boss"—also, *Tooh*, meaning "River," referring to the San Juan River.

Shiprock is on the San Juan River at the junction of US-666 and US-64 (95 miles north of Gallup). Shiprock was founded in 1903 as the San Juan (agricultural) School and Agency. This school became the third boarding

(Continued on page 208)

Side Trip from Teec Nos Pos to Four Corners Monument

Take US-160 north for about 4 miles to the Four Corners Monument.

Four Corners Monument (elev. 4,800 ft.)

Navajo: *Tsé 'Íí'áhí,* meaning "Rock Spire."

A Navajo tribal monument was erected here in 1964 where Arizona, New Mexico, Utah, and Colorado meet. Ute mountain reservation and the Navajo reservation also meet here. There has been a longstanding controversy between Navajos and Utes over a strip of land twenty-five miles long and one hundred yards wide on this boundary. The original 1868 survey of this area was proved to be in error in 1925. The courts decided to stay with the 1868 survey, and the tribes have contested that decision to the present time (Linford 2000).

Side Trip from Shiprock to Two Gray Hills

Two Gray Hills is located south off US-666 (the old US-491) halfway between Twin Lakes and Shiprock. Shiprock is at the junction of US-64 and US-666.

Two Grey Hills (elev. 5,900 ft.)

Navajo: *Bis Dah Kitso,* meaning "Yellow Clay at an Elevation."

Two Grey Hills is one of the most famous Navajo trading centers, noted for its distinctive natural-hued rugs. There are many prehistoric Anasazi and early Navajo sites in the area. Narbona, an influential Navajo, was killed in this area.

Shiprock (continued)

school on the reservation in 1907. Franciscan missionaries and Christian Reformed Churches came into the area around the same time. Several trading posts were opened. The superintendent of both school and agency was William Shelton ("Tall Boss").

Navajos had been irrigating land here for many years, according to Shelton. There were 275 Navajo farms, using some twenty-five ditches to draw water from the San Juan River between Shiprock and Farmington. Shelton improved and extended the irrigation system and developed a dairy herd. He was instrumental in starting the Shiprock Fair and in building a sawmill. A coal mine was opened in the Shiprock Hogback. Shelton, a hard taskmaster, was respected throughout the region for his championship of Navajos and for his efforts in adding the Utah-Colorado extension to the reservation (ibid.).

Oil, gas, and helium were found near Shiprock in 1920, eventually making the tribe one of the richest in the country. A large uranium mill was located in Shiprock in the l970s.

The Northern Fair is held in Shiprock in October. Yei Bei Chei dances are held, including dances such as the Night Chant, Mountain Chant, and an Enemy Way ceremony. Like other major fairs on the reservation, it is an event lasting the whole weekend. There are few services in Shiprock; stay in Farmington twenty-eight miles east on US-64.

Directions from Shiprock to Farmington
Continue east on US-64. It is 28 miles from Shiprock to Farmington.

Farmington (elev. 5,308 ft.)

Navajo: *Tóta'*, meaning "Between the Waters," referring to the San Juan and Animus rivers, which meet here.

The northeast corner of the Navajo reservation is 12 miles west of Farmington. Navajos have lived on the south side of the San Juan River for a long time. They come to Farmington to barter their products for the excellent fruit grown in the area, and they shop in town regularly.

Farmington is an area of ancient history; both Anasazi and later Navajos farmed near the rivers. The Soil Conservation Service identified a possible Chacoan road in the area in 1932. At the present time the Navajo Indian Irrigation Project oversees the farming of 60,000 acres. There are plans to irrigate a total of 110,630 acres. Navajo crops and livestock are marketed throughout the United States and Mexico under the trademark "Navajo Pride."

There are excellent galleries, shops, and trading posts that sell beautiful rugs, jewelry, and arts and crafts in Farmington. Of particular interest is the Totah Festival (800-448-1240) held September 3–4 at the Farmington Civic Center (200 W. Arrington). There are rug auctions and fine arts for sale. For more information, contact the local visitor bureau (800-448-1240 or 505-326-7602). Three tribes seek prominence here—the Navajo, Ute, and Jicarilla. To ensure you get all the information on Navajo ceremonies, genuine Navajo rugs, and arts and crafts, contact the Navajo Tourism Department in Window Rock, AZ (928-871-6436 or 928-871-7371). Farmington Museum and Visitor Center (see below) provides an excellent opportunity to learn about the cultures of all three tribes.

Farmington Museum and Visitor Center

This museum is located at Gateway Park, 3041 E. Main Street. It has a wide variety of exhibits related to the various cultures in the area and traveling exhibits and juried art shows. Admission is free. Open 8 a.m. to 5 p.m. You can observe birds and animals from large windows overlooking areas where food and water attracts wildlife.

Accommodations

Anasazi Inn
903 W. Main Street
(505) 325-4564
60 rooms, 8 suites.

Best Western Inn and Suites
700 Scot Avenue
(505) 327-5221
192 rooms, indoor pool, Jacuzzi, sauna, and restaurant.

Holiday Inn
600 E. Broadway
(505) 327-9811
148 rooms, pool, whirlpool, sauna, and exercise room.

Holiday Inn Express
2110 Bloomfield Boulevard
(505) 325-2545 or (800) Holiday
100 rooms, heated indoor pool, whirlpool, and laundry.

Casa Blanca Bed and Breakfast
505 E. La Plata Street
(505) 327-6503 or (800) 550-6503
Upscale, some rooms with fireplace and/or whirlpool.

Comfort Inn
555 Scott Avenue
(505) 325-2626 or (800) 228-5150
60 rooms and 19 suites.

Courtyard by Marriott
560 Scott Avenue
(505) 325-5111 or (800) 528-1234
121 rooms, 4 suites, pool, whirlpool, and exercise room.

Days Inn
1901 E. Broadway
(505) 325-3700
63 rooms, some with kitchenette.

La Quinta
675 Scott Avenue
(505) 327-4706 or (800) 531-5900
106 rooms, heated outdoor pool.

Super 8 Motel
1601 E. Broadway
(505) 325-1813 or (800) 800-8000
60 rooms.

Super 8 Motel
4751 Cortez Way
(505) 564-8100 or (800) 800-8000
67 rooms, pool.

Travelodge
510 Scott Avenue
(505) 327-0242 or (800) 578-7878
98 rooms, outdoor heated pool.

Restaurants

3 Rivers
101 East Main
(505) 324-2187
Classic 1912 building, 100-item menu and 12 handcrafted beers.

The River's Edge Café
560 Scott Avenue (located in Courtyard by Marriott)
(505) 325-5111
Open for breakfast, lunch, and dinner. Salad bar, steak, seafood, and pastas served. Cocktails.

Spare Rib BBQ Company
1700 East Main
(505) 325-4800
Hickory smoked beef ribs, sausage, chicken, and catfish.

Denny's
600 Scott Avenue
(505) 324-8415

K. B. Dillons
101 W. Broadway
(505) 325-0222
Steaks, seafood, and poultry; cocktails.

River Walk
700 Scott Avenue (located in the Best Western Motel)
(505) 325-0222
Open for breakfast, lunch, and dinner.

RV and Campgrounds

Dad's RV Park
202 E. Pinon, Farmington
(505) 564-2222
15 full hookups, cable TV, laundromat, picnic tables, and security gate.

The Downs RV Park
5701 US-64, Farmington
(505) 325-7094
31 full hookups, tent spaces, laundromat, restrooms, and showers.

KOA Campground
1900 E. Blanco Boulevard, Bloomfield
(505) 632-8339 or (800) 562-8513
75 full hookups, shaded grass tent sites, Kamping Kabins, cable TV, restrooms, showers, and laundromat.

Lee Acres RV Park
63 CR 5500, Farmington (located next door to Sun Ray Park & Casino and McGee Park)
(505) 326-5207
Full hook-ups, ample space for pull-throughs and back-ins.

Mom and Pop's RV Park
901 Illinois, Farmington (off US-64)
(800) 748-2807
35 full hookups and tent spaces, restrooms, showers, dump station, toy soldier store, and outdoor electric train layout.

Aztec Ruins Road RV Park
312 Ruins Road, Aztec, NM
(505) 334-3160; www.ruinsroadrvpark.com

Navajo Lake State Park
1448 NM-511 #1, Navajo Dam, NM (45 miles east of Farmington on NM-511)
(877) 644-7787; www.nmparks.com

Recreation and Camping Areas

Pine River Site
157 sites, 54 with electric hookups. Features a boat ramp, docks, marina, and general store.

Sims Mesa Campground
43 sites, 20 with electric hookups. Features a boat ramp, docks, marina, and general store.

San Juan River Site
48 sites, 24 with electric hookups. Located on both sides of the San Juan River below the dam. Modern, handicapped-accessible facilities, including campsites, picnic areas, elevated fishing platforms, and paved trails.

Airlines

America West Express
Four Corners Airport, service to/from Phoenix
(505) 326-4494 or (800) 235-9292

Great Lakes Airlines
Four Corners Airport, service to/from Denver
(800) 554-5111; www.greatlakesav.com

Mesa Airlines
Four Corners Airport
(505) 326-3338 or (800) 637-2247

Public Golf Courses

Pinon Hills
2101 Sunrise Parkway, Farmington, NM
(505) 326-6066
Rated the best municipal course in the U.S. by *Golf Digest* in 2002.

Civitan Municipal
2200 N. Dustin, Farmington, NM
(505) 599-1194
Par-three course.

Hidden Valley Golf Club
29 CR 3025, off CR 3000 (Southside River Road) Aztec, NM
(505) 334-3248
New eighteen-hole golf course, full-service pro shop, bar and grill.

Riverview Golf Course
4146 US-64, Kirtland, NM
(505) 598-0140

CHAPTER 21

FROM FARMINGTON TO CHACO CULTURE NATIONAL HISTORICAL PARK AND CROWNPOINT

The area south of Farmington, on both NM-371 and US-550, is in the Checkerboard Area, an area inhabited by both Navajos and whites. The Checkerboard Area is east of and contiguous to the New Mexico portion of the Navajo reservation. Santa Fe Railroad was granted alternating sections (square miles) of land prior to the expansion of the reservation into this region. The grants extended forty miles on both sides of the railroad tracks. Navajos occupied much of this area prior to 1868 when the reservation was established. The Navajo Nation acquired some tracts by grant or purchase; individual Navajos have acquired quarter-section tracts by federal allotment and by purchase; and other tracts have been sold to non-Indian interests (Linford 2000).

Note: Fill your tank and carry lots of water, a lunch, and snacks; there are no services in Chaco Canyon and surrounding area. Avoid the area on rainy days because dirt roads are often impassable when wet. Have an emergency supply of food and water in case you are caught in a storm. Not recommended for RVs.

Directions from Farmington to Chaco Canyon
Note: *It is approximately 130 miles from Farmington to Chaco Canyon. Access to Chaco Culture Park is easier via US-550. There are only 20 miles of rough dirt roads using this route. There are 33 miles of rough dirt roads if you access Chaco Park from NM-371. Both options and the sites you see along each route are given: Option 1 (NM-371) starts below; Option 2 (US-550) starts on page 217.*

Option 1: NM-371 Route from Farmington to Chaco Canyon via Bistí/De-Na-Zin
Take NM-371 south from Farmington for about 37 miles to Bistí/De-Na-Zin wilderness area. You will travel down 2 miles of dirt road to the parking area.

Bistí/De-Na-Zin (elev. 7,200–6,300 ft.)

Navajo: *Bistahí*, "Among the Adobe Formations"

Linford (2000) calls this area the "Bistí Badlands." He goes on to say this area was "an ancient lake bed, now broken badlands and low hills" (176).

Scattered among the numerous colorful land forms and unique geological features are petrified logs and other fossils. If you hike two miles east from the Bistí parking area, you will see the most interesting formations. No services are available—a true wilderness.

Option 1: NM-371 Route from Bistí/De-Na-Zin wilderness to Chaco Canyon
Continue south on NM-371 to IR-9. Follow IR-9 east to Pueblo Pintado (IR-9 is paved; thereafter you travel on dirt roads). Turn north onto IR-46 (for 10 miles), left on CR-7900 (for 7 miles), and left on CR-7950 (for 16 miles) to the entrance of the park. The road inside the park is paved.

Chaco Culture National Historic Park (elev. 6,100 ft.)

Navajo: *Tségai* can mean "home" to many Navajos, especially if their ancestors come from this area.

The canyon is ten miles long and about a half-mile wide. It contains eighteen major ruins and thousands of smaller units—all Anasazi in origin (ibid.). Long winters, short growing seasons, and marginal rainfall make this high desert country an unlikely place to support a major culture. Nevertheless, Chaco Canyon flourished and was the center of a thriving culture a thousand years ago. The National Park Service describes this unique community:

> The monumental scale of its architecture, the complexity of its community life, the high level of its community social organization, and its far-reaching commerce created a cultural vision unlike any other seen before or since.
>
> The cultural flowering of the Chacoan people began in the mid-800s and lasted more than 300 years. We can see it clearly in the grand scale of the architecture. Using masonry techniques unique for their time, they constructed massive stone buildings ("great houses") of multiple stories containing hundreds of rooms much larger than any they had previously built. The buildings were planned from the start, in contrast to the usual practice of adding rooms to existing structures as needed. Construction on some of these buildings spanned decades and even centuries. Although each is unique, all great houses share architectural features that make them recognizable as Chacoan.

The sphere of influence of this ceremonial, administrative, and economic center was extensive by 1050. Throughout the region roads connected more than 150 great houses. These great houses may not have been traditional farming villages occupied by large populations, but rather may have been erected as examples of public architecture that were used periodically during times of ceremony, commerce, and trading when temporary populations came to the canyon for these events. The question is asked, "What was the heart of this great social experiment?" According to Pueblo descendents, Chaco was the gathering place where many peoples and clans converged to share ceremonies, traditions, and knowledge.

Linford writes: The "Chaco Phenomenon" was an Anasazi "integrated system of cooperating towns and villages that produced and assembled goods for local consumption and for widespread distribution. A turquoise distribution center is believed to have branched out from here. The Anasazi abandoned Chaco Canyon around 1275. Navajos appear to have arrived in the Canyon by 1720" (184).

According to some historians, Chaco Canyon was one of four regions of continuous Navajo occupation since the early 1700s (ibid.). It is central to the origins of several Navajo clans and ceremonies. Many Southwest Indians look upon Chaco as an important stop along their clans' sacred migration path. The Chaco culture site is respected and honored by the Hopi, the Pueblo peoples, and the Navajo as part of their sacred homeland.

Visitor Center

505-786-7014. Open 8 a.m. to 5 p.m. daily. Call the visitor center for weather conditions before setting out. Begin your sightseeing at the visitor center, where you can view an informative short film. Rangers will answer your questions, and the exhibits will help you to understand Chaco and its people. The best way to see Chaco is on a ranger-conducted walk. Information about these tours and the evening programs is available at the center and at www.nps/gov.chcu.

Hiking

All backcountry hiking requires a free permit available at the visitor center. Camping and fires are not permitted in the backcountry. All trails and Chacoan cultural sites are closed from sunset to sunrise.

At an elevation of 6,200 feet, winters are cold and summers are hot, with very little shade; brief, violent thunderstorms occur in the summer. Trails are steep, uneven, and icy in winter. Wear good hiking boots and appropriate clothing. Drink plenty of water and prepare for extremes.

Camping

Gallo Campgrounds

Not recommended for RVs over thirty feet long because of rough dirt roads. Located one mile east of the visitor center. There are neary fifty sites with picnic tables and fire grates but no firewood. Available on a first-come basis. Restrooms and drinking water are available, but there are no showers.

Option 1: NM-371 Route from Chaco Canyon to I-40
Retrace your steps to NM-371 (follow directions on page 214), approximately 23 miles. Continue south on NM-371 for almost 29 miles to I-40 at Thoreau. You can travel west to Arizona or east to Albuquerque from this point.

On your way, Crownpoint, near the junction of IR-9 and NM-371, is interesting because of the rug auctions conducted here. From Crownpoint continue south on NM-371. You will cross over the Great Divide (8,620 ft.) a few miles south of Crownpoint. Pick up I-40 here, either east to Albuquerque or west to Arizona.

Crownpoint (elev. 6,943 ft.)

Navajo: *T'íístʼóóz Ńdeeshgizh*, meaning "Narrow-Leafed Cottonwood Gap."

This small administrative town, located at the junction of NM-371 and IR-9, includes public schools, a BIA boarding school, and an Indian Health Service medical center. Pueblo Bonito Indian School, the sixth on the reservation, was established in 1909 (Linford).

Crownpoint is important to tourists for its three hundred to four hundred hand-woven rugs auctioned each month, sponsored by the Crownpoint Rug Weavers Association. Viewing is from 4 p.m. to 6 p.m., and the auction is at 7 p.m. at the Crownpoint Elementary School (72 miles south of Farmington and 24 miles north of Thoreau on I-40).

Directions from Farmington to Chaco Canyon
Option 2: US-550 Route
Travel east from Farmington on US-64 for about 12.5 miles to Bloomfield. Continue south on US-550. This is an area of cultural significance for the Navajo people. You will see Huerfano Mesa, Hosta Butte, Gobernador Knob, and Blanco Canyon on your way. Huerfano is 25 miles south of Bloomfield. CR 7900, the access road to Chaco Culture National Historic Monument, is 38 miles southeast of Bloomfield. (CR 7900 is about three miles east of Nageezi.)

You will see Angel Peak on your way south on US-550. It is the chief landmark in the "Garden of Angels," an eighty-square-mile area of tortured landscape with formations resembling a group of angels (ibid.).

Huerfano Mesa (elev. 7,470 ft.)

Navajo: *Dził Náʼoodiłii,* meaning "People Encircling Around Mountain," refers to a legend in which people moved around a mountain.

The mesa is steep walled and angular with one arm extending east and the other south. It is topped with four cupola-like sandstone crags. Huerfano Mesa dominates all the country south of the San Juan River. Traditional Navajos prefer that only their medicine men climb to the top of this mesa. However, the top of the mesa is now covered with "radio and microwave towers," an affront to Navajos, as the towers were placed there without their consent. The Bureau of Land Management (BLM) proposed establishing a recreation area in the east wing of the mesa, but Navajo Singers protested. The Navajo tribe was successful in negotiating a land exchange with the BLM. Now it is a "sacred wilderness" accessible only to Navajo Singers and those accompanying them (ibid., 219).

Hosta Butte (elev. 8,620 ft.)

Navajo: *Akʼiih Nástʼání,* meaning "Mountain That Sits on Top of Another Mountain."

A sacred Navajo peak, this butte can be seen for many miles from the north and east. It is said to be the home of Hadahoniye' 'Ashkii (Mirage Stone Boy) and Hadahoniye' 'At'ééd (Mirage Stone Girl) and is mentioned in the Night and Blessingway ceremonies (ibid.).

Gobernador Knob (elev. 7,100 ft.)

Navajo: *Chʼóolʼį́ʼí,* meaning "Fir Mountain."
Ceremonial name: *Ntłʼiz Dziil,* meaning "Hard Goods Mountain."

Gobernador Knob is a cone-shaped pinnacle above the broken mesas sloping west from the Continental Divide, five miles west of the Jicarilla reservation. It is sacred to the Navajo because of a number of ancient Navajo remains found in the area. According to Blanco Canyon Navajos, the Ta'neeszahnii, "Tangle People Clan," were supposed to have lived here at one time. Navajos have many traditions associated with this site (ibid.).

Blanco Canyon and Blanko Wash (elev. 6,400–5,700 ft.)

Navajo: *T'iistah Diiteelí*, meaning "Spread Among the Cottonwoods."

As with other washes, this area is important in Navajo history, and today because of the seepages and shallow wells that provide irrigation for agriculture. This is a Checkerboard Area, so white ranchers also live here. "Constellation glyphs" have been found here, giving rise to theories of ancient Navajo archaeoastronomy (ibid.).

Directions from Blanco Canyon to Chaco Canyon

Watch for CR-7900, 3 miles east of Nageezi. Follow the signs south on CR-7900 for 5 miles (paved), then turn right on CR 7950 (16 miles unpaved) to the Chaco Canyon boundary. The park road is paved. *See page 214 for information on Chaco Canyon.*

Directions to I-40 with destinations east to Albuquerque and west to Arizona

To return to Albuquerque, retrace your steps to NM-550. Follow NM-550 through many Pueblo communities to the junction of I-25. Take I-25 south to Albuquerque.

To return to Arizona from Chaco Canyon, take CR-7950 (unpaved) for 16 miles. Turn right on CR-7900 (unpaved) for 7 miles. Go south on IR-46 (unpaved) for 10 miles until you meet IR-9 (paved). Follow IR-9 southwest to NM-371 and Crownpoint, and continue south to I-40.

PART III

THE NAVAJO LANGUAGE[1]

1. Sources used in preparing this chapter include the following:
Navajo-English Dictionary, by Leon Wall and William Morgan. New York: Hippocrene, 2004
The Navajo, by Clyde Kluckhohn and Dorothea Leighton. New York: Doubleday, 1962
www.geocities.com/Athens/9479/Navajo.html?20061
www.omniglot.com/writing/Navajo.htm (2/1/2006)
http://hometown.aol.com/tg3907/navlit.html (2/1/2006)

CHAPTER 22

THE NAVAJO LANGUAGE

Navajo (*Diné Bizaad)* is a member of the Athabaskan branch of the *Na-Dené* language family. Under the Athabaskan branch, there are two language groups: Northern and the Athabaskan-Eyak-Tlingit family to which Navajo belongs. Other language family members within the Apachean language group are Mescalero, Chiricahua, Western Apache, Jicarrilla, Lipan, and Kiowa-Apache. Whereas Navajo is closely related to these Apache languages, it has little or no relationship to other Native American languages. (See www.omniglot.com/writing/Navajo.htm for more on this.)

Today, Navajo is the language of some 200,000 people, living on and around their historic homeland, extending across northeastern Arizona, northwestern New Mexico, and southeastern Utah. Its speakers outnumber those of other Native American or First Nation languages north of the United States–Mexican border. As far as it is known, pre-Columbian Navajos had not developed any written version of their tongue, and Navajo, like most of the world's languages, was unwritten until recent times. When the Spanish colonized Nueva Mexico they made no effort to learn or document the Navajo language. This was in obvious contrast to what they had done when they arrived in Mexico, which was to learn the local language and develop a Latin alphabet for it. It was not until the United States took over the Southwest in the 1840s that the first attempt was made to develop a written version of the Navajo language (http://hometown.aol.com/tg3907/navlit.html).

Advent of Written Version

Navajo first appeared in writing in 1849 in the form of a Navajo word list published in the *Journal of a Military Reconnaissance* by Lieutenant James H. Simpson. About the same time, Colonel J. H. Eaton was compiling a Navajo vocabulary. A few years later, Dr. Washington Matthews transcribed various Navajo religious ceremonies and legends. At the beginning of the twentieth century, missionaries were turning out religious texts, dictionaries, and grammar guides in Navajo. Noteworthy contributors were the Franciscan friars, who arrived at St. Michael's Mission in 1898. As noted previously, the Mission of St. Micheal claims that Father Anselem Weber compiled the first dictionary of the Navajo language. The friars discovered that there were few natives whose English vocabulary held more than a few words, and if they were to succeed in their work among the Navajo, they would have to learn their language (*Padre's Trail Magazine*, Franciscan Friars, Albuquerque, 1998). This motivated friars Berard Haile and Leopold Ostermann to work on constructing a written form for Navajo. By 1912, they had succeeded in producing three notable works in the Navajo language: a *Navajo-English Catechism*, an *Ethnologic Dictionary*, and a *Vocabulary* (two volumes) *of the Navajo Language.*

As one could imagine, each of these pioneers of written Navajo tended to invent his own alphabet. As a result, there emerged several different ways to write Navajo. Over the next few years little interest was expressed in developing a standardized form of the language. American government policy at the time was more focused on eradicating Native American languages and culture, which were seen as obstacles to assimilating Indians into mainstream American society. The primary tool used in this effort was that of isolating them from all influences of their tribe. Navajo children were compelled, often by force, to attend boarding schools both on and off the reservation where the Navajo language was prohibited. It was not until after the election of President Franklin Roosevelt in 1932 and the appointment of John Collier as head of Indian Affairs and Willard Beatty as head of Indian Education that any significant policy change toward Native Americans occurred. Collier, a reformer, believed that Indian culture had much to teach Anglo-American society, and he set out to save it from extinction. Beatty, a leader in the progressive education movement, was determined to shift from English-only boarding schools to day schools and bilingualism. Both decided that a standard Navajo alphabet was needed, and they commissioned a team, including Robert Young and William Morgan, to create a consistent alphabet and publish Navajo language materials (http://hometown.aol.com/tg3907/navlit.html).

By 1939, the new alphabet was finished, and during the 1940s, the first bilingual primers and dictionary were published. Initially, the Navajos showed little support for their newfound literacy. Historians tell us that this was partly the result of their anger at the government's policies on livestock reduction, for which they blamed Collier. Nonetheless, Navajo as a written medium has progressed in the years since with achievements of many literacy milestones. More recently, the United States Congress passed the Native American Languages Act of 1990, affirming support for the use of Native languages as a medium of instruction and acknowledging the right of Native American governing bodies to give official status to their languages (http://hometown.aol.com/tg3907/navlit.html).

Difficult Language for Non-Navajos

Navajo is described as a difficult language for non-Navajos to learn and pronounce. It has many sounds that are not found in English. It is also a tonal language, which means the vowels rise and fall when pronounced, changing meaning with pitch. There are four separate tones of voice used: low, high, rising, and falling. Two separate words with different meanings may therefore have the same pronunciation but with different tones. Some Navajo words are also nasalized, meaning that the sound comes through the nose instead of the mouth (http://library.thinkquest.org/J002073F/thinkquest/Language.htm).

The ′ over a vowel means the sound rises a note higher. The ˛ under a letter means the sound is carried somewhat through the nose.

As is by and large the case with speakers of other languages, the Navajo worldview—how they think, act, and react in relation to the world around them—is very evident in the way they speak. For example, one would not say in Navajo, "I am drowning," but instead "water is killing me." Similarly, the Navajo language prefers the active, personalized "hunger is killing me" to "I am hungry." According to Kluckhohn and Leighton, such examples give one an immediate insight into the Navajo manner of conceiving events: "To the People, hunger is not something which comes from within but something to which the individual is subjected by an outside force. Indeed, if an articulate Navajo is pressed for an explanation of this linguistic idiom he is likely to say, 'The spirit of hunger sits here beside me'" (Kluckhohm and Leighton 1962, 253–254).

The Navajo language is also more intricate and complex than languages of the Indo-European family, for example, Celtic and Italian. It is also very descriptive and very specific. One word can describe physical features; movement; first, second, and third person; and singular or plural (two, three, or more). A Navajo noun is often a verb transformed into a noun so that it is never left void of character. It is also very different from other languages in its grammatical and phonetic structure, which may be difficult for the learner to grasp.

The basic challenge with learning the Navajo language can be recognized in the following quotation from Robert Young and William Morgan (1994–2003):

> The pattern of Navajo thought and linguistic expression is totally unlike that of the European languages with which we are most commonly familiar. We learn such foreign languages as Spanish, French, Italian, and German with a minimum of difficulty because there exist so many analogies, both with respect to grammar and to words, with our own native English. Moreover, the pattern according to which we conceive and express our thoughts in English and in these common European languages is basically the same throughout. We translate readily from one to the other, often almost word for word. And lastly, similar or very closely related sound systems prevailing throughout make the words easy to pronounce and to remember.
>
> On the other hand, the Navajo language presents a number of strange sounds which are difficult to imitate, and which make the words very hard to remember at first. Secondly, the pattern of thought varies so greatly from our English pattern that we have no small difficulty in learning to think like, and subsequently to express ourselves like the Navajo. An understanding of the morphology and structure of the language, and an insight into the nature of the thought patterns involved can go far in aiding to solve the puzzle. (40)

The Navajo language, being entirely different from English, can be an ordeal for non-Navajos when they make an effort to learn it. This is not only because of its unfamiliar and difficult sounds, but also because Navajos are accustomed to respond to small variations, which in English are either ignored or used merely for expressive emphasis. For example, a small clutch of the breath (glottal closure), which the speaker of European languages scarcely notices, often differentiates Navajo words. *Tsin* means "log," "stick," or "tree," whereas *ts'* (the ' representing glottal closure) means "bone" (Kluckhohn and Leighton, 256).

Navajo Language Sounds: Vowels

There are four vowels in Navajo: *a, e, i,* and *o*. Vowels may be either long or short in duration. The long or doubled vowels are pronounced the same, but the sounds are held longer. Each of the vowels may occur as the following (Wall and Morgan 2004, 11):

Short, as in *a* and *e*
Long, as in *aa* and *ee*
Nasalized, as in *ą* and *ę*

Or with one of four tones:

High, as in *áá* and *éé*
Low, as in *aa* and *ee*
Rising, as in *aá* and *eé*
Falling, as in *áa* and *ée*

The following is a simplified guide to the pronunciation of vowels:

The short vowels are pronounced as follows:

a as in the word *father*
gah (rabbit)
gad (juniper)

e as in the word *west*
dego (up)
abe' (milk)

i as in the word *sit*
sis (belt)
sin (song)

o as in the word *low*
sodizin (prayer)
dikos (cough)

The long duration vowel is stated by a doubling of the letter, which never affects the quality of the vowel except that the long duration *i* is always pronounced as in the English word *see*.

aa as in the word *yaw*
baa (about it)
naadiin (twenty)

ee as in the word *they*
nee (concerning you)

ii as in the word *see*
biith (into it)

oo as in the word *so*
doobish (it will boil)

Examples: in **sis** (belt) the vowel is short. In **siziiz** (my belt) the second vowel sound is long.

Combined vowels are pronounced as follows:
ai as in *my*
ao as in *cow*
ei as in *say*
oi as *chewy*

Vowels with a hook (*ą*) beneath the letters are nasalized. This means that some of the breath passes through the nose when sound is produced. All vowels following *n* are nasalized, though not marked. A mark above the letter *ó* indicates that the voice rises on that letter. When only the first element of a long vowel has a mark above it the tone falls. If only the last element is marked, the tone rises.

Navajo language sounds: Diphthongs

ai as in the English *y* in *my*	**hai** (winter)
ao as in the English *ow* in *now*	**ao'** (yes)
oi as in the English *ewy* in *chewy*	
ei as in the English *ei* in *weight*	**ei** (that, those)

Parts of Speech: Nouns

There are few true Navajo nouns in comparison to the English language. Most words, which the English speaker is apt to term as nouns, are really nominalized verbs. Navajo nouns, except for some kinship terms, have the same form for singular and plural. For example, *tł'ízí* can mean either "goat" or "goats"; the distinction is made in the verb. Adjectives are almost entirely the third-person forms of neuter verbs that denote quality, state, or condition. In the formal sense, Navajo has no adjectives. Other parts of speech are pronouns, postpositions, and particles. Many pronouns are absorbed in verbs, but they are also used independently or prefixed to nouns and postpositions. Navajo pronouns express features of usage and nuances of meaning, which are difficult for the English speaker to grasp. For example, *it* as the object of a verb has several different forms, dependent upon whether *it* is thought of as definite or indefinite or as a place[2] (Kluckhohn and Leighton 1962).

Parts of Speech: Verbs

Navajo has a peculiarly intricate construction of verbs. Navajo sentences are built from verb stems; the resulting verb structures then function as complete sentences. The verb stems are based on about five hundred verb roots. For each root there is an underlying conceptual meaning of the verb, as well as numerous extensions and meanings, some metaphorical. For instance, the root *kaad*, with the underlying meaning of "flatness" or "expansiveness," can have extended meanings, such as the following.[3]

2. Kluckhohn and Leighton, 261.
3. http://college.hmco.com/history/readerscomp/naind/html/na_025300_navaj 2/4/2006.

Na'nish*kaad*.	I am herding sheep.
Ahésh*kad*.	I am clapping.
Si*kaad*.	It is spread out flat.
Násh*kad*.	I am sewing it.

Establishing Good Relations

Navajo may be a difficult language to grasp, but this should not discourage non-Navajos from making an earnest effort to learn it. Having knowledge of some conversational aspects of the Diné language helps provide an understanding of the Diné ways of speech, while speaking to the Navajo in his language when traveling on the reservation is a gesture of good will, an implied compliment on the part of the visitor. Using the language even a little helps to build up easy and confident relations between the Anglo-American visitor and Navajos. A few words of greeting and farewell: **didoochííł** (it will start to snow); **deesk'aaz** (it is cold); **ch'ééh déyá** (I am exhausted); **ahéhee'** (thank you) (Kluckhohn, 286).

The person who makes the effort necessary to gain a general orientation of the language will not only find the information intensely interesting but will also discover that he or she can use even this limited knowledge very effectively. Taking the further step of talking a bit, in spite of the mistakes that will certainly be made, the speaker will be rewarded for this venture considerably beyond any expectations.[4] Do not hesitate to inform your Navajo conversationalist of your interest in learning the Navajo language. Navajos greatly appreciate this, and while they may initially chuckle at your ambition, they will nevertheless be more than obliging.

The aim of this section is to provide a sketch of some of the structural features to show the reader how response and way of thinking created by the Navajo language are different from those created by English. To further assist the reader in acquiring a familiarity with the Navajo language, provided is a selection of everyday conversational phrases and frequently used words translated from English to Navajo.

---

4. Kluckhohn and Leighton, 256.

CHAPTER 23

CONVERSATIONAL PHRASES TRANSLATED FROM ENGLISH TO NAVAJO

English	Navajo
a year completely passed	**náàhai**
A year is going by.	**Yihah.**
all of you	**t' áá ' ánółtso**
as time goes on	**hoolzhishgo**
Come here.	**Hágo.**
Do not bother me.	**T' áadoo shaa nánit' íní.**
federal government	**wááshindoon**
has been sold	**nahaaznii'**
He/she/it died.	**Daastsaah.**
He/she/it does not want it.	**Yinízin da.**
He/she/it forgot about it.	**Yooznah, yaa.**
He/she/it gave me a piece of his mind. *(idiom)*	**Shíí'įįd.**
He/she/it is elusive/or hiding.	**Nanit' in.**
He is not interested. *(refers to activities)*	**Doo bizhneedlįį da.**
He/she/it is searching for it.	**Hazhnitá.**
He/she/it is unreliable.	**Doo ba'jóolíí' 'at ' ée da.**
He/she knows us.	**Nihééhósin.**

English	Navajo
He/she shook hands with him.	**Yilák' edoolnii'.**
He/she spoke.	**Haadzíí'.**
He/she told his story.	**Nahase'.**
He/she will return.	**Nádááh.**
He/she will relay the information to him.	**Yił hodoolnih, yił.**
Hello.	**Yá' át'ééh.**
I am anticipating it or him.	**Neíníshłį.**
I am interested in it. *(activities)*	**Bíneeshdlį.**
I am thinking about it.	**Baa ntséskees.**
I am tired.	**Ch' ééh déyá.**
I am tracking it.	**Naashkaah.**
I am watching.	**Ha' asíid.**
I am working on something.	**Naashnish, baa.**
I can do it.	**Bíínishghah.**
I cannot do it.	**Doobíínishghahdá.**
I don't know.	**Hóla.**
I have confidence in you.	**Na jóshłí.**
I hear you. (*not* I understand you.)	**Ndiists' a'.**
I helped him.	**Biká 'eeshwod.**
I made some coffee.	**Gohwééh shéłbéézh.**
I said a prayer.	**Sodeezin.**
I shall go.	**Deeshááł.**
I went back and forth. *(made a round-trip)*	**Nisíyá.**
I washed it.	**Ségis.**
I will make a picture of you.	**Ini'deeshkił.**
I will paint a picture.	**N' deeshch' ąh.**
I will pick them up. *(objects)*	**Ńdideeshjih.**
I will tell him this.	**Bidideeshniił.**
I'll go with you.	**Nił deesh'ash.**
in the future	**náásgóó**
Is that true?	**Da' t'áá 'aaníí?**
It hurts.	**Neezgai.**
It is cool. *(weather)*	**Honeezk'àází.**
It is not correct.	**Doo ákót'éé da.**
It is raining.	**Nahałtin.**
It is useful.	**Choo'į.**

English	Navajo
It is very fun.	**Bíhoneedlí, 'ayóo.**
It is very warm.	**Honeezdo.**
It/he is alive.	**Hiná.**
me	**shí**
She is driving it.	**Oołbąs.**
Show me./Let's see.	**Háá 'í yee'.**
Sit down.	**Dah ńdah.**
Thank you.	**Ahéhee'.**
The weather is cooler./It's cooling down.	**Honiik'aaz.**
Their names are ...	**Dawolyé/daolyé ...**
There is work being finished.	**Nda 'ńíísh.**
They are hunting.	**Ndaalzheeh.**
They are investigating it.	**Ndeiłkaah.**
They are playing.	**Ndaané.**
They are working.	**Ndaalnish.**
They are cheap.	**Doo da' íłįį da.**
They spoke.	**Hadaasdzíí'.**
They will be sold/bought.	**Ndahidoonih.**
We went away.	**Dá' d'iikai.**
We will buy it from you.	**Naa nahiilniih.**
We will spend the night.	**Nihiidoołkéááł./ Nihiidoołkááł.**
We will tell him.	**Bididii'niił.**
What happened?	**Haa lá hoodzaa?**
What is the matter with you? *(idiom)*	**Haa lá yinidzaa?**
What is your name?	**Haash yinílyé?**
What time is it?	**'Oolkił, Íkwíígóó?**
when the sun sets	**i'íí'áahgo**

CHAPTER 24

FREQUENTLY USED ENGLISH WORDS TRANSLATED TO NAVAJO

Fruits and Vegetables

English	Navajo	English	Navajo
apple	**bilasáana**	peach	**didzétsoh**
banana	**hashk'aan**	pear	**bitsee'hólóní**
beans	**naa'ołí**	peas	**naa'ołí dootł'izhígíí**
cantaloupe	**ta'neesk'ání**	potatoes	**nímasii**
carrot	**chą́ą́sht'eezhiitsoh**	squash	**naayízí**
corn	**naadą́ą́**	sweet potatoes	**naahooyéí**
fruit	**tsin bineest'ą'**	vegetables	**ch'il daadánígíí**
lettuce, cabbage	**ch'il łigaii**	watermelon	**ch'ééjiyáán**
onion	**tł'ohchin**		
orange	**ch'il łitsxooí**		

Meats and Fish

beef	**béégashii bitsį'**	liver	**'azid**
chicken	**naa' ahóóhai bitsį'**	meat	**'atsį'**
fish	**łóó'**	mutton	**dibé bitsį'**
goat meat	**tł' ízí bitsį'**	mutton stew	**dibé bitoo'**
ham	**bisoodí bitsį'**	rabbit	**gah**
lamb	**dibé yázhí**		

Milk Products

butter	**mandagíiya**	ice cream	**abe' yistiní**
cheese	**géeso**	milk	**abe'**

Grains

bread	**bááh**	rice	**alóós**
corn	**naadáá'**	wheat	**tł' oh naadáá'**
oatmeal	**taaskaal**		

Miscellaneous

coffee	**áhwééh**	salt	**áshįįh**
cookie	**bááh łikaní**	soup, stew	**atoo'**
egg	**ayęęzhii**	sugar	**áshįįh łikan**
flour	**ak'áán**	tea	**dééh**
fried bread	**dahdíníilghaazh**	tortilla	**náneeskaadí**
jam	**jélii**		

Table Items

chair	**bikáá' dah'asdáhí**
coffee pot	**jaa' í/gohwééh beebézhí**
cup	**bee' adlání/bąą' íízhahi**
fork	**bíla' dįį' ii, bíla' táá'ii**
frying pan	**tsee' é**
glass *(drink with)*	**tózis/bee' adlání**
knife	**béésh**
paper towel	**naaltsoos bee 'ádít 'oodí**
plate, bowl	**łeets' aa'**
pot	**ásaa'**
spoon	**béésh ádee'/béésh adee'**
table	**bikáá' adání**

Animal and Bird Terms

badger	**nahashch'id**	fish	**łóó'**
bear	**shash**	frog	**ch'ał**
beaver	**chaa'**	goat	**tł'ízí**
buzzard	**jeeshóó'**	horse	**łįį'**
calf	**béégashii yáázh**	jackrabbit	**gahtsoh**
cat	**mósí**	lamb	**dibé yázhí**
cow	**béégashii**	mountain lion	**náshdóítsoh**
coyote	**mą'ii**	mouse	**na'asts'oosí**
crow	**gáagii**	owl	**né'éshjaa'**
deer	**bįįh**	pig	**bisóodi**
dog	**łééchąą' í**	sheep	**dibé**
eagle	**'atsá**	snake	**tł'iish/na'ashó'įį**
elk	**dzééh**		

Family Relationship and Kinship Terms

Note: Kinship terms always have the prefix "a-" meaning "someone's"

baby	**awéé'**
boy	**ashkii**
boys	**ashiiké**
brother *(older)*	**ánaaí**
brother *(younger)*	**átsilí**
children	**ałchíní**
clan	**dóone'é**
daughter	**ach'é'é** *(woman speaking)*
father	**azhé'é** *(someone's father)*
girl	**at'ééd**
girls	**at'ééké**
man	**hastiin**
mother	**amá**
sibling	**alah** *(opposite sex)*
sibling	**ak'is** *(same sex)*
singer *(medicine man)*	**hataałii**
sister *(older)*	**hádí**
sister *(younger)*	**adeezhí**
woman	**asdzą́ą**

Anatomical Terms

Note: Here again the prefix "a-" means "someone's

arm	**agaan**
ear	**'ajaa'**
eye	**anáá'**
hair	**atsii'**
leg	**ajáád**
toes	**akédiníbiní**
tooth	**awoo'**

Numbers

one	**láa' ii/t'áálái**	six	**hastáá**
two	**naaki**	seven	**tsosts'id**
three	**táá'**	eight	**tseebíí**
four	**dįį'**	nine	**náhást' éí**
five	**ashdla'**	ten	**neeznáá**

Miscellaneous

air, breeze	**nílch'ih**	final/that's all	**t'aa ákódí**
Anglo	**Bilagáana**	fire	**ko'**
ant *(red)*	**wóláchíí'**	firewood	**chizh**
area/space	**haz'ą**	gasoline	**chidi bitoo´**
Arizona	**Hoozdoh bił hahoodzo**	guard	**ha'ásídí**
arrow	**k' aa'**	guide/ according to	**bik'ehgo**
automobile	**chidí**	halt	**t'áá ákwe' é**
axe	**tsénił**	hat	**ch'ah**
baggage	**héél**	home	**hooghan**
beads	**yoo'**	hospital	**azee'ál'**
boulder	**tsétsoh**	house	**kin**
brush shelter	**chaha'oh**	hunger	**dichin**
buckskin	**'abaní**	instruct	**ná' íntin**
cactus	**hosh**	interfere	**na'niłtł'ah**
cave	**tsé' áán**	labor	**na 'anish**
cliff	**tsé nít'i'**	land	**kéyah**
cliff dwelling	**tsé bii' kin**	leader	**naat'áanii**
dawn	**hayoolk'aał**	medicine	**'azee'**
distribute	**na'nii**	money	**béeso**
document	**naaltsoos**	moon	**tł' éhonaa' éí, ooljéé'**
Earth	**Nahasdzáán**		
emergency	**nisihvviiinídéél**	morning	**abíní**
engine	**chidi bitsiits'iin**	mosquito	**ts'í'ii (danineezí)**
equipment	**bee na' anishí**	mountain	**dził**
field	**dá' ák'eh**	Navajo country	**diné bikéyah**
feather	**ats'os**	necklace	**yoo'**

needle	**tsah**	sky	**yá**
now	**k'ad**	smoke	**łid**
oil	**ak'ahko'**	springtime	**daango/dąągo**
outside	**tłóo'di**	sun	**jóhonaa'eí**
people	**diné**	thunderstorm	**ní't'il'ch'ił**
petrified wood	**tsé nástánii**	truck	**chiditsoh**
policeman	**siláo**	turquoise	**dootł´ izhii**
proceed	**náásoo**	valley	**tééh**
question	**ná'ídíkid**	water	**tó**
quick	**tsxíįłgo**	white	**łigai**
ravine	**bikooh**	wood	**chizh**
road	**atiin**	wool	**aghaa'**
rug	**diyogi**	yesterday	**adąądąą'**
school	**ólta'**	zone	**hoodzo**
shirt	**deiji'éé**		

APPENDIX

TREATY OF 1868

ANDREW JOHNSON, President of the United States of America, to all and singular to whom these presents shall come, greetings:

Whereas a Treaty was made and concluded at Fort Sumner, in the Territory of New Mexico, on the first day of June, in the year of our Lord one thousand eight hundred and sixty-eight, by and between Lieutenant General W.T. Sherman and Samuel F. Tappan, Commissioners, on the part of the United States, and Barboncito, Armijo, and other Chiefs and Headmen of the Navajo tribe of Indians, on the part of said Indians, and duly authorized thereto by them, which Treaty is in the words and figures following, to wit:

June 1, 1868
15 Stat. L. 677.
Ratified July 25, 1868.
Proclaimed Aug. 12, 1868

Articles of a treaty and agreement made and entered into at Fort Sumner, New Mexico, on the first day of June, one thousand eight hundred and sixty-eight, by and between the United States, represented by its commissioners, Lieutenant General W.T. Sherman and Colonel Samuel F. Tappan, of the one part, and the Navajo Nation or tribe of Indians, represented by their chiefs and head-men, duly authorized and empowered to act for the whole people of said nation or tribe, (the names of said chiefs and head-men being hereto subscribed), of the other part, witness:

Peace and friendship

ARTICLE 1. From this day forward all war between the parties to this agreement shall forever cease. The Government of the United States desires peace, and its honor is hereby pledged to keep it. The Indians desire peace, and they now pledge their honor to keep it.

Offenders among the whites to be arrested and punished.

If bad men among the whites, or among other people subject to the authority of the United States, shall commit any wrong upon the person or property of the Indians, the United States will, upon proof made to the agent and forwarded to the Commissioner of Indian Affairs at Washington City, proceed at once to cause the offender to be arrested and punished according to the laws of the United States, and also to reimburse the injured persons for the loss sustained.

Offenders among the Indians to be given up to the United States.

Rules for ascertaining damages.

If the bad men among the Indians shall commit a wrong or depredation upon the person or property of any one, white, black, or Indian, subject to the authority of the United States and at peace therewith, the Navajo tribe agree that they will, on proof made to their agent, and on notice by him, deliver up the wrongdoer to the United States, to be tried and punished according to its laws; and in case they willfully refuse so to do, the person injured shall be reimbursed for his loss from the annuities ore other moneys due or to become due to them under this treaty, or any others that may be made with the United States. And the President may prescribe such rules and regulations for ascertaining damages under this article as in his judgment may be proper; but no such damage shall be adjusted and paid until examined and passed upon by the Commissioner of Indian Affairs, and no one sustaining loss whilst violating, or because of his violating, the provisions of this treaty or the laws of the United States, shall be reimbursed therefore.

Reservation boundaries.

Who not to reside thereon.

ARTICLE 2. The United States agrees that the following district of country, to wit: bounded on the north by the 37th degree of north latitude, south by an east and west line passing through the site of old Fort Defiance, in Canon Bonito, east by the parallel of longitude which, if prolonged south, would pass through Old Fort Lyon or the Ojo-de-oso, Bear Spring, and west by a parallel of longitude about 109 degree 30' west of Greenwich, provided it embraces the outlet of the Canon-de-Chilly, which canon is to be all included in this reservation, shall be, and the same is hereby, set apart for the use and occupation of the Navajo tribe of Indians, and for such other friendly tribes or individual Indians as from time to time they may be willing, with the consent of the United States, to admit among them; and the United States agrees that no persons except those herein so authorized to do, and except such officers, soldiers, agents, and employees of the Government, or of the Indians, as may be authorized to enter upon Indian reservations in discharge of duties imposed by law, or the orders of the President, shall ever be permitted to pass over, settle upon, or reside in, the territory described in the article.

Buildings to be erected by the United States.

ARTICLE 3. The United States agrees to cause to be built, at some point within said reservation, where timber and water may be convenient, the following buildings: a warehouse, to cost not exceeding twenty-five hundred dollars; an agency building for the residence of the agent, not to cost exceeding three thousand dollars; a carpenter-shop and blacksmith-shop, not to cost exceeding one thousand dollars each; and a schoolhouse and chapel, so soon as a sufficient number of children can be induced to attend school, which shall not cost to exceed five thousand dollars.

Agent to make his home and reside where.

ARTICLE 4. The United States agrees that the agent for the Navajos shall make his home at the agency building; that he shall reside among them, and shall keep an office open at all times for the purpose of prompt and diligent inquiry into such matters of complaint by or against the Indians as may be presented for investigation, as also for the faithful discharge of other duties enjoined by law. In all cases of depredation on person or property he shall cause the evidence to be taken in writing and forwarded, together with his finding, to the Commissioner of Indian Affairs, whose decision shall be binding on the parties to this treaty.

Heads of family desiring to commence farming may select lands, etc.

Effect of such selection.

ARTICLE 5. If any individual belonging to said tribe, or legally incorporated with it, being the head of a family, shall desire or commence farming, he shall have the privilege to select, in the presence and with the assistance of the agent then in charge, a tract of land within said reservation, not exceeding one hundred and sixty acres in extent, which tract, when so selected, certified, and recorded in the "land book" as herein described, shall cease to be held in common, but the same may be occupied and held in the exclusive possession of the person selecting it, and of his family, so long as he or they may continue to cultivate it.

Persons not heads of families.

Any person over eighteen years of age, not being the head of a family, may in like manner select, and cause to be certified to him or her for purposes of cultivation, a quantity of land not exceeding eight acres in extent, and thereupon be entitled to the exclusive possession of the same as above directed.

Certificates of selection to be delivered, etc., To be recorded.

For each tract of land so selected a certificate containing a description thereof, and the name of the person selecting it, with a certificate endorsed thereon, that the same has been recorded, shall be delivered to the party entitled to it by the agent, after the same shall have been recorded by him in a book to be dept in his office, subject to inspect, which said book shall be known as the "Navajo Land Book."

Survey.

The President may at any time order a survey of the reservation, and when so surveyed, Congress shall provide for protecting the rights of said settlers in their improvements, and may fix the character of the title held by each.

Alienation and descent of property.

The United States may pass such laws on the subject of alienation and descent of property between the Indians and their descendants as may be thought proper.

The Navajo People must give up the education of their children, between the ages of 6 and 16, to the white man (by attending school).

Duty of agent.

Schoolhouses and teachers.

ARTICLE 6. In order to insure the civilization of the Indians entering into this treaty, the necessity of education is admitted, especially of such of them as may be settle on said agricultural parts of this reservation, and they therefore pledge themselves to compel their children, male and female, between the ages of six and sixteen years, to attend school; and it is hereby made the duty of the agent for said Indians to see that this stipulation is strictly complied with; and the United States agrees that, for every thirty children between said ages who can be induced or compelled to attend school, a house shall be provided, and a teacher competent to teach the elementary branches of an English education shall be furnished, who will reside among said Indians, and faithfully discharge his or her duties as a teacher. The provisions of this article to continue for not less than ten years.

Seeds and agricultural implements.

ARTICLE 7. When the head of a family shall have selected lands and received his certificate as above directed, and the agent shall be satisfied that he intends in good faith to commence cultivating the soil for a living, he shall be entitled to receive seeds and agricultural implements for the first year, not exceeding in value one hundred dollars, and for each succeeding year he shall continue to farm, for a period of two years, he shall be entitled to receive seeds and implements to the value of twenty-five dollars.

Delivery of articles in lieu of money and annuities.

ARTICLE 8. In lieu of all sums of money or other annuities provided to be paid to the Indians herein named under any treaty or treaties heretofore made, the United States agrees to deliver at the agency house on the reservation herein named, on the first day of September of each year for ten years, the following articles, to wit:

Indians to be furnished with no articles they can make.

Clothing, etc.

Census.

Such articles of clothing, goods, or raw materials in lieu thereof, as the agent may make his estimate for, not exceeding in value five dollars per Indian—each Indian being encouraged to manufacture their own clothing, blankets, etc.; to be furnished with no article which they can manufacture themselves. And, in order that the Commissioner of Indian Affairs may be able to estimate properly for the articles herein named, it shall be the duty of the agent each year to forward to him a full and exact census of the Indians, on which the estimate for year to year can be based.

Annual appropriation in money for ten years.
May be changed.
Army officer to attend delivery of goods.

And in addition to the articles herein named, the sum of ten dollars for each person entitled to the beneficial effects of this treaty shall be annually appropriated for a period of ten years, for each person who engages in farming or mechanical pursuits, to be used by the Commissioner of Indian Affairs, in the purchase of such articles as from time to time the condition and necessities of the Indians may indicate to be proper; and if within the ten years at any time it shall appear that the amount of money needed for clothing, under the article, can be appropriated to better uses for the Indians named herein, the Commissioner of Indian Affairs may change the appropriation to other purposes, but in no event shall the amount of this appropriation be withdrawn or discontinued for the period named, provided they remain at peace. And the President shall annually detail an officer of the army to be present and attest the delivery of all the goods herein named to the Indians, and he shall inspect and report on the quantity and quality of the goods and the manner of their delivery.

Stipulations by the Indians as to outside territory.

ARTICLE 9. In consideration of the advantages and benefits conferred by this treaty, and the many pledges of friendship by the United States, the tribes who are parties to this agreement hereby stipulate that they will relinquish all right to occupy any territory outside their reservation, as herein defined, but retain the right to hunt on any unoccupied lands contiguous to their reservation, so long as the large game may range thereon in such numbers as to justify the chase; and they, the said Indians, further expressly agree:

Railroads.

1st. That they will make no opposition to the construction of railroads now being built or hereafter to be built across the continent.

2nd. That they will not interfere with the peaceful construction of any railroad not passing over their reservation as herein defined.

Residents, travelers, wagon trains.

3rd. That they will not attack any persons at home or traveling nor molest or disturb any wagon trains, coaches, mules, or cattle belonging to the people of the United States, or to person friendly therewith.

Women and children.

4th. That they will never capture or carry off from the settlements women or children.

Scalping.

5th. They will never kill or scalp white men, nor attempt to do them harm.

Roads or stations.

6th. They will not in future oppose the construction of railroads, wagon roads, mail stations, or other works of utility or necessity which may be ordered or permitted by the laws of the United States; but should such roads or other works be constructed on the lands of their reservation, the government will pay the tribe whatever amount of damage may be assessed by three disinterested commissioners to be appointed by the President for that purpose, one of said commissioners to be a chief or head man of the tribe.

Military posts and roads.

7th. They will make no opposition to the military posts or roads now established, or that may be established, not in violation of treaties heretofore made or hereafter to be made with any of the Indian tribes.

Cession of reservation not to be valid unless, etc.

ARTICLE 10. No future treaty for the cession of any portion or part of the reservation herein described, which may be held in common, shall be of any validity or force against said Indians unless agreed to and executed by at least three-fourths of all the adult male Indians occupying or interested in the same; and no cession by the tribe shall be understood or construed in such manner as to deprive, without his consent, any individual member of the tribe of his rights to any tract of land selected by him provided in article 5 of this treaty.

Indians to go to reservation when required.

ARTICLE 11. The Navajos also hereby agree that at any time after the signing of these presents they will proceed in such manner as may be required by them by the agent, or by the officer charged with their removal, to the reservation herein provided for, the United States paying for their subsistence en route, and providing a reasonable amount of transportation for the sick and feeble.

Appropriations, how to be disbursed.

ARTICLE 12. It is further agreed by and between the parties to this agreement that the sum of one hundred fifty thousand dollars appropriated or to be appropriated shall be disbursed as follows, subject to any condition provided in the law, to wit:

Removal.

1st. The actual cost of the removal of the tribe from the Bosque Redondo reservation to the reservation, say fifty thousand dollars.

Sheep and goats.

2nd. The purchase of fifteen thousand sheep and goats, at a cost not to exceed thirty thousand dollars.

Cattle and corn.

3rd. The purchase of five hundred beef cattle and a million pounds of corn, to be collected and held at the military post nearest the reservation, subject to the orders of the agent, for the relief of the needy during the coming winter.

Remainder.

4th. The balance, if any, of the appropriation to be invested for the maintenance of the Indians pending their removal, in such manner as the agent who is with them may determine.

Removal, how made.

5th. The removal of this tribe to be made under the supreme control and direction of the military commander of the Territory of New Mexico, and when completed, the management of the tribe to revert to the proper agent.

Penalty for leaving reservation.

ARTICLE 13. The tribe herein named, by their representatives, parties to this treaty, agree to make the reservation herein described their permanent home, and they will not as a tribe make any permanent settlement elsewhere, reserving the right to hunt on the lands adjoining the said reservation formerly called theirs, subject to the modifications named in this treaty and the orders of the commander or the department in which said reservation may be for the time being; and it is further agreed and understood by the parties to this treaty, that if any Navajo Indian or Indians shall leave the reservation herein described to settle elsewhere, he or they shall forfeit all the rights, privileges, and annuities conferred by the terms of this treaty; and it is further agreed by the parties to this treaty, that they will do all they can to induced Indians now away from reservation set apart for the exclusive use and occupation of the Indians, leading a nomadic life, or engaged in war against the people of the United States, to abandon such a life and settle permanently in one of the territorial reservations set apart for the exclusive use and occupation of the Indians.

In testimony of all which the said parties have hereunto, on this the first day of June, one thousand eight hundred and sixty-eight, at Fort Sumner, in the Territory of New Mexico, set their hands and seals.

W.T. Sherman
Lieutenant General,
Indian Peace Commissioner.

S.F. Tappan,
Indian Peace Commissioner.

Navajo Chiefs:
(Each signed with an X)

Barboncito, Principal Chief
Chiqueto
Armijo
Muerto de Hombre
Delgado
Hombre
Manuelito
Narbona
Largo
Ganado Mucho
Herrero
Narbono Segundo

Navajo Head Men:
(Each signed with an X)

Riquo
Torivio
Juan Martin
Despendado
Serginto
Juan
Grande
Guero Inoetenito
Gugadore
Muchachos Mucho
Cabason
Chiqueto Segundo
Barbon Segundo
Cabello Amarillo
Cabares Colorados
Francisco

ATTEST

Geo. W.G. Getty, Colonel Thirty-Seventh Infantry, Brevet Major – General U.S. Army

B.S. Roberts, Brevet Brigadier – General U.S. Army, Lieutenant – Colonel Third Cavalry

J. Cooper McKee, Brevet Lieutenant – Colonel, Surgeon U.S. Army

Theo. H. Dodd, United States Indian Agent for Navajos

Chas. McClure, Brevet Major and Commissary of Subsistence, U.S. Army

James F. Weeds, Brevet Major and Assistant Surgeon, U.S. Army

J.C. Sutherland, Interpreter

William Vaux, Chaplain U.S. Army

In Executive Session, Senate of the United States

Resolved, (two-thirds of the senators present concurring) That the Senate advise and consent to the ratification of the treaty between the United States and the Navajo Indians, concluded at Fort Sumner, New Mexico, on the first day of June, 1868.

Attest:

Geo. C. Gorham,
Secretary

By W.J. McDonald,
Chief Clerk

Now, therefore, be it known that I, ANDREW JOHNSON, President of the United States of America, do, in pursuance of the advice and consent of the Senate, as expressed in its resolution of the twenty-fifth of July, one thousand eight hundred and sixty-eight, accept, ratify, and confirm the said treaty.

In testimony whereof, I have hereto signed my name, and caused the seal of the United States to be affixed.

Done at the City of Washington, this twelfth day of August, in the year of our Lord one thousand eight hundred and sixty-eight, and of the Independence of the United States of America, the ninety-third.

ANDREW JOHNSON

By the President:
W. Hunter
Acting Secretary of State

TIMELINE OF EVENTS

9000 B.C.	Athabasken-speaking people migrate from Asia to North America.
1000–1500 A.D.	Descendents of the Athabasken-speaking people—the Apacheans—migrate from the Great Plains into New Mexico.
1540	Discovery of earliest known hogan site shows Navajos living in the Governador, New Mexico, area as early as this period.
1540	Explorer Francisco de Coronado enters the Southwest searching for the fabled Seven Golden Cities of Cibola.
1627	Alonso de Benavides establishes a mission at Santa Clara, the Tewa village on the west side of the Rio Grande below San Juan, to service the "Apaches of Navaju."
1774	Father Carlos Delgado and Father Jose Yrigoyen journey to the rancherias of Dinétah to explore missionary work.
1805	The Spanish, determined to extend the reach of their authority deep into Diné' bikéyah, undertake a series of military operations against the Navajo.
1821	Mexico gains its independence from Spain.

1835 Navajos ambush a column of men from Santa Fe at Narbona Pass, killing the leader, Blas de Hinojos.

1846 The Mexican-American War begins; General Kearny annexes New Mexico to the United States.

1846 Colonel Alexander Doniphan succeeds in convincing some Navajos to sign a peace treaty at Bear Springs, near Fort Wingate. It is the first of seven treaties signed between the Navajo and the United States between 1846 and 1848.

1848 War ends when Mexico and the United States sign the Treaty of Guadalupe Hidalgo.

1851 Fort Defiance is constructed in the heart of Diné' bikéyah.

1860 More than one thousand Navajo warriors launch an attack on Fort Defiance. The army's artillery is too powerful against the bows and arrows of the Navajos, and after a two-hour battle the Diné retreat.

1863 Colonel Kit Carson, mountain-man-turned-soldier, marches into the heart of Navajo country at the head of a regiment of seven hundred soldiers, destroying crops and livestock and rounding up Navajos.

1864 An estimated eight thousand Navajos are rounded up by Carson's men and herded like cattle on the infamous three-hundred-mile walk from Canyon de Chelly to exile at Bosque Redondo on the Pecos River in New Mexico.

1865 Smallpox epidemic strikes the Navajo at Bosque Redondo; some 2,321 Navajos die within a few months.

1867 Conditions at Bosque Redondo are investigated by General William Sherman; findings result in Carlton being removed as commander of the Department of New Mexico.

1867	Control over the Navajos at Bosque Redondo is taken from the army and turned over to the Indian Service.
1868	Treaty allows the Navajo to return to a defined portion of their home territory and begin a new life in their homeland.
1869	President Grant initiates "Grant's Peace Policy" aimed at correcting the deplorable management of native affairs.
1882	President Chester A. Arthur signs an executive order that creates a joint-occupation reservation for both Navajos and Hopis in Arizona.
1882	The Bureau of Indian Affairs opens the first Navajo boarding school at Fort Defiance. This school is fashioned on the pioneering efforts of General Richard H. Pratt, who founded the Carlisle Indian School in Pennsylvania in 1878.
1902	Franciscans found St. Michael's Mission School about twenty-five miles east of Ganado, near Fort Defiance.
1924	Indian Citizenship Act passes. United States citizenship, however, does not secure voting rights for Navajos until much later.
1934	Indian Reorganization Act passes, ending the allotment era and creating tribal constitutions and form of self-government.
1941–1945	More than 3,600 Navajos serve in the military and over 10,000 Navajos go to work in military-related factories.
1942	First wave of Navajo code talkers are recruited from the Indian Boarding School in Fort Defiance, Arizona.
1947	While the United States is helping to rebuild Europe, a report compiled by the Bureau of Indian Affairs discloses that 50 percent of Navajo children were starving to death.

1948 The state of Arizona grants Navajos the right to vote.

1950 Congress passes the Navajo Hopi Rehabilitation Act, which, among other benefits, provides money to build roads and infrastructure across the reservations.

1951 Uranium is discovered on the Navajo reservation.

1951 Annie Dodge Wauneka, daughter of Henry Chee Dodge, is the first woman elected to the Navajo Tribal Council. She holds the post until 1973.

1953 The state of New Mexico grants Navajos voting rights.

1957 The state of Utah grants Navajos voting rights.

1959 The *Navajo Times* (formally the *Navajo Times Today*) is copyrighted and published by the Navajo Tribe in Window Rock, Arizona.

1963 The Presidential Medal of Freedom is presented to Annie Dodge Wauneka by President Lyndon B. Johnson.

1964 The U.S. Civil Rights Act, Title VII, is passed. The act prohibits discrimination for reasons of race, religion, or national origin.

1965 The U.S. Voting Rights act is passed. The act ensures equal voting rights to all U.S. citizens.

1968 The Navajo Community College is established, the first community college on an Indian reservation. It is now known as Diné College.

1969 The Navajo Tribal Council resolves that the Navajo should officially call themselves the "Navajo Nation," not "Navajo Tribe." Further, the Spanish style *Navajo* is officially preferred to the English style *Navaho*.

1972 KTDB-FM in Ramah, New Mexico, is the first Indian-owned and -operated noncommercial radio station to go on the air in the nation.

1974 Congress passes the Hopi Land Settlement Act, which eventually forces the relocation of more than 12,000 Navajos who lived over the coal deposits in the Navajo-Hopi Joint Use Area. It became the largest Indian relocation since the 1880s.

1975 George Patrick Lee, a Navajo, becomes the first (and only) American Indian to hold a high office in the Latter-day Saints (Mormon) Church by being sustained to the First Quorum of the Seventy. He was later excommunicated.

1978 The Indian Education Act is passed, giving greater decision-making powers to American Native school boards.

1979 The largest nuclear accident (including Three Mile Island) in the United States occurs at a United Nuclear Company milling plant on the Navajo reservation in Church Rock, New Mexico, on July 16. More than 1,100 tons of uranium waste from a ruptured dam release more than 100 million gallons of radioactive water into the Rio Puerco.

1993 Navajo Tribal Chairman Peter MacDonald goes to prison, having been convicted of conspiracy to commit kidnapping and burglary of tribal buildings as well as for receiving kickbacks in a Navajo Nation land deal.

1994 Navajo Roberta Blackgoat, a seventy-seven-year-old grandmother, is named "America's Unsung Woman" by the National Women's History Project for her unwavering leadership in the pursuit of environmental and human rights issues on Native American reservations.

1999 The results of a 1997 study by the Bureau of Indian Affairs estimates the total number of Navajo tribal members to be

212,319. Of this total, 165,614 live on the Diné' bikéyah. These results differ from a 1995 study by the Navajo Division of Community Development, which listed 259,556 Navajos.

2000 President Clinton visits the Navajo Nation at Shiprock, New Mexico.

2001 Code talkers are finally decorated for their heroic deeds in WWII.

GLOSSARY

Anasazi: Ancestors of the Pueblo Indian tribes who lived in and around the Four Corners area but disappeared around A.D. 1300.

Athabaskan: Navajo ancestors who lived around Lake Athabaska, Canada, but migrated southward, beginning around the year A.D. 1000.

Athabaskan languages: A group of related languages spoken by Indian peoples whose ancestors were native to the region of Lake Athabaska in northwestern Canada. Included in the languages of this group are those of the Navajo, the Hupa, and the Mescalero Apaches.

Blessingway rite: The core ritual of the traditional Navajo beliefs.

Bureau of Indian Affairs: A federal government agency established in 1824 and merged into the Department of the Interior in 1849. Its original mission was that of managing Indian affairs and supervising tribes on reservations. More recently, its mission has become that of encouraging Indians to manage their own affairs and improve their economic well-being.

Changing Woman: In Navajo mythology, Changing Woman, a supernatural being, had much to do with the creation of the Earth Surface People and with the meeting at which they were taught how to control the wind, lightning, storms, and animals and how to keep all these forces in harmony with each other.

Chantways: Also a "sing"; a Navajo religious ceremony used to cure illness or restore balance.

Chindi: An evil spirit or demon associated with the dead.

Clan: A multigenerational group with common identity, organization, and property and that claims descent from a common ancestor.

Code talkers: A group of several hundred Navajo men who were selected by the Marine Corps during World War II to send coded messages, using the Navajo language, to Pacific combat zones.

Cradleboard: A device made from a wooden board that supports babies so that their mothers can work with free hands.

Diné: The Navajo word meaning "the People." It is the term the People use to refer to themselves.

Dinétah: The Navajo word meaning "The Land of the People."

Four Corners: The point in the United States where Colorado, Utah, Arizona, and New Mexico meet.

Fry bread: The staple food made by combining flour, water, salt, and baking powder and then frying the dough in hot oil.

Hand tremblers: Men or women who determine the source of a person's illness or trouble.

Hataalii: Also called a Singer; a person trained to carry out Navajo chant ceremonies.

Hogan: A traditional Navajo dwelling: cone- or dome-shaped dwelling with a frame made of logs and bark and covered with a thick coat of mud.

Hozho: The Navajo word meaning "beauty, happiness, harmony, and goodness." It summarizes the basic goal and ultimate value of the Navajo world and everything in it.

Joint Use Area: A parcel of Arizona land reserved for the use of both Hopi and Navajo people.

Kinaalda: The four-day ceremony conducted for a Navajo girl when she reaches puberty. During the kinaalda, the young novice receives instruction from female elders as to what her duties and responsibilities as a Navajo woman will be.

Long Walk: The grueling 250-mile journey forced upon more than 8,000 Navajos from their homeland to the Bosque Redondo area in northwestern New Mexico Territory in 1863–64.

Matrilineal: A society in which heritage is traced through the mother.

Mutton: The meat of a mature sheep; traditional Navajo food.

Na'tanii: A person in which a group of people place their trust; a leader.

Native American Church: A religious organization whose practices combine elements of Christianity with rituals of traditional Indian religions. Many of these rituals involve the consumption of the hallucinogenic peyote cactus.

Origin story: The People's story of how the Diné emerged into this world after a long and difficult journey that first took them through three other worlds. It defines for the Navajo many of their basic conceptions of life.

Prayer stick: A Navajo sacred object.

Querechos: The name given to Navajos by Spaniards who first encountered them in the sixteenth century.

Reservation: A tract of land set aside by treaty for the occupation and use of Indians. Some reservations were for an entire tribe; many others were for several tribes of unaffiliated Indians.

Sandpainting: A Navajo art form that depicts sacred beings and is made by "drawing" with colored sand.

Spider Woman: The figure in Navajo mythology that taught the Diné how to weave.

Termination: The proposed governmental policy whereby present federal support would cease and Native Americans would become wholly self-sufficient.

Tribe: A community or group of communities that occupy a common territory and are related by bonds of kinship, language, and shared traditions.

The following sources were perused in compiling this glossary:

Marcello, Patricia Cronin 2000. *The Navajo.* San Diego: Lucent Books.
Iverson, Peter 1990. *The Navajos*. New York: Chelsea House.

REFERENCES

American Automobile Association (AAA) 2005. *Arizona and New Mexico Tour Book.*

Beck, Warren A. 1971. *New Mexico: A History of Four Centuries.* Norman: University of Oklahoma Press.

Benedek, Emily 1995. *Beyond the Four Corners,* Norman: University of Oklahoma Press.

Bial, Raymond 2003. *The Long Walk.* New York: Benchmark Books.

Boman, Mary Beth, ed. 2005. *Fodor's Arizona 2005.* New York: Random House.

Brown, Kenneth A. 1996. *Four Corners.* New York: Harper Perennial.

Brugge, David M. 1994. *The Navajo-Hopi Land Dispute.* Albuquerque: University of New Mexico Press.

Bryant, Kathleen 2003. *The Four Corners.* Flagstaff, AZ: Northland Publishing.

Collier, John, Jr. 2002. *Photographing Navajos.* Albuquerque: University of New Mexico Press.

Cordell, Linda S. 1984. *Prehistory of the Southwest.* Boston: Academic Press.

Eichstaedt, Peter H. 1994. *If You Poison Us.* Santa Fe, NM: Red Crane Books.

Evans, Will 2005. *Navajo Trails.* Logan: Utah State University Press.

Faris, James C. 1994. *The Highway.* Albuquerque: University of New Mexico Press.

Fergusson, Erna 1980. *New Mexico.* Albuquerque: University of New Mexico Press.

Franciscan Fathers. *An Ethnologic Dictionary of the Navajo Language*. St. Michael's, AZ: Franciscan Fathers.

Goodman, James M., 1971. *The Navajo Atlas*. Norman: University of Oklahoma Press.

Goossen, Irvy W. 1983. *Navajo Made Easier: A Course in Conversational Navajo*. Flagstaff, AZ: Northland Press.

Goossen, Irvy W. 1995. *Diné Bizaad*. Flagstaff, AZ: The Salina Bookshelf.

Gregg, Josiah 1968. *The Commerce of the Praries*. New York: Citadel Press.

Haile, Berard 1951. *A Stem Vocabulary of the Navajo Language,* Vol. 2. St. Michael's: St. Michael's Press.

Haile, Father Berard 1998. *Tales of an Endishodi,* Santa Fe: University of New Mexico Press.

Heisey, Adriel, and Kawano, Kenji 2001. *In the Fifth World*. Tucson, AZ: Rio Nuevo.

Hillerman, Tony and Hillerman, Barney 1991. *Hillerman Country: A Journey Through the Southwest with Tony Hillerman*. New York: Perennial Press.

Hooker, Kathy Eckles 2002. *Time among the Navajo*. Flagstaff, AZ: The Salina Bookshelf.

Houk, Rose 1995. *Navajo of Canyon de Chelly*. Tucson, AZ: SW Parks and Monument.

Iverson, Peter 1990. *The Navajos*. New York: Chelsea House.

Iverson, Peter 2002a. *Diné: A History of the Navajos*. Albuquerque: University of New Mexico Press.

Iverson, Peter, ed. 2002b. *For Our Navajo People*. Albuquerque: University of New Mexico Press.

Keeney, Bradford 2001. *Walking Thunder*. Philadelphia: Ringing Rocks Press.

Kluckhohn, Clyde, and Dorothea Leighton 1962. *The Navajo*. Cambridge, MA: Harvard University Press.

Knaut, Andrew L. 1995. *The Pueblo Revolt of 1680*. Norman: University of Oklahoma Press.

Kosik, Fran 1996. *Native Roads*. Tucson, AZ: Rio Nuevo.

Lavin, Patrick 2001. *Arizona, An Illustrated History*. New York: Hippocrene.

Linford, Laurance D. 2000. *Navajo Places: History, Legend, Landscapes*. Salt Lake City: University of Utah Press.

Link, Martin A., ed. 1968. *Navajo: A Century of Progress 1868–1968.* Window Rock, Arizona: Navajo Tribes.

Lipps, Oscar H. 1989. *A Little History of the Navajos.* Albuquerque: Avanyu.

Luey, Beth, and Stowe, Noel, eds. 1987. *The Next Twenty-five Years.* Albuquerque: University of Arizona Press.

MacDonald, Peter 1993. *The Last Warrior.* New York: Orion Books.

Marcello, Patricia Cronin 2000. *The Navajo.* San Diego: Lucent Books.

McCarty, Teresa L. 2002. *A Place to Be Navajo.* Mahwah, NJ: Lawrence Erlbaum Associates.

McNitt, Frank 1972. *Navajo Wars.* Albuquerque: University of New Mexico Press.

McPherson, Robert S. 2001. *Navajo Land, Navajo Culture.* Norman: University of Oklahoma Press.

Melendez, A. Gabriel, Moore, Patricia, Pynes, Patrick, Young, M. Jane eds. 2001. *The Multicultural Southwest.* Tuscon: University of Arizona Press.

Noble, David Grant 2000. *Ancient Ruins of the Southwest.* Flagstaff, AZ: Northland Publishing.

Pratt, Richard Henry 1987. *Battlefield and Classroom: Four Decades with the American Indian, 1867–1904.* Lincoln, Nebraska: University of Nebraska Press.

Reichard, Gladys A. 1970. *Navajo Religion.* Princeton, NJ: Princeton University Press.

Richardson, Gladwell 1986. *Navajo Trader.* Tucson: University of Arizona Press.

Roberts, David 2004. *Pueblo Revolt.* New York: Simon and Schuster.

Schwarz, Maureen Trudelle 2001. *Navajo Lifeways.* Norman: University of Oklahoma Press.

Sheridan, Thomas E., and Parezo, Nancy J., eds. 1996. *Paths of Life.* Tucson: University of Arizona Press.

Sherry, John W. 2002. *Land, Wind, and Hard Words.* Albuquerque: University of New Mexico Press.

Simmons, Mark 1988. *New Mexico: An Interpretive History.* Albuquerque: University of New Mexico Press.

Simonelli, Jeanne M. 1997. *Crossing Between Worlds.* Santa Fe, NM: School of American Research Press.

Spicer, Edward H. 1997. *Cycles of Conquest.* Tucson: University of Arizona Press.

Sundberg, Lawrence D. 1995. *Dinétah.* Santa Fe, NM: Sunstone Press.

Trennert, Robert A. 1998. *White Man's Medicine.* Albuquerque: University of New Mexico Press.

Trimble, Marshall 1997. *Roadside History of Arizona.* Missoula, MT: Mountain Press.

Trimble, Stephen 2000. *The People.* Santa Fe, NM: School of American Research Press.

Trockur, Fr. Emanual, OFM 1998. "The Vision Begins" from *Padres' Trail,* 1898–1998. St. Michael's.

Underhill, Ruth M. 1985. *The Navajos.* Norman: University of Oklahoma Press.

Walker, Paul Robert, *The Southwest.* National Geographic Society: Washington, DC.

Wall, Leon, and Morgan, William 2004. *Navajo-English Dictionary.* New York: Hippocrene.

Wilson, Dave 1999. *Hiking, Ruins Seldom Seen.* Guilford, CT: Globe Pequot Press.

Young, Robert W. 1978. *A Political History of the Navajo Tribe.* Tsille, Navajo Nation, AZ: Navajo Community College Press.

Young, Robert W., and Morgan, William 1998. *Colloquial Navajo.* New York: Hippocrene.

Young, Robert W., and Morgan, William, Sr. 1987. *The Navajo Language: A Grammar and Colloquial Dictionary,* revised edition. Albuquerque: University of New Mexico Press.

INDEX